THE UNIVERSITY OF
WINCHESTER

Martial Rose Library
Tel: 01962 827306

To be returned on or before the day marked above, subject to recall.

sport ethics in context

DEBRA SHOGAN

Canadian Scholars' Press Inc.
Toronto

Sport Ethics in Context
by Debra Shogan

First published in 2007 by
Canadian Scholars' Press Inc.
180 Bloor Street West, Suite 801
Toronto, Ontario
M5S 2V6
www.cspi.org

Canadian Scholars' Press Inc. gratefully acknowledges financial support for our publishing activities from the Government of Canada through the Book Publishing Industry Development Program (BPIDP).

Library and Archives Canada Cataloguing in Publication

Shogan, Debra A., 1951–
    Sport ethics in context / Debra Shogan.

Includes bibliographical references and index.
ISBN 978-1-55130-332-1

    1. Sports—Moral and ethical aspects. I. Title.

GV706.3.S56 2007   175   C2007-904550-2

Book design: Susan MacGregor/DigitalZone

07 08 09 10 11   5 4 3 2 1

Printed and bound in Canada by Marquis Book Printing Inc.

For my parents,
Myrle and Lloyd Shogan

TABLE OF CONTENTS

ACKNOWLEDGEMENTS

In the context of the difficult lives of so many in this world, taking advantage of my own good fortune to think and write about sport seems, on the surface, to be ethically suspect. It is my contention, however, throughout *Sport Ethics in Context* that the intensity of interpersonal interactions in sport can provide an important site to better understand the ethical domain itself. I am grateful for having had the luxury to read and think about these issues over the course of my career and hope that in some small way what I have written may contribute to refusing an unjust world.

During 30-plus years as a coach and then as a professor at the University of Alberta, I have had an opportunity to work with and learn from a number of students. I particularly want to acknowledge the impact on me personally and on my scholarship of the doctoral students with whom I worked, especially in the last 10 years.

Over the years my work has been supported by grants, sabbaticals, and honours from the University of Alberta and from four grants from the Social Sciences and Humanities Research Council. Without this support, I would not have been able to secure time to do my research.

I have dedicated this book to my parents, Myrle Shogan and Lloyd Shogan, who, while not always aware of the details and concerns of my work, have nevertheless supported me in all my endeavours throughout my life. Finally and eternally, I want to thank Gloria Filax, my connection to all that is important.

INTRODUCTION

It is common for sport organizers, coaches, and educators to claim that sport is a unique environment for participants to become better people. This claim is understood in part to mean that sport is a context, unlike all others, for participants to learn ethical values and become ethical people. Competitive sport no doubt has had life-altering effects on many people, effects that might even fall into the ethical domain. Yet, we do not need to look far to see that abuses of rules, opponents, teammates, and officials abound at all levels of sport. Despite claims for sport as a special ethical environment, evidence from actual sport occurrences clearly shows that mere participation in sport does not bring about ethical conversion and may in fact be a context for people to disregard ethics.

That there is no guarantee that people become more ethical merely by being in a sporting environment is a crucial realization. Without this realization, attention will not be paid to ways in which ethical development might be facilitated by participating in sport. If sport is to be a context for a better understanding of and appreciation for ethical behaviour, it is necessary to pay attention to just what is at stake in the ethical domain, including the components of an ethical response and how sport leaders might facilitate ethical responses in a sport environment.

This book is a collection of selected articles written by me over almost 20 years of thinking about what constitutes the ethical domain, ethical practice, ethics education, and ethics in the context of sport. The title of the book, *Sport Ethics in Context,* is to be understood in a number of different ways. First, the issues I have written about and how I have theorized them reflect my own intellectual context: my doctoral studies were in philosophy and philosophy of education, but I have spent most of my scholarly career in Sport and Leisure Studies after 11 years as a high performance coach. While my writing over the years has included work in ethics, ethics education, feminist ethics, disability studies, and cultural studies, I have often turned my attention to thinking about ethics in the context of sport and sport in the context of ethics. My coaching experience together with my experiences as a professor across a number of academic programs, including Women's Studies, have influenced what I find interesting about ethics and ethical issues in sport as well as how I theorize them. No doubt what I find interesting and how I have chosen to think about what I find interesting will often have a different focus from other sport ethicists, who also work from their own intellectual histories and social contexts.

I also intend the title of the book to signify that there are a number of contexts in which to consider sport ethics. In *Sport Ethics in Context* I consider ethical issues in the context of responsibilities to opponents and the less considered context of responsibilities to those on the same team, including athletes, coaches, trainers, and administrators. As importantly, I understand the domain of ethics to be a context in which issues in sport can be understood. In this introductory chapter I reprise an argument about what the ethical domain entails that I first began to think about in my book *Care and Moral Motivation* (1988). How ethics is distinguished from other domains, what comprises components of an ethical response, and what needs to be paid attention to if sport leaders want to be taken seriously when they claim that sport provides a context for ethics education are all important factors in contextualizing sport ethics.

THE ETHICAL DOMAIN

Ought, Right, and Good

Dictionary definitions of what ethics entails indicate that ethics is concerned with good and bad, right and wrong, and with what people ought to or are obligated to do. What these definitions miss is that words such as *ought, obligation, right*, and, *good* have both ethical and non-ethical uses. Something may be aesthetically good, for example, or mathematically right. Moreover, obligations are acknowledged that at least on the surface have nothing to do with the ethical domain. For example, I feel that I ought to make my bed in the morning, but this obligation is not an ethical obligation. *Ought, good*, and *right* are ethical terms when reference is made to significant effects on welfare or fair treatment of sentient beings. A sentient being is a being that can physically or psychically suffer, whose welfare or fair treatment can be harmed, and who, therefore, can be assisted in some way.

The terms *good*, *right*, and *ought* are also used to describe actions that are purely self-interested or prudential. Prudence is, of course, absolutely necessary as a motivation for human beings if we are to live satisfying, productive lives. We must make decisions about housing, food, education, and relationships and these decisions must focus on ourselves if we are to continue to live and thrive. We often refer to these decisions as *good* decisions, or the *right* thing to do, or indicate that we *ought* to pursue a particular action in order to do well. What is important to understand is that prudence is its own domain, with its own internal logic and that, while prudence (self-interest) may not conflict with the ethical domain, it often does.

Ethical Motivations

As I have said, *good* and *bad*, *right* and *wrong*, and *obligation* in the ethical domain concern motivation and actions that affect the welfare or fair treatment of sentient beings. What might be called ethics discourse or talk about ethics has something to say about the improvement of the lives of sentient beings rather than how to better promote oneself. Of course, since we are also sentient beings, we are often in situations in which our own welfare or fair treatment is at stake. In some of these situations, the ethically appropriate response is to pay attention to our own welfare or fair treatment. It is unethical to allow oneself to be bullied, for example, for fear of hurting the bully's feelings or to give up one's legitimate claim to compensation or acknowledgement in order to avoid conflict.

Even when the ethical thing to do is to ensure one's own welfare or fair treatment, if the response is to be an *ethical* response, the focus of the response must be on how someone's welfare or fair treatment can be improved. This means that not just any reason counts as an ethical reason for responding in an ethical situation. As Beehler says, "only *some kinds* of reasons, only *some kinds* of considerations are [ethical] reasons.... Of course, if one doesn't find these reasons compelling, well, one doesn't. But this does not make the reasons one does find compelling [ethical] reasons by default..." (1977, p. 60).

When attempting to convince someone that an action or motivation is ethical, reference is made to the importance of minimizing suffering and enhancing welfare and fair treatment. If, however, these ethical reasons do not matter to the person you are trying to convince, appealing to these ethical reasons will have no impact. When you realize that he is only interested in promoting himself and you then try to convince him to behave ethically by appealing to his self-interest, you have only managed to convince him to continue to be self-interested. For example, if someone wants to tell a blind vendor that she has given him a $10 bill when she has actually given him a five, arguing that this action harms the vendor won't be persuasive to a self-interested person. Trying to convince her by offering reasons that justify an ethical response will not be persuasive because ethical reasons don't count for this person. However, to say something like, "you should be careful about saying this is a ten when it is a five because all transactions are on videotape" while persuading her not to deceive the vendor is not also to persuade her to be *ethical*. This is because she has responded to reasons that enhance her self-interest. To abstain from deception for this reason is self-interested and not ethical behaviour.

Other Motivations in Ethical Situations

There are other motivations for responding in situations in which welfare or fair treatment is at stake that on the surface seem to be ethical reasons. These include

1. Responding so that in a similar situation others will reciprocate (do unto others as you would have others do unto you).
2. Responding so that you will be rewarded (or not punished) by God, the state, the school, the coach, or other authorities.
3. Responding to uphold one's own integrity; to be a virtuous person.
4. Responding to uphold ethical principles or responding from a sense of duty.

Responses one through three focus on the person acting and not on the recipient of the response. In the first of the examples, the response is motivated by a belief that to "help" will be of personal benefit ("honesty pays"). In the second example, there is motivation to "help," not because someone needs help but because of the prospect of a personal reward or unpleasant personal consequences (not going to Heaven, going to jail, being expelled from school). Because integrity and virtue are terms with ethical implications, these are often thought to be legitimate ethical motivations. It is clear, however, that the focus of this motivation—to uphold one's own integrity or to be a virtuous person—is only indirectly, if at all, on those who might benefit from a response. It is inadequate to act only from concern about "some 'moral state' of oneself." If one's concern is to be a "certain sort of person," others are then "simply occasions for ['ethical'] action" (Beehler 1977, p. 31).

Responding in order to uphold ethical principles, while not focusing on oneself, as the others in the list do, does not focus on those in the ethical situation either. Consider this example:

> You are very bored and restless and at loose ends when Smith comes in once again. You are now convinced more than ever that he is a fine fellow and a real friend—taking so much time to cheer you up, traveling all the way across town, and so on. You are so effusive with your praise and thanks that he protests that he always tries to do what he thinks is his duty, what he thinks will be best. You at first think he is engaging in a polite form of self-deprecation…. The more you two speak, the more it becomes clear that he was telling the literal truth: that it is not essentially because of you that he came to see you, not because you are friends, but because he thought it his duty. (Stocker 1976, p. 462)

There are times, however, in which it is not possible to be motivated to respond directly to individuals in ethical predicaments. We are simply not in a position to be aware of the particulars of every ethical predicament. In some ethical situations, it may be very difficult, even when one is aware of another's predicament, to be motivated by the welfare or fair treatment of this person. For example, if I am asked to adjudicate a conflict between a vendor who is known to exploit his workers and one of the workers who is the neighbourhood bully, I may have no particular desire that these particular people are treated fairly. However, because I recognize a principle of fairness, I respond in this instance to a duty to be fair. The focus shifts from the people in the conflict to the duty itself.

The Scope of the Ethical Domain

There are ethical debates about the limit of the domain of ethics. Said differently, there is not agreement about the extent to which one should acknowledge sentience. Many limit the ethical domain to family and friends. The scope of ethics for others includes people like themselves or people who share the same community or nationality. Still others regard human beings to be the limit of ethical concern. For others, the scope of ethical concern is a series of concentric circles with oneself at the middle and working out to family, personal friends, age-group, colleagues, race, social class, nation, species, and the biosphere (Midgley 1983, p. 29). According to this position, the interests of those in the inner circles override interests in the outer circle, especially in the event of conflict. Still others maintain that, sentience cannot be put into a hierarchy. If one can be physically or psychically harmed, then one is a legitimate subject of ethical concern. As Utilitarian philosopher, Jeremy Bentham, wrote in the 1770s,

> [A] full grown horse or dog is beyond comparison a more rational, as well as a more conversable animal, than an infant of a day or week, or even a month, old. But suppose they were otherwise, what would it avail? The question is not, Can they *reason*? nor, Can they *talk*?, but Can they *suffer*? (1948, p. 311n)

We often work out conflicts between humans and animals or between species of animals based on the supposition that suffering and enjoyment increase as nervous systems grow progressively more complex (Midgley 1983, p. 90). If this is the only criterion, however, conflicts between humans and animals will always be resolved in the favour of humans.

In a conflict between non-human sentient beings and human sentient beings, fair treatment requires that both are assisted according to the type of life appropriate to each. We do not find credible someone who argues that the interests of her social class should override the interests of those of another social class, while using the perceived attributes of her class as evidence of its higher ethical standing. We might also consider suspect the argument that humans should always take precedence over animals in ethical situations because the attributes of humans are more important than those of the particular animal. This is like saying, "I am more important because I am more important."

Ethically Trivial

Not every situation we encounter involves an ethical dilemma. To claim that ethical situations are to be found at every turn is to trivialize what actually affects welfare and fair treatment. To see every event in life as an ethical situation is to create conflicts and difficulties where none exist. Potentially any action taken can adversely affect someone else. For example, I may decide against getting on the bus because I might occupy the spot of someone else who wants to get on at a later stop. To make life decisions in this way would be to make any action impossible.

To react to every event as if it is an ethical situation is also to deny the value of many non-ethical attributes and events. When considering the characteristics of someone, "one would hope that they would be [ethically] good … but one would hope, too, that they are not just [ethically] good, but talented, or accomplished, or attractive in non-[ethical] ways as well" (Wolf 1982, p. 422). There are many attributes that are ethically neutral. Attributes such as courage, industry, fortitude, patience, and temperance may be of assistance to someone in an ethical situation. Courage, for example, is an important attribute in those ethical situations that involve personal risk. However, ethically neutral attributes can also be useful to someone who wants to take advantage of a situation for personal gain. "Courage will aid the thug, determination the pirate, patience the cracksman, gentleness the jewel thief and so on…. for these attributes can make a bad man more effective in the same way as they fortify the good man in what he attempts" (Attfield 1978, p. 76).

To note that not every situation encountered in life is an ethical situation leaves open the question: what are the ethically significant issues in sport? It seems obvious that it is ethically trivial to avoid playing tennis because one will have to deceive one's opponent into thinking that the ball will be lobbed when the intention is to drive it. But, is it ethically trivial to deliberately break a rule to stop a game, as occurs when a "good foul" is committed? Is it ethically trivial for coaches to pare down a roster by telling some participants that they can't play on a particular team? For some, the answer to these questions and others affecting interpersonal interactions in sport will be: it depends. It may depend, for example, on the age of the participants, how competitive the game or team is or on the expectations of the competitors involved. For others, there may be no ethically significant questions in sport because, for them, sport itself is insignificant. According to this view, in the context of war, famine, environmental degradation, poverty, and violence, the situations affecting people in sport are so trivial as to be not worth mentioning.

If there are ethical issues related to sport, is it because other more important human endeavours become implicated? For those who hold this view, cheating in sport became a national concern in Canada not because Ben Johnson failed his drug test at the 1988 Seoul Olympics but because Canada's reputation as an honest, fair-playing country was undermined. Similarly, interpersonal relations in sport became an issue of public concern in Canada not because people were suddenly upset about the power coaches wield in relation to athletes but because Graham James's abuse of Sheldon Kennedy was an instance of predation of children by adults.

Still others might argue that it is not sport *per se* that makes something ethically significant but, like any human endeavour that consists of interactions among people, there are opportunities or situations for people (and in some sport, animals) to be significantly affected by the actions of others. It is to these situations I now turn.

COMPONENTS OF AN ETHICAL RESPONSE

An Ethical Situation

What types of situation or problem tend to be those that require an ethical response as opposed to a prudential response? Ethical situations tend to be of two general types: situations involving welfare and situations involving fairness.

Situations Involving Welfare

Situations involving welfare include those in which others are injured, starved, homeless, distraught, lost, confused, tormented and the like, or when they do not suffer but there is an opportunity to help them flourish in some way. In this type of ethical situation, welfare is at stake as a result of some predicament or circumstance that requires that someone help. Because it is impossible to be in a position to help everyone who requires help, ethical situations also include those in which one desires that someone in a position to help does help. This may entail a commitment to changing both social structures and people so that others can be helped in those situations in which a personal action is not possible.

In those situations where helping makes it possible for someone to *flourish*, it is necessary that a helper knows what counts as flourishing for another. To desire that a specific individual flourish is dependent upon knowing something about that individual. Less information is needed to know what counts as *suffering* for another sentient being because we share with others the potential to suffer. We do not, however, share particular life circumstances. Because of this, it is often difficult to desire (except in a general way) flourishing for others whose circumstances are unlike our own and whose interests and needs are not apparent.

Situations Involving Fair Treatment

Situations involving fair treatment are those in which there is a conflict between sentient beings or between sentient beings and a standard the fair resolution of which requires adjudication. Many but not all situations requiring fair adjudication occur while fulfilling an institutional role, as an official or a judge, for example. When one fulfills an institutional role, the interests of everyone in a conflict must be treated impartially. It is not fair, for example, to select a family member to a position within an institution by virtue of that relationship. Since people often have difficulty being impartial toward family and friends, or because it is perceived that they would have difficulty being impartial, formal adjudicators are usually expected to withdraw when friends or family members are involved in conflicts that would be adjudicated by them. However, there are many less formal situations in which one is called upon to adjudicate conflicts that involve others one has not met before and conflicts that involve friends and family members.

Adjudication of a conflict may result in an enhancement of another's welfare. Often, however, adjudication will result in diminished welfare for one or more in a conflict, even though fair treatment is achieved for all. If, for example, a student is denied her university degree because her grades have not been accurately recorded by the registrar's office, fair adjudication of the problem would result in her obtaining credit for her courses and being awarded her degree. This would also enhance her welfare. But when two people conflict over a parking spot, fair adjudication may result in one person losing any claim to the parking spot. They can both be treated fairly even though one's welfare is decreased as a result of having to look for another parking spot.

Appraisal of an Ethical Situation

We are often so busy or rushed or too self-centered to recognize when someone's welfare or fair treatment is at stake. In order to respond in an ethical situation, one must recognize an ethical situation *as* an ethical situation. Ethical failure is often the result of the narrow range of a person's perception and discrimination (Hampshire 1965, p. 222). In order to respond ethically, someone must have knowledge about what makes a situation an ethical situation. He or she must recognize a situation as one in which someone requires help or fair treatment. As an example, someone will not offer to help another looking at room numbers above classroom doors, unless this person is also recognized as someone who is lost. It is only if the person is appraised as being lost that she can be helped.

Appraising a situation as one in which another requires help or fair treatment is a necessary but not sufficient condition for an ethical response. This is because those who have no interest in responding ethically also require an ability to recognize when another is in need of help or fairness. A sadist, a thief, or an embezzler also requires an ability to recognize when others are vulnerable in some way but not in order to help or fairly adjudicate but to take advantage of the situation.

Motivation That Those in an Ethical Situation Are Treated Well or Fairly

In order to respond ethically, the focus of one's motivation in an ethical situation must be on those in the predicament rather than on how a response might enhance oneself. An ethical person is someone who, given the ethical situation, desires that sentient beings receive fair treatment or their welfare is improved. An ethical person may not actually be the one who acts to change another's circumstances because there are times when it is impossible to change the circumstances that affect others. Even so, desiring that circumstances change for others is to ethically respond to them. A benevolent or just desire is part of both the description of an ethical person's motivation to respond in an ethical situation and part of the description of the response itself.

There are ethical situations in which a desire that another's circumstances change is an ethically significant response, even if an action is not possible. Someone who desires the welfare of another in an uncontrollable fire ethically responds to this person even if the smoke and flames make it impossible to act. That this is so becomes more clear when contrasted with someone who watches the fire indifferent to the suffering of others. Even though neither acts, the one who desires the welfare of the person in the fire responds to this person, and this response is ethically significant even if there is no action possible.

The ethical significance of a response cannot be determined by action alone. If George visits Sam in the hospital, the nature of George's visit is different if he desires that Sam recover from his illness than it is if he desires to do his duty or he has designs on Sam's fortune. Similarly, if Mary desires that Jane be treated fairly, this is a different response from Mary desiring that she benefit somehow from Jane receiving fair treatment. To assess the ethics of a response, it is necessary to understand as much as you can about the response. George assisting Sam because it is in George's self-interest to help Sam is a different response from George assisting Sam because George desires Sam's welfare. The action and the motivation for the action are both components of the description of a response.

Other things that we desire often complicate whether we are able to respond ethically. When conflicting desires are stronger than a desire we have to help or adjudicate fairly, this conflicting desire will override. For example, on the way to a concert that I have been anticipating for months, I see someone who has fallen in the street and realize that this person is hurt. Even though I want to help and do hope that someone else will help, my conflicting desire to get to the concert on time overrides and I continue on my way. Acting from self-interest in ethical situations is something most of us do from time to time. If, however, acting from self-interest is something I regularly do when faced with ethical situations, I would be hard pressed to claim that I am an ethical person.

Practical and/or Social Skills

Someone who recognizes an ethical situation as an ethical situation and desires another's welfare or fair treatment often will also require certain skills in order to act. It is conceivable that a person who recognizes an ethical situation and who has no conflicting desires may still not act even when an action is possible because this person is without some relevant know-how or skill. Someone who desires to help another who is choking, drowning, cut, burned, or otherwise injured but who knows nothing about lifesaving or first aid will not be able to help. It is inconsistent to say that I desire that others not suffer from injuries but I don't care to know how to alleviate the effects of injuries. Likewise, if I say that I desire that those who are lost, lonely, confused, embarrassed, bereaved, disappointed, discouraged, or unhappy be assisted, then there is some further responsibility placed on me to acquire social skills to communicate with people in these situations.

An Action

I have indicated that an action is not always possible in ethical situations and that someone may still respond ethically, even without an action, if he or she desires that others are treated well or fairly. However, an action is an essential part of an ethical response in those situations in which an action is possible. Having only a desire to change another's circumstance without an attempt to do something, when it is possible to do something is an inadequate response. For example, if I desire your safety but am unwilling to fend off your attackers because of a desire for my own well-being, while justified on prudential grounds, my response is inadequate as an ethical response.

Emotion

When an ethical situation is recognized as an ethical situation and the person who recognizes this desires another's welfare or fair treatment, he or she will experience an emotion during the ethical situation and as a result of how the situation is resolved. For example, if I desire that you receive fair treatment and you are not treated fairly, I will experience disappointment or anger, depending on the severity of the situation. If you are treated fairly, I will experience satisfaction or joy, again depending on the particulars of the situation. Similarly, if I desire your welfare and am not able to help you in your predicament, I experience regret or sorrow. If I desire your welfare but have not acted because I have a conflicting desire to get to the concert, for example, I will experience guilt or remorse.

An emotion is part of an ethical response and is ethically significant to the recipient of the response. The emotion is significant because, if properly displayed, it is an indication that the person who responds actually desires the recipient's welfare or fair treatment. The sincere display of emotion indicates whether someone's behaviour is a result of motivation directed at another in a predicament or conflict.

A display of emotion in response to an ethical situation, while ethically significant, may, however, get in the way of helping or adjudicating fairly. If someone experiences extreme despair as a result of another's situation, the emotional experience may be harmful if it is incapacitating. An adjudicator who becomes overwhelmed by the plight of others in conflict situations may have an ability to adjudicate problems but be unable to shift attention from his or her emotional experience to the task at hand. Similarly, if someone has the ability to provide first aid to an accident victim but is overwhelmed by emotions and is unable to utilize these skills, the skills are useless.

ETHICAL RESPONSES IN SPORT

It should be evident from the descriptions in the previous sections that there is more to ethical achievement in sport than merely having someone participate in sport. Nevertheless, sport does have an advantage as a vehicle for ethics education over other enterprises: participants encounter a number of ethical situations that they would not normally encounter in the same time period elsewhere. There are numerous ethically problematic situations that arise in the practice of sport to which participants can respond ethically, prudentially, and/or unethically. These include situations participants face that involve opponents, often while the game is being played, and those situations faced in the context of being a member of a team, a league, or a representative of a community.

Ethical Situations in Sport

Both types of ethical situations—those involving welfare and those involving fairness—occur in sport. They arise in relation to opponents, during and in preparation for competition, and in interactions among coaches, athletes, and administrators and league officials, some of which occur in preparation for competition and others that occur during competition.

Responsibilities to Opponents

Do competitors in sport have ethical responsibilities to opponents and, if they do, how are these responsibilities to be understood? Is it possible to care about opponents in the same way one might care about a teammate or is there something else that governs these relationships? There are a number of situations that arise during competition and in preparation for competition that involve consideration of opponents. Each sport is made up of rules that must apply in the same way to each person in the contest if it is to be fair. However, fair treatment of participants is not guaranteed by the rules. Participants can accept or reject the extent to which rules will govern their behaviour. They can decide whether to deliberately break game rules in order to gain an advantage over opponents. Not all deliberate rule breakage occurs during competition. Many also occur in preparation for competition. These situations include decisions to take banned perform-ance-enhancing drugs, to alter equipment and playing fields, to disguise eligibility, to skew playing schedules, and so on. These offences may be even more serious than decisions to break rules during the heat of a competition because they require premeditation.

Sport is an environment in which it is at least possible to expose partic-ipants to instances in which fairness is important but it is often not possi-ble to learn from these situations because coaches and officials make decisions for athletes. Since all but the most recreational games of sport are officiated, many opportunities for participants to respond fairly to others are taken away. Participants are not often, if ever, responsible for reporting their own rule breakages. If not discovered by the official, they are expected to play on. The message from this both legally and ethically is that something is wrong only if it is found out. Moreover, if expecta-tions by leaders are that participants are merely to conform to rules rein-forced by officials and coaches, the only lesson (problematically) learned is that authorities must be obeyed. The potential to learn ethical responses from situations requiring fairness may be lost if participants are not expected to make decisions about their own behaviour.

There are not as many opportunities for participants to help oppo-nents in sport even though the physical nature of sport makes it likely that, at least in some contests, participants will be physically hurt. There are, of course, instances in which players have opportunities to avoid hurting other players. These include refraining from striking opponents in retaliation or refraining from initiating excessive force in order to intim-idate. Most decisions of this kind, however, are actually instances of abid-ing by rules that establish fair behaviour in relation to physical contact.

There are occasions for participants to help each other during stop-pages of play when, for example, someone falls or has been hit or even if someone is dejected. These helping situations will more often that not be expectations of teammates rather than opponents. There are not, however, as far as I can see, occasions for helping behaviours to occur during an actual play sequence. If, for example, a defensive player falls with an obvious knee injury while defending someone driving to the basket, the offensive player cannot both stop to help the fallen player and continue the drive to the basket. To help someone in this type of situation is to cease to be involved in carrying out the prescribed movements of the game. If someone stops to help an opponent in this type of situation, he or she, in effect, is deciding that helping is more important than playing the game at this time. While ceasing to play in order to help an opponent is not unheard of in sport—for example, the Canadian sailor who pulled himself out of an Olympic race to help an opponent who had capsized—continuing to play is certainly the expectation.

Responsibilities to Team Members

I have said that sport is limited as a vehicle for the development of responses to opponents with respect to issues of fairness both during and in preparation for competition. It is also limited with respect to responding to opponents who need help. Opponents are not the only people with whom athletes, coaches, and administrators engage during competition and in preparation for competition. Participants in sport spend a significant proportion of each day with teammates, coaches, and trainers, and sometimes with administrators. These interpersonal relationships are as often fraught with conflict as they are characterized by goodwill. Indeed, my research has revealed that competitors at every level of sport identify relationships with teammates, coaches, and administrators associated with their own teams to be more likely to yield ethical dilemmas than interactions with opponents. Athletes frequently reported that they thought coaches and administrators treated them unfairly in team selections and in not paying attention to their legitimate concerns about the day-to-day operation of the team. High-profile cases of athlete abuse by coaches underline that ethical situations are prevalent in sport at all levels and are not only perpetrated by opponents on the playing field (Kirby, Greaves & Hankivsky 2001; Robinson 1998). Section 2 of *Sport Ethics in Context* is concerned with ethical responsibilities to those on the same team and whether these responsibilities are different from responsibilities to opponents.

ETHICS EDUCATION IN SPORT

Sport is a fertile environment for ethical responses to occur because of the prevalence of ethical situations that confront participants. To say that something can happen is different, however, from saying it will happen.

The fact that there are a number of ethical situations that sport participants face is no guarantee that they will respond ethically or that they will
learn ethical behaviour. This is because, as we have seen, people do not
always or perhaps often respond ethically merely by being confronted with
an ethical situation.

Central to any educational endeavour is how to "teach" someone to
see the point of an enterprise—to have them be motivated to act because
to do so matters to the person—and not for other reasons such as fear of
punishment or in order to conform. Since it is possible that someone can
both recognize an ethical situation as one in which help or fairness is at
stake and still not care about this, it is clear that "teaching" ethical behaviour is not a straightforward matter of explaining ethical reasons for
responding in a certain way. If the concern is ethical behaviour and not
merely legal behaviour (see "Rules, Penalties, and Officials" in Section
1), participants must not only be instructed to follow the rules. Attention
must be paid to the effect breaking rules will have on the people in the
contest who may or may not be counting on others to play by the rules.

If sport is to be a vehicle for ethical development, participants must be
able to recognize ethical situations when they arise. As I have said, it is
not possible to respond ethically in an ethical situation if one does not
recognize it as an ethical situation. It is not always obvious, particularly
to young participants, when they might help others or respond fairly or
what might be ethically problematic about their actions. A leader who is
concerned with ethics in sport must take the time to point out these situations to participants. It is important that participants' attention is regularly drawn not just to ethically problematic behaviour. Attention needs
to be drawn as well to those situations in which participants act out of
respect for each other and for officials. Since these situations are less
frequent in sport, a leader will need to be actively engaged in creating
opportunities for these situations to occur.

People often learn about ethical behaviour by attending to the lives
and actions of ethical people. Someone who is admired, as a leader in
sport often is, can change the significance of what might otherwise go
unnoticed. Attempting to see what is compelling to someone who is
admired is an important step in the process of ethics education.

Since participation in sport is only one of many enterprises in which
people engage, it can only be one of many vehicles for the development of
ethical responses. Whether sport will be one of these enterprises largely

depends on the type of environment leaders create and whether leaders are involved both through example and in a deliberate effort to draw attention to the ethical importance of ethical situations as they arise in sport.

BOOK ORGANIZATION

The essays in the first section of this book reflect ethical situations that arise in relation to opponents, while the essays in the second section are concerned with situations that arise from relationships with those on the same team. While there is some overlap in conceptualization with Section 2, the essays in the third section take a different approach. Rather than focus on questions of justification for responding ethically—questions about what is ethically right or good, or what one ought to do—the essays in this section and the essay "Racism As an Ethical Issue in Sport," in Section 2, are concerned, in part, with how some ethical issues and not others gain prominence. It should be clear by the end of Section 3 that sport ethics cannot be limited to the maintenance of game rules or even to obligations to opponents, nor can an understanding of ethics be limited to philosophical ethics. Section 3 and parts of Section 2 explore Sport Ethics through a number of different lenses, including philosophy, sociology, and cultural studies.

If, as I argue in various places in this text, the very structure and expectations of sport create ethical issues for participants both while competing and in preparation for competition, a "new sport ethics" calls upon sport participants to more actively question the commonly held expectations of sport and to refuse them, as well as to call for inclusion into the ethical domain issues that sport ethicists have typically ignored.

REFERENCES

Attfiled, D. (1978). Problems with virtues. *Journal of Moral Education 7*, 75–80.

Beehler, R. (1977). *Moral life*. Oxford, Basil Blackwood.

Bentham, J. (1948). *An introduction to the principles of morals and legislation*, intro. L.J. Lafleur. New York, Hafner Publishing Co.

Kirby, S., Greaves, L. & Hankivsky, O. (2001). *The dome of silence: Sexual harassment and abuse in sport*. Zed Books.

Midgley, M. (1983). *Animals and why they matter*. New York: Penguin Books.

Robinson, L. (1998). *Crossing the line: Violence and sexual assault in Canada's National Sport*. Toronto: McClelland and Stewart.

Shogan, D. 1988. *Care and moral motivation*. Toronto: OISE Press.

Shogan, D. 1999. *The making of high performance athletes: Discipline, diversity, and ethics*. Toronto: University of Toronto Press.

Stocker, M. (1976). The schizophrenia of modern ethical theories. *The Journal of Philosophy* 6: 453–66.

Wolf, S. (1982). Moral saints. *The Journal of Philosophy 77*, 419–39.

RESPONSIBILITIES TO OPPONENTS

INTRODUCTION

Many of the ethical questions in sport ethics are focused on ethical responsibilities opponents have to each other. Issues range from the ethics of taking banned performance-enhancing substances, to acts of violence against opponents, to taking the "good" foul. Responsibilities to opponents in these situations are thought to be based on an agreement by participants to play by the rules of a sport in order to test skills. According to this view, a competitor's ethical responsibility to an opponent emanates from the shared agreement to play by the rules of the game. This agreement to be subjected to the rules, in turn, legitimates the rules and hence the contest itself. That responsibilities to opponents are dependent upon and follow from an agreement to abide by the rules is considered to be analogous to responsibilities people have to each other as a consequence of agreeing to be governed by a social contract (Fielding 1976). Indeed, sports are often seen as exemplary of a social contract (Eassom 1998).

There are a number of difficulties with reducing ethical relationships between opponents to a social contract. There are significant issues related to the structure of rules in sports and how competitors relate to these rules, but it is important not to assume that games of sports can be fully understood by virtue of understanding rules (Eassom 1998, p. 57). Eassom asks why an agreement to play by the rules of a game of sports should "take precedence over other duties that might exist as a result of people already realizing some sort of social existence necessary for the contract condition" (p. 63)? For example, coaches and athletes are often more implicated in a sporting culture that demands that athletes strive to reach the limits of performance than they are with the logic that agreement to play by the rules legitimates the activity in which they are engaged (Shogan 1999, p. 77).

In the last chapter in this first section, "Ethics for Strangers in Sport," I argue that relationships with opponents are governed neither by contract nor often by friendship. Contracts require independent individuals who are able to carry out an agreement without the aid of others (Kittay 1999; Williams 1991). Yet many decisions about keeping or breaking rules in sports are made by those who exercise more power than athletes on teams, such as coaches and administrators. In other words, athletes aren't always in a position to contract to play by the rules by virtue of their position within team structures. If a social contract is the only way to understand one's responsibilities to opponents, athletes cannot be held ethically responsible for actions that may be undertaken at the request of a coach or administrator. On the other hand, expecting athletes to respond to opponents as if they are friends assumes that opponents are important enough to them to care about them as individuals. Unless opponents are also friends, it is not possible to know enough about them to care that, as individuals, they are treated well and fairly. It is possible, however, to be concerned about fulfilling a duty to respond to the principles of fair treatment and helping.

As I indicate in "Ethics for Strangers in Sport," strangers in sports are not only those one meets in competition. They are also those who are affected by decisions as one prepares for competition—people one may not ever encounter as a consequence of decisions one makes to, say, take banned performance-enhancing substances or recruit illegally. As I show in "Ethics for Strangers in Sport," an ethic of duty does not require that someone else enter into an agreement with you before an ethical responsibility is recognized. Responding to a recognized duty to fulfill principles of fairness and helping can be carried out by individuals regardless of what others do.

When responsibilities to opponents are reduced to a social contract, notice is not given to what a contract actually expects people to do or not do. When the ethical injunction is related to the fact that an agreement was made to abide by the rules—no matter what the rules require—compliance with the rules may be ethically problematic. Since the content of what is required by rules may be harmful in some way to others, it is necessary to assess what the rules expect participants to do or not do. For example, for some the actions required by bullfighting or kick-boxing are ethically problematic as are rules that disallow certain people from participating. Whites-only representative teams in apartheid South Africa were legal according to the laws of the land, but also unethical. Similarly, it is possible to question the ethics of sports that rule out children by utilizing equipment that is too heavy or too large or playing fields that are too big.

Eassom (1998) is correct to say that rules don't tell us everything of importance about games of sports. However, games of sports can tell us a great deal about how rules work, not just in sports but as exemplars of how other constraints work in our everyday lives, including our interactions with others. As I explain in the first two chapters in this section— "Rules, Penalties, and Officials" and "Characterizing Constraints of Leisure"—rules or constraints set the parameters within which actions and experiences occur. They set these parameters by prescribing certain actions, proscribing other actions, and describing boundaries or contexts within which these actions make sense. This does not mean that in sports or other life endeavours that these constraints bind people without any room to manoeuvre. It does mean, however, that human culture is bound or constituted by constraints. There is no such thing as a human activity without rules or constraints. By understanding how rules work in games of sports, it is possible to have a better understanding of how other enterprises are constituted by constraints and how these in turn affect how we interact with each other. "Characterizing Constraints of Leisure" revisits the logic of game rules presented in "Rules, Penalties, and Officials," but with a different emphasis. In this chapter I am interested in elaborating how rules as constraints enable actions (in this case skills) as well as how they limit action and how the introduction of enabling rules (constraints) can be utilized to improve opportunities for participation in sports.

Rather than recognize ethical responsibilities to opponents, many competitors see opponents as obstacles to out-manoeuvre.[1] Regardless of the level of intensity of competitive sports, players are usually interested in achieving the goal of the activity. In a basketball contest, for example, the goal is to score points while stopping the opponent from scoring points. Most of the decisions a player will make in a basketball contest are decisions about how to enhance the likelihood of achieving this goal. That is to say that almost all decisions are self-interested or prudential decisions. Acting from self-interest in most of these situations is not ethically problematic since decisions to achieve the goal of a game do not usually significantly affect the welfare or fair treatment of others. If a player decides to drive to the basket rather than shoot the ball from a distance, there is an effect on the opponent, but the effect is of no ethical importance. To refrain from making a decision to enhance oneself in a situation of this type is to trivialize ethics. Prudential decisions are ethically problematic, however, when others are harmed or treated unfairly as a result of self-interested decisions.

Both prudential and ethical decisions can be said to be rational decisions if they coincide with one's goals. If a football player says, for example, that his goal is to compete with others while respecting their rights, but he regularly harms others in order to gain an advantage, we can say that the means that this person uses are not rational given his stated goal. However, if his goal is to always be at an advantage regardless of harm to others, then decisions to achieve this goal, including decisions to harm others, are rational decisions. To deliberately harm another is to do something that is unethical, but it is not to do something that is irrational as long as the player's goal is to be declared the winner of the contest. To deliberately harm another is irrational when one's goal is to compete while taking into account the welfare and fair treatment of others.

There are times, however, when acting to fulfill a goal based on self-interest paradoxically turns out to be irrational. There are instances when an attempt by two opposing individuals or groups to maximize outcomes leads to a situation that is not the best outcome for either. This paradox, called the prisoner's dilemma after the anecdote used to describe the game, has the following features:

Two prisoners are charged with the same crime of which they will be convicted only if one of them confesses. The prisoners are told that if they both confess to the crime, they will both receive five years in jail. If neither confesses, some trumped-up evidence will put them both in jail for three years. If one confesses while the other does not, the one who confesses will receive one year in jail and the one who does not confess will receive 10 years in jail.

If both confess, the worst outcome for each prisoner is to spend five years in jail. The best outcome is to spend one year in jail, but this will occur only if one prisoner can trick the other into confessing while he or she does not. By not confessing, the worst outcome is to spend 10 years in jail. This happens when one prisoner believes that the other prisoner will not confess and is duped into not confessing while the other prisoner confesses. The best outcome for both is to spend three years in jail. This can happen only if neither confesses.

	Best Outcome	Worst Outcome
Confess	One year in jail	Five years in jail
Don't confess	10 years in jail	Three years in jail

Since each prisoner attempts to create the best self-interested outcome, each confesses to the crime and each receives five years in jail. The paradox is that by attempting to create the best possible self-interested outcome, each prisoner is left with an outcome that is not the best for anyone. The best outcome for both would be not to confess and receive three years in jail, but because each prisoner knows that the other is attempting to create the best possible self-interested outcome, each chooses to confess for fear that the other will confess. Each knows that if one confesses and the other does not, the one who does not confess will be sentenced to 10 years in jail while the other will be released after only one year. Neither wants to be trapped in this outcome.

Although the example of the prisoner's dilemma is contrived to make the point, one does not need to look far to see the paradox of the prisoner's dilemma in actual situations in our lives. Problems with pollution, overpopulation, conservation, and disarmament are all exacerbated by the fact that individual decision makers do not trust others. For example, for a large company to spend the millions of dollars it would cost to control pollution emissions, those in charge would have to trust that competing companies will also control their emissions. If a competing company does not control emissions, this company will be able to produce products for less money. Company managers do not trust decision makers in other companies to spend the money necessary for pollution control, so they make decisions that result in pollution of our air, rivers, and oceans. Everyone, including those who make the decisions, is in a worse position since everyone is affected by the pollution of the Earth's resources.

When the goal of participants in competitive sports is to be declared the winner of a contest regardless of the effects of their decisions on others, they become game theorists in the mathematical sense of that term. When win–loss records, medals, and trophies accumulate, and championships and scoring races won are what are important in sports, participants are likely to become trapped in the prisoner's dilemma. Prudential decision making requires you to take advantage of others before they take advantage of you. An environment is created in which no one trusts anyone else. Banned performance-enhancing substances may be a good example in sports of how these work. Some athletes who use banned substances do not trust that opponents will refrain from using them and consequently feel compelled to use banned substances for fear of being less competitive. To refrain from using these substances is to risk having one's strategy weakened and one's outcome minimized. Paradoxically, however, participants who feel that they must use banned substances in order to compete may be in a worse position with respect to other concerns such as health. It may very well be that there are few individuals competing in international weightlifting and throwing events who do not take banned substances with the effect that someone who chooses not to use these substances may have difficulty staying competitive.

Chapter 3, "The Paradox of Sport Activities in the Wilderness"[2] demonstrates the paradox of acting solely from self-interest. I have included this chapter in this section because it exemplifies how rational attempts to maximize personal benefits can sometimes lead to consequences that are paradoxically neither personally beneficial nor beneficial for others. Moreover, in some situations acting ethically by paying attention to the welfare and fair treatment of all sentient beings in the situation leads to greater benefits for oneself. While this chapter is not about responsibilities to opponents in games of sports, it is about responsibilities to others with whom we share the Earth.

Chapter 2, "Characterizing Constraints of Leisure" is reprinted as it appeared in *Leisure Studies* in 2002. Chapters 1 and 3 have been revised in minor ways and with updated examples. If I were writing these pieces for the first time now, I would situate participants' decision making within the cultural contexts within which these decisions are made. For those in high-performance sport, for example, it is important to understand how the discipline of sport narrows the range of decisions available to athletes (Shogan 1999). This is similar to the point I made earlier in this introduction that athletes are not enabled within sport structures to make independent decisions—either to contract with opponents to abide by rules or to outwit them in an attempt to maximize self-interest. Even so, these three chapters do capture some of the ethos of winning in competitive sports, even if it isn't often athletes who make the decisions. Chapter 4, "Ethics for Strangers in Sport," is reprised from an earlier essay (Shogan 1993) in which I explored responsibilities to people one may never know and seldom encounter but to whom one nevertheless may have ethical responsibilities.

NOTES

1   This section is abridged from Shogan (1988a).
2   This chapter has been adapted from Shogan (1988b).

REFERENCES

Brown, W. (1980). Ethics, drugs, and sport. *Journal of the Philosophy of Sport 7*, 15–23.

Brown, W. (2001). Paternalism, drugs, and the nature of sport. In W.J. Morgan, K. Meier, and A. Schneider (Eds.), *Ethics & sport*, 130–141. London and New York: E & FN Spoon.

Eassom, S. (1998). Games, rules, contracts. In M. McNamee and S. Perry (Eds.), *Ethics in sport* (pp. 57–78). Champaign: Human Kinetics Publishers.

Fielding, M. (1976). Against competition. *Proceedings of the Philosophy of Education Society of Great Britain 10*, 140–141.

Kittay, E. (1999). *Love's labor*. New York: Routledge.

Shogan, D. (1988a). The prisoner's dilemma in competitive sport: Moral decision-making vs. prudence. In P.J. Galasso (Ed.), *Philosophy of sport and physical activity* (pp. 343–351). Toronto: Canadian Scholars' Press Inc.

Shogan, D. (1988b). The paradox of physical activity in the wilderness. In P.J. Galasso (Ed.), *Philosophy of sport and physical activity* (pp. 210–215). Toronto: Canadian Scholars' Press Inc.

Shogan, D. (1993). A feminist ethics for strangers. In D. Shogan (Ed.), *A reader in feminist ethics* (pp. 171–184). Toronto: Canadian Scholars' Press Inc.

Shogan, D. (1999). *The making of high-performance athletes: Discipline, diversity, and ethics*. Toronto: University of Toronto Press.

Teuber, A. (1982). Simone Weil: Equality as compassion. *Philosophy and Phenomenological Research 43*, 221–237.

Williams, P. (1991). *The alchemy of race and rights*. Boston: Harvard University Press.

1

RULES, PENALTIES,

AND OFFICIALS

In this chapter I show how examples from sport can be helpful in clarifying conceptual distinctions between what is legal and what is ethical. To accomplish this I say something about constitutive rules, the role of officials, and the logical status of penalties including the "good" penalty. As well, I consider whether there is ever any justification for breaking rules.

RULES

There are a number of different rules associated with games of sport. Regulatory rules, which indicate such things as size and placement of numbers on uniforms and stipulations regarding submission of team line-ups prior to contests, make it possible to administer games of sport more efficiently. Regulatory rules are very important in highly competitive contests and are much less important in casual contests. All games, whether highly competitive or casual, are distinguished by their *constitutive* rules. Constitutive rules have descriptive, prescriptive, and proscriptive functions all of which serve to outline what a particular game is. *Descriptive rules* describe the dimensions of the playing area and specifications about equipment size and shape. Descriptive rules in basketball, for example, describe the dimensions of the court, the height of the basket, the size of the ball, and so on. The game of basketball would be much differently constituted if these features were described in significantly different ways— for example, a 12-foot or a 6-foot basket. *Prescriptive rules* prescribe those actions that a participant may perform when engaged in a particular game. Prescriptive rules in basketball indicate what entails a shot at the basket, what dribbling the ball is, what a sideline throw-in is, and so on. *Proscriptive rules*, on the other hand, proscribe actions that a participant must *not* perform when engaged in a particular game. Proscriptive rules in basketball include that one must not go outside of certain boundaries, that one must not stand in the key area longer than three seconds, and that one must not bump one's opponent when he or she is shooting the ball at the basket.

There is an important relationship among descriptive, prescriptive, and proscriptive rules. When James Naismith invented the game of basketball there were no sidelines. Players often chased the ball into the running track adjacent to or above the gym. Significant time was spent chasing, and sometimes wrestling for the ball rather than on attempting to shoot it into one of the peach baskets. The creation of descriptive rules that set out boundaries within which the game was to be played, as well as proscriptive rules that indicated that players must not cause the ball to go outside these specified boundaries, made it possible for players to attend to the prescriptive skills of the games such as dribbling, passing, and shooting.

In most sports, the number of proscriptive rules has increased as participants devise ways of making it difficult for opponents to carry out prescriptive skills. I am reminded of a Herman comic in which Herman, prone in front of the golf pin, says, "there's nothing in the rule book that says I can't stay here." By stretching out in front of the pin, Herman prevents his opponent from carrying out the prescriptive rule that indicates that players are to play the ball into the hole by successive strokes. If Herman, and others, do this action often enough, it forces rule makers to add a proscriptive rule prohibiting lying in front of the pin as well as an indication of how someone who breaks the rule will be penalized.

The descriptive, prescriptive, and proscriptive rules of most sports are ethically neutral. In most sports, rules constitute activities that are ethically neutral—jumping over bars, throwing implements, aiming for targets. Actions that harm others are proscribed in almost all sport. In hockey, for example, hitting others with your hockey stick is a proscribed action. In boxing actions that may harm others are, on the other hand, prescribed by rules. By definition someone is not boxing unless he or she directs blows toward another's body, or at least, this person cannot win at boxing unless these actions are undertaken. Those who box and, in doing so, conform to the prescriptive rules of boxing are engaged in legal behaviour. Some would argue, however, that by conforming to the prescriptive rules of boxing, the boxer, while doing nothing illegal, is nevertheless engaged in an activity that is ethically problematic, since the rules prescribe actions that are potentially harmful. The rule-governed practice of boxing helps us to see that rules as such do not confer ethical status on a practice.

PENALTIES, PUNISHMENT, AND THE ROLE OF THE OFFICIAL

Penalties and Punishment

Whereas proscriptive rules (Do not do this) can be broken, it is more appropriate to refer to the *non-performance* of prescriptive rules and the *non-compliance* with descriptive rules than indicate that prescriptive or descriptive rules can be broken. The non-performance of a prescriptive rule may be an indication that a player is unskilled or unknowledgeable about when to use a skill in a game. For example, a participant in a basketball game may not shoot the ball at the basket when unguarded because he doesn't recognize that he is not defended or because he is unable to shoot the ball well enough from that distance. Non-performance of certain skills may also be a tactic used in certain game situations. In basketball, for example, not attempting to shoot the ball at the basket late in the game to avoid giving up the ball to the opponent is a tactical non-performance of prescriptive rules. However, while an individual may not perform a skill or a team may decline to perform specific skills in tactical situations, some players must be performing at least some of the prescribed skills of the game during each play phase or we would be hard pressed to say that there was a game happening.

There are a number of potential ethical issues that arise from the non-performance of skills in particular situations. For example, it is ethically problematic for athletes not to perform skills in expected situations in order to fix a game. It is ethically suspect to not perform to the level one is capable of performing in order to lose a match and receive a better match-up in a tournament or draw, as sometimes happens in curling. In the final game of the 2006 NBA season, the Los Angeles Clippers were alleged to have deliberately lost a game in order that in the first round of the playoffs they would be matched up against the Denver Nuggets, a team they had consistently defeated in the regular season. In the playoff series with the Phoenix Suns, Los Angeles Lakers' star, Kobe Bryant, was charged with quitting on his teammates when, in the final game of the series, he shot the ball only three times. On the other hand, in the 2006 Winter Olympics, the Canadian Women's Hockey Team was criticized for running up the score against weaker teams. There was an expectation by some that they should not fully perform their prescriptive skills against these teams.

In almost all sports, the non-performance of prescriptive rules does not have a concomitant penalty. The basketball rule book, for example, indicates what entails a shot at the basket. There is no penalty for not taking a shot during a game, or for missing a shot when one is attempted. Although there are occasions when not shooting the ball is tactically inappropriate, there are no penalties administered by game officials for not recognizing when a prescriptive rule of this kind is appropriate. There is at least one exception to this relationship between prescriptive rules and penalties. In synchronized swimming there are required elements by each individual or team. If a required element is attempted but not completed according to the prescription, a penalty is assigned.[1]

To break a proscriptive rule is to do something the rules indicate must not be done. If a proscribed rule is broken with no loss to the rule breaker, the rule is empty. If, for example, a proscriptive rule indicates that a player must not touch the game ball with the feet, but the game is allowed to proceed whenever the game ball is touched with the feet, it quickly becomes clear to players that this is not a proscriptive rule at all or, at least, not one to be taken seriously. If, however, the rule is not taken seriously and players use their feet, the game is no longer the same game. In order that proscriptive rules will be taken seriously, a penalty must be invoked when a proscriptive rule is broken.

Penalties ensure that the game, as circumscribed by its proscriptive rules, can continue within those boundaries at that time and in the future. Logically, a penalty is a good penalty if it corrects the inequity created when the rule is broken. In other words, game penalties must be *retributive* in order to restore order to the game.[2] Order is restored to a game when rule breakers are punished. Although they are conceptually related, a penalty and punishment are not the same. A penalty is concomitant to a proscriptive rule, both of which are written into the rule book. There must be a formal indication of what the punishment will be in the event that a rule is broken so that participants understand that proscriptive rules are to be taken seriously as proscriptive rules. This formal indication is the penalty that is indicated in the rule book. The penalty is invoked by punishing an offender when a proscriptive rule is broken.

It is important to note that penalties are invoked both for infractions (such as stepping out of bounds) and for fouls (such as bumping someone attempting a shot in basketball) and they are invoked for both accidental and deliberate rule breakages. Someone cannot avoid the punishment stipulated by a penalty by claiming that a rule breakage is accidental.

The outcome of games can be affected by altering equipment and boundaries established by descriptive rules, and consequently proscriptive rules have been enacted that prohibit alterations to playing dimensions and equipment size. In addition to the descriptive rule in ice hockey that stipulates the thickness of goalie pads, for example, there is a proscriptive rule that indicates that this thickness must not be altered. And, since there is a proscriptive rule prohibiting alteration of pad size, there is also a penalty that specifies what will be the punishment if the proscriptive rule is transgressed.

The "Good" Penalty

Among the tactics of coaches and players in highly competitive games of sport is calculating how and when to deliberately break certain rules with the intention of being detected by an official for doing so. When reference is made to the actual rule breakage, this tactic is called a "good" foul or a "good" infraction and, when reference is made to the penalty that is invoked, the tactic is called a "good" penalty. When, for example, a basketball player deliberately fouls an opponent near the end of a game and, by doing so, sends this person to the foul line, this is often referred to as a "good" foul because, if the opponent misses the foul shots, there is an opportunity for the fouling team to regain possession of the ball for another attempt to score a basket. The penalty for breaking the rule is thought to be a "good" penalty to take under the circumstances because there is a chance that the team will benefit from doing so and because the team will be at a disadvantage if the rule is not broken and the penalty is not invoked. The violator wants to be discovered breaking the proscriptive rule because it is to his or her advantage to have the penalty invoked rather than to have play go on.

These situations arise because the punishment incurred by invoking the penalty may not be as severe as the consequences if the rule is not broken (bringing a player down on a breakaway in hockey), or because the administration of the penalty makes possible a benefit (obtaining ball possession from missed foul shots late in a basketball game). "Good" fouls occur in games and "good" penalties are accepted because the penalties are not commensurate with the rule breakage. They are not retributive. There would be no "good" penalty if, for example, the penalty for deliberately fouling in order to stop the clock was to award the opponent the two free shots as well as ball possession; nor would there be a "good" penalty if, after taking a player down on a breakaway, a goal was awarded to the fouled team. If players were punished rather than potentially rewarded, as the logic of penalties demands, there would be no "good" penalties. There may be other very good reasons for not changing the rules to make all penalties retributive. These are not related to the logic of rules but to the culture of the sport in which having the knowledge and skill to utilize rule breakage to gain an advantage adds to the excitement of the sport.

The Role of the Official

The legal conduct of game players can be achieved through retributive penalties, but the ethical conduct of game players cannot. Ethical retribution cannot be achieved in games because there is no independent system of ethical punishment apart from the legal system of punishment. Officials are responsible for legal transgressions, but not for ethical transgressions. Even if punishment for an ethical offence operated independently from the punishment of a legal offence with independent authorities responsible for ethical breaches, it is not clear what, if anything, would qualify as punishment for an ethical wrongdoing. Commensurability of punishment occurs when the punishment is severe enough to ensure that the rule breaker is at a disadvantage for having broken a game rule, but without making the penalty so severe that participants are discouraged from playing the game at all. It is not possible to construct a system of ethically retributive penalties in a game because it is not clear just what type of punishment is equal to the harm experienced by someone for, say, bringing an opponent down on a breakaway or by deceiving someone by moving your golf ball by hand up the fairway.

When a game rule is deliberately broken, ethical wrongdoing often coincides with legal wrongdoing, but punishment administered by officials is legal punishment and not ethical punishment. The individual is punished for breaking a game rule and not for treating an opponent unfairly. In some instances, the breaker of the rule may be judged ethically, but penalties associated with game rules do not attribute ethical blame.

Retributive penalties do not assure the ethical conduct of game players, although they do assure legal conduct. Ethical conduct is based on motivation to respond in such a way that others are treated well or fairly. Ethical conduct of game players is a complex process that involves much more than the administration of game penalties. A coach concerned with ethical development might further punish a player for an ethical transgression by benching the player. Or, the coach may discuss the incident with the player, pointing out the ethical harm. In either case, the purpose is not necessarily to punish the player but to teach. The purpose of the legal authority—the official—is to punish the wrongdoer.[3]

DELIBERATELY UNDERMINING RULES: LEGALITY AND ETHICS

In this section I am interested in whether there is ever any legal or ethical justification for breaking game rules. There is no legal justification for someone to break a game rule whether deliberately, accidentally, or from ignorance. This is because rules are to apply equally to everyone involved in an enterprise. It is not, therefore, the prerogative of someone to decide that a particular rule will not apply to her in a particular situation while it is to apply to others. There is, however, ethical justification for breaking or undermining rules when rules prescribe activities that harm people in some way or when rules proscribe some people from accessing activities.

The way in which rules may be justifiably undermined differs according to whether the ethically objectionable rule is prescriptive or proscriptive. When one breaks a proscriptive rule for ethical reasons, it is important to continue to show respect for legal procedures. When breaking a rule, the rule must be broken publicly and not surreptitiously. This is accomplished by accepting the punishment dictated by the penalty. Punishment is accepted in order to respect legal procedures and to force those who would punish the illegal action to engage in a discussion about the ethics of the rule. When Kathrine Switzer broke the proscriptive rule against women participating in the Boston Marathon, for example, she did something illegal, but in doing so she forced sport officials to engage in discussion about the ethics of excluding women from this event.

The Kathrine Switzer example shows that in some situations there may be justification in breaking proscriptive rules when they unjustly prevent certain people from being participants.[4] While there may be prudential or cultural justification for breaking game rules, there is no ethical justification for breaking rules, as long as abiding by the rules does not conflict with something of ethical importance. For example, there is obviously justification for a race car driver to break the rule that drivers must stay on the racetrack in order to avoid hitting someone who has wandered onto the track, whereas there is no ethical justification for deciding that the rule against moving one's golf ball by hand up the fairway will not apply to oneself while it applies to everyone else.

I am interested in whether there are opportunities in sport for acts of civil disobedience when one believes that a rule is unethical. It is helpful to explore this issue by looking at rules proscribing performance-enhancing substances. Some argue on ethical grounds that there should be no rule against taking performance-enhancing substances because the rule abrogates an individual's freedom to make choices about how far he or she wishes to push the limits of performance. If someone exhausts the normal procedures for changing rules that proscribe performance-enhancing substances such as appeals to governing bodies and motions at rules meetings, the next step is to deliberately break the rule in a public way in order to show respect for rules generally and in order to make those who enforce the subsequent penalty to discuss the ethical justification of the rule. Someone is not engaged in civil disobedience if he or she believes that rules against performance-enhancing drugs are unethical, but nevertheless disguises their use in order to avoid punishment. I know of no cases of someone using a banned substance for purposes of civil disobedience, nor am I aware of anyone who has used performance-enhancing drugs in order to be punished, thus opening up a discussion about whether it is unethical to limit adults' choices about these substances.

If one disagrees on ethical grounds with prescriptive rules of an activity, he or she must withdraw from the activity and attempt to undermine the rules from the outside. To participate is to perform the prescribed skills one finds ethically objectionable. It would be impossible to take up boxing, for example, with the intent of "breaking" the prescriptive rules of boxing because to take up boxing is to perform these prescriptive rules and to "break" these rules is to not box at all. Action designed to alter or abolish perceived unethical prescriptive rules must occur outside the practice itself. If one believes that certain practices or enterprises are unethical, withdrawal or separation from the activity is what is ethically required. To continue to be involved is to be complicit since it entails participating in the very prescriptive rules that one finds objectionable. One can only choose not to participate—a response that is ethically significant.

CLOSING REMARKS

Ethics courses, including sport ethics courses, can help with conceptual distinctions between what is ethical and what is legal. It is important to note, however, that being able to make these distinctions is not a guarantee of how someone will act. An ethical conversion from taking an ethics course is as unlikely as an ethical conversion from participating in sport. Ethical behaviour involves regular attention to matters that might include ethics courses and sport participation, but go beyond these as well. Using sport examples may help to understand ethics, but understanding ethics is not sufficient or perhaps even necessary to being an ethical person in sport or elsewhere. This is because to understand the ethical domain is an intellectual ability that both ethical and unethical people may possess. Much depends on whether this understanding counts with a person and whether it counts enough to motivate behaviour.

NOTES

1   I am grateful to Vanessa Bray for this example.
2   There is no agreement that penalties for breaking societal laws should be retributive. Some argue, for example, that the purpose of "punishment" is rehabilitation.
3   In some other legal systems the role of the legal authority is similar to the role of the legal authority in games. If someone plagiarizes another's work in university, for example, there must be a penalty if a rule against plagiarism is to be taken seriously. It is the role of the official to punish those who plagiarize. The role of a legal authority with respect to state laws is not as straightforward. Some argue that the purpose of legal procedures, including the role of legal authorities, is to rehabilitate and not to seek retribution.
4   Some activities are interesting only as contests because of rules that proscribe certain participants from taking part. For example, rules that create weight divisions in wrestling make it possible for a wide range of people to wrestle.

2   CHARACTERIZING CONSTRAINTS

OF LEISURE

INTRODUCTION

This chapter's title, "Characterizing Constraints of Leisure," has two meanings that underscore two purposes for this chapter. The title is intended to suggest that constraints structure or characterize leisure and to invite other ways of understanding or characterizing constraints. Both these meanings are explored in this paper by taking up French intellectual Michel Foucault's (1926–1984) work on social constraints.

While there has been a recognition in the leisure constraints literature that constraints function in more than one way to intervene between a leisure experience and participation (Jackson 1988), constraints are typically understood in this literature as restricting or limiting. In 1988, Jackson proposed that "constraints per se are best viewed as a subset of reasons for not engaging in particular behaviour" (1988, p. 211) and, more than 10 years later, Shaw (1999, p. 274) agreed that constraints are factors that may prevent, reduce, or modify participation, or may adversely affect the quality of enjoyment of leisure activities.[1]

Challenges to the assumption that leisure constraints restrict leisure participation have taken into account the ways in which people negotiate constraints, but constraints in these accounts nevertheless have been understood as wholly negative or restricting (Kay & Jackson 1991; Shaw et al. 1991). Feminist work, like that of Henderson et al. (1996), has made it possible to begin to conceptualize constraints differently by recognizing that a constraint such as an "ethic of care" both enables and restricts women in their leisure. In this chapter, I extend this insight about constraints as potentially enabling as well as restricting and argue that enhancing leisure experiences may at times involve ensuring that certain enabling constraints are present rather than merely removing restricting ones.

In order to provide a theoretical backing for the claim that constraints are enabling as well as restricting, the work of Michel Foucault is examined.

The focus of Foucault's work was on the emergence of modern institutions, such as asylums, prisons, hospitals, and schools, and the forms of governance associated with them (Usher & Edwards 1994, p. 82). For Foucault, modernity signalled a shift to a modern form of power comprised of procedures, practices, and expert inquiries. By detailing these procedures, Foucault (1980a, p. 104) showed how modern or disciplinary power is "possessed of highly specific procedural techniques ... [and] presupposes a tightly knit grid of material coercions rather than the physical existence of a sovereign." Power, according to Foucault, is to be understood in relation to social constraints (Fraser 1989, p. 20). Whereas constraints are often thought to be restrictions imposed by someone who possesses more power and who uses these constraints to limit the actions of others who have less or no power, Foucault argued that power and hence social constraint is productive. Foucault (1980b, p. 119) showed that power "produces things, it induces pleasure, forms knowledge, produces discourse." Social constraint as power is productive and, therefore, never wholly limiting.[2]

The enabling and restricting effects of social constraints can be demonstrated by first examining how leisure activities and experiences are structured. By looking at the structure of leisure activities and experiences, it is possible to see how the constraints that comprise structures impact on whether and how participants will be restricted or enabled in their experience of a particular leisure activity. As a way to emphasize that social constraints may be enabling of leisure experience, Foucault's work is used to demonstrate how constraints enable skill within a structure. Finally, the structural constraints of identity that impact on participation prior to engagement with a leisure experience are examined.

Barriers to leisure and not the structure[3] of leisure experiences have been the focus of most research on leisure constraints. As Goodale and Witt (1989, p. 421) note, "concern about barriers, nonparticipation in recreation activities, and lack of leisure opportunities have always been an important progenitor of park, recreation, and leisure services." Since identification and amelioration of restrictions to leisure was the purpose of researchers interested in these services, it was not part of their project to also conceptualize constraints as enabling. What I hope to show is that by thinking about barriers as structures that enable and restrict, it may be possible to think about constraints differently.

CONSTRAINTS OF STRUCTURE:
THE EXAMPLE OF RULES OF GAMES

It is not the absence of socially produced rules and constraints that characterize leisure: rather it is their presence. (Gruneau 1984, p. 120)

Like constraints that structure other enterprises, rules of games set the
parameters within which actions and experiences occur. They do this by
prescribing certain actions, *proscribing* other actions, and *describing*
boundaries or contexts within which these actions make sense. Prescriptive
rules or constraints of the game of table tennis, for example, produce
particular actions by specifying what is to count as a skill, say, a volley
or a serve. Proscriptive rules or constraints circumscribe these skills by
placing limitations on what counts as a serve or a volley: hitting the net
when serving, for example, does not count as a legitimate serve.
"Descriptive rules" circumscribe action by controlling the space and time
in which the game is to be played and by placing stipulations on the equipment to be used. In table tennis the length of the table, height of the net,
and texture and size of the ball circumscribe participants' actions.

"Proscriptive constraints" restrict participants by virtue of ruling out
certain experiences from a particular leisure practice. If one is golfing, for
example, one is restricted from throwing the ball toward the hole. But this
restriction also enables someone engaged in this leisure experience to test
his or her skills of hitting the golf ball with a golf club. Although prohibiting some actions, proscriptive constraints make other actions possible. The
extent to which options are restricted for participants by proscriptive
constraints depends upon how many of these constraints are imposed and/or
accepted by a participant and just what experiences are proscribed. Too
few proscriptions will likely result in chaos (anything goes) yet too many
proscriptions create such rigidity that the experience may not be worth
participation. What actions are proscribed is also important. A single
constraint that proscribes leaving one's home after 7:00 p.m. may be more
limiting of action than 10 traffic rules. Likewise, a few proscriptive game
rules that severely limit movement are more limiting of action than a number
of rules that prohibit movement in relation to boundary lines.

Increasing options for participation is not just a matter of removing (in
this case) proscriptive constraints since at least some proscriptive constraints
are necessary in order that prescribed actions can be undertaken in an

unchaotic environment. When a chaotic environment impedes participants' actions, adding proscriptive constraints enables participants as they attempt the prescribed experiences of the leisure practice.

Proscriptive rules have been added to games over a period of time, not in order to inflict participants with ever more limitations on their actions (although this has been an effect) but to enable participants to perform prescribed actions. Accepting limitations on actions in order to enable other actions is not unique to games, of course. Drivers of automobiles accept limitations on their actions as they drive in order to enable them to arrive unscathed at desired destinations; musicians accept limitations on what notes they will play in order to be able to play a particular musical score; academics rule out certain kinds of writing in order to make an academic text possible.

For each person in each activity or experience, there are an optimum number and kind of proscriptive constraints that enable the prescriptive skills of the endeavour to be attempted with some level of challenge. What this optimum is varies with abilities or skills participants already have. Some will find certain proscriptive constraints more limiting of their action than will others. For example, a strong skater in ice hockey benefits from a proscription that limits holding an opponent in a race for the puck whereas a weaker skater will be restricted.

Prescriptive constraints are enabling of action because they create the actual experiences in which a participant engages. The effect of removing all prescriptive constraints would be the elimination of action or experience altogether. For example, prescriptive constraints of the game of chess set out what is a legitimate move and prescriptive constraints of bird watching set out certain experiences to be constitutive of this practice (sighting a bird in a tree rather than on a television show). Prescriptive constraints enable action by establishing the specifications of actions. If prescriptive constraints were removed from an activity, there would literally be nothing to do.

Prescriptive constraints do also limit action, however, by circumscribing the range of actions possible. The prescriptive rules of basketball, for example, limit possible actions performed with the basketball to dribbling, passing, and shooting. Heading the ball, although not proscribed in basketball, is not an actual possibility for action as long as participants are serious about attempting to shoot the ball into the basket more times than the opponent. Prescriptive constraints set out experiences in which a participant may engage and, in doing so, a range of other experiences are excluded as possibilities.

Removing certain prescriptive constraints might enable some to act more skillfully in sport in which they are unskilled—removing, for example, the rule that prescribes "spiking" in volleyball may make it possible for longer rallies. It is also possible to enable skill by *adding* prescriptive constraints that correspond to abilities some participants already have. For example, prescribing skills that require flexibility rather than strength may enable more women to engage in leisure experiences.

Descriptive constraints are those constraints that establish the contextual, physical boundaries within which a leisure practice occurs as well as the equipment that is used. Like prescriptive constraints, descriptive constraints can restrict participants by eliminating other possibilities (one shoots the ball at the net in soccer in the way one does and not in other ways because of the size and shape of the net). As well, by creating certain physical boundaries for participation, descriptive constraints often make it difficult for some to participate. Many activities requiring physical skill are activities whose descriptive constraints create actions in which only a few people of a certain body size and strength can attain enjoyment or hope to remain as participants at championship levels. The 10-foot vertical target in basketball restricts the participation of children and shorter adults, for example.

Since descriptive constraints both restrict and enable leisure choices, increasing opportunities for leisure experiences cannot simply be a matter of removing these constraints. Changing, not removing, the field, goal, and ball size constraints in soccer, for example, is enabling of children's participation. As with proscriptive and prescriptive constraints, removing some descriptive constraints and adding others may enable some while restricting other participants. Three-par golf courses, for example, make it possible for some participants to experience some success while restricting the experiences of those players who have a range of golf skills.

Descriptive constraints of leisure go beyond the particular boundaries and equipment constraints of a leisure experience. Descriptive constraints also include the social context within which a leisure experience occurs. An experience of downhill skiing, for example, is not often only a matter of performing requisite constitutive skills and not others with certain pieces of necessary equipment on a hill with snow. Skiing and other leisure experiences often occur in a context of consumerism in which leisure experiences are purchased. What options are available is dependent on how much variation is created by commercial leisure agencies. Moreover, other social categories such as class, race, and gender affect whether particular social constraints will be enabling or restricting for a particular individual. I say more about these constraints of identity later in the chapter. First, however, in order to emphasize further the enabling effects of constraints, I say something about constraints that enable abilities within a structure.

CONSTRAINTS OF SKILL

In the previous section, it was outlined how what counts as an action in a game and other enterprises is circumscribed by constraints that frame possibilities for participants' actions. However, acquiring skill to undertake these actions requires still other constraints. Foucault showed how large numbers of people became skilled participants in factories, schools, workplaces, armies, hospitals, and prisons by being subjected to constraints, which organized the time and space within which they performed designated tasks. In this section, some of the constraints that control time, space, and movement are detailed in order to show that constraints are essential to the acquisition of even minimal skill in order to enable participation in leisure activities or experiences.

The acquisition of skills in a leisure pursuit relies on the organization of space or what Foucault (1979) referred to as an "art of distribution." Constraints that make up "the art of distribution"—constraints that organize enclosure, partitioning, function, and rank—make it possible for participants to learn and use skills continuously and without interruption. Participants must understand ways in which boundary lines, target dimensions, and equipment constrain the use of space and consequently how skills, then, are enabled and limited by these constraints.

In order for participants to acquire a bodily understanding of the space within which they engage, they accept constraints that separate the practice space from those not engaged in the learning session. It is important to *enclose* space and in so doing specify it as different from other space to "derive the maximum advantages and to neutralize the inconveniences" (Foucault 1979, p. 142). This enclosed practice space is often further subdivided when skills are acquired with others. *Partitioning* eliminates "the uncontrolled disappearance of individuals, their diffuse circulation, their unusable and dangerous coagulation" (Foucault 1979, p. 143). The advantages of partitioning, as Foucault describes it, are that it aims to "establish presences and absences, to know where and how to locate individuals, to set up useful communications, to interrupt others, to be able at each moment to supervise the conduct of each individual, to assess it, judge it, calculate its qualities of merits" (Foucault 1979, p. 143).

By accepting constraints that distribute them into spaces within the larger enclosure, participants are enabled to increase opportunities for practice of skills. Instances are avoided in which they watch others perform while they wait their turn. As well, movements that are extraneous to the skill are eliminated. When practising shooting at the basket in basketball, participants accept constraints that station them close to baskets, thus eliminating the necessity of moving to the basket for each shot or shooting from a spot that would not likely occur in a game. And, in accepting these partitioning constraints, participants are enabled to hone their skills.

Enclosures within larger enclosures are *functional sites* (Foucault 1979, p. 144). Participants accept constraints that make it possible for them to acquire skills in relation to their function in the dance, in the orchestra, or on the team. Constraining participants into designated spaces for skill acquisition allows the *ranking* of participants for intervention by instructors, which further enables skill development. For example, in a weight-training room, the particular exercise sites remain fixed and participants move as they acquire skill or need remedial work on skill.

Participants not only accept constraints of space in order to acquire skill, they accept constraints that manipulate *time*. In most activities there are temporal constraints that must be understood if one is to be a skilled participant. Constraints of time allow participants to learn and embody the tempo at which skills are to be performed and coordinate these with others if participating in a group. In order to acquire skill, participants accept time constraints so that nothing "remain[s] idle or useless: everything [is] called upon to form the support of the act required" (Foucault 1979, p. 152). Foucault described these time constraints as timetables, temporal elaboration of the act, correlation of the body and the gesture, body–object articulation, and exhaustive use.

> 8.45 entrance of the monitor, 8.52 the monitor's summons, 8.56 entrance of the children and prayer, 9.00 the children go to their benches, 9.04 first slate, 9.08 end of dictation, 9.12 second slate, etc. (Tronchot in Foucault 1979, p. 150)

In order to ensure efficient use of time, participants accept timetable constraints that make it possible to rule out unnecessary actions and concentrate effort on activities designed to improve skill. Timetable constraints make possible "totally useful time ... a time of good quality, throughout which the body is constantly applied to its exercise" (Foucault 1979, pp. 150–151).

> The length of the short step will be a foot, that of the ordinary step, the double step and the marching step will be two feet, the whole measured from one heel to the next; as for the duration, that of the ordinary step and the marching step will last one second, during which two double steps would be performed; the duration of the marching step will be a little longer than one second. (Ordonnance in Foucault 1979, p. 151)

Most skills require a temporal sequencing that a participant must incorporate to perform correctly. A tennis serve, a basketball lay-up shot, a placing of a piton in the ice, or a dance sequence all require that participants accept constraints that sequence in time the movements required to perform these activities.

> Good handwriting ... presupposes a gymnastics—a whole routine whose rigorous code invests the body in its entirety, from the points of the feet to the tip of the index ringer. (Foucault 1979, p. 152)

Time is used correctly when movement is efficient—when "everything is called upon to form the support of the act required" (Foucault 1979, p. 152). Shooting a basketball, for example, is not merely a matter of performing a series of particular gestures. To become a skilled shooter, a participant must accept constraints that will achieve the "best relation between a gesture and the overall position of the body, which is its condition of efficiency and speed" (Foucault 1979, p. 152).

> Bring the weapon forward. In three stages. Raise the rifle with the right hand, bringing it close to the body so as to hold it perpendicular with the right knee, the end of the barrel at eye level.... At the second stage, bring the rifle in front of you with the left hand, the barrel in the middle between the two eyes.... At the third stage, let go of the rifle with the left hand, which falls along the thigh, raising the rifle with the right hand, the lock outwards and opposite the chest. (Ordonnance in Foucault 1979, p. 153)

Most leisure activities involve the articulation of the body with one or more objects or implements. Rowers articulate with their boats and oars;

piano players with their pianos, synchronized swimmers with the water and their props; even runners must articulate with a running surface.

For a participant to become skilled in relation to the object to be manipulated, she or he accepts constraints that break down the total gesture into two parallel series: the parts of the body to be used and the object to be manipulated. Once each of these is mastered, constraints are introduced to correlate them together "according to a number of simple gestures" and in a "canonical succession in which each of these correlations occupies a particular place" (Foucault 1979, p. 153). Beginner tennis players, for example, agree to constraints that allow them to acquire basic skills of footwork, then constraints that allow the acquisition of racquet skills, followed by constraints that combine the two.

Practice sessions are organized to "extract ... from time, ever more available moments and, from each moment, ever more useful forces" (Foucault 1979, p. 154). In order to accomplish this, participants accept constraints that require them to repeat actions at a particular tempo. As a consequence, participants come to feel bodily discomfort as "unnatural" when they have not followed the temporal sequence and intensity for a particular skill.

Constraints of space and time constrain *movement*, which enables participants to perform skills not otherwise possible. What Foucault refers to as *"the organization of geneses"* (Foucault 1979) involves the gradual progression and acquisition of knowledge in segments, building on each other and making possible coordination with others. Through repetitive, different, and graduated exercise, tasks are imposed on the body. It is not necessary for me to detail these constraints here since the preceding examples of space and time constraints make the point that accepting constraints on space, time, and movement makes possible the acquisition of abilities to engage in leisure activities and experiences.

CONSTRAINTS OF IDENTITY

I have shown that leisure activities and experiences are produced by constraints that enable these activities and experiences to occur and that the skills required to competently engage in these activities and experiences require subjection to specific spatial and temporal constraints on movements. Constraints also produce expectations for who will engage in particular leisure activities and experiences. These expectations are often differentiated according to gender, race, class, age, and disability categories. In this section I show that improving opportunities for leisure participation is not merely a matter of removing obstacles associated with expectations for a social group. This is because what counts as a category of identification is also produced by constraints that, in turn, serve to constrain (enable and restrict) participation in structured activities by those who identity with the group. To the extent that individuals engage identity categories and practise the "skills" of comportment and behaviour associated with them, these constraints characterize or produce what they are able to do and hence their success with leisure activities and experiences in which they engage. For example, those actions that are identifiable in a culture as conventionally feminine or masculine are produced through particular prescriptive, proscriptive, and descriptive constraints. These constraints set out what counts as appropriate skills for conventionally appropriate men and women in a culture, just as the prescriptive, proscriptive, and descriptive constraints of a game set out what counts as the skills of that particular game. Commenting on the photographs of masculine and feminine body posture by photographer Marianne Wex, Bartky (1990, p. 68) notes the following:

> Women sit waiting for trains with arms close to the body, hands folded together in their laps, toes pointing straight ahead and turned inward, and legs pressed together. The women in these photographs make themselves small and narrow, harmless; they seem tense; they take up little space. Men, on the other hand, expand into the available space; they sit with legs far apart and arms flung out at some distance from the body. Most common in these sitting male figures is ... the "proffering position": the men sit with legs thrown wide apart, crotch visible, feet pointing outward, often with an arm and casually dangling hand resting comfortably on an open, spread thigh.

Like acquiring competent skills to perform in games, skills for bodily comportment of conventional masculinity and femininity are produced through spatial and temporal constraints on movement. Constraints that go into producing conventional femininity and masculinity produce bodies that in "gesture and appearance" are recognizably gendered (Bartky 1990, p. 65). As detailed by Foucault, spatial and temporal constraints produce particular modalities of movement, which, in the case of gender "skills" are manifested in particular ways of walking, standing, sitting, getting in and out of vehicles, and particular facial expressions. These gestures, movements, and expressions are embodied as a result of daily, disciplined repetition within particular spatial and temporal constraints. And, like the embodiment of musical or sport skills, improper or inadequate performance of required gender skills feels "wrong" or "unnatural" to the performer.

Like practising skills of a game, practising the skills of femininity or masculinity require an "investment of time, the use of a wide variety of preparations, the mastery of a set of techniques and ... the acquisition of a specialized knowledge" (Bartky 1990, p. 71). Just as skilled performers of games are rewarded for their skill, conventional women and men are rewarded or enabled for conforming to the constraints of femininity and masculinity. However, they also may be limited or restricted. Conventionally feminine women, for example, are often unable to participate in activities that are regarded as standards of competency in a culture. Many of these activities are leisure activities. These girls and women are ill equipped for leisure activities that require forceful, space-occupying movements associated with conventional masculinity.

Constraints of masculinity enable engagement in forceful, space-occupying movements. Boys who have accepted constraints that produce conventional masculinity do better than conventionally feminine girls when exposed to forceful, space-occupying leisure activities. A boy who is not skilled at conventional masculinity may have similar difficulties in certain leisure environments as conventionally feminine girls.

Whether the constraints that produce conventional gender are enabling or restricting for a particular individual is relative to the activities and experiences in which they do or wish to engage and the extent to which the constraints of gender have shaped the individual's identity. Nevertheless, because constraints of gender produce identity, these constraints do not merely intervene between an individual and a leisure activity or experience. It is not, then, a matter, of improving leisure opportunities for, say, girls and women by removing external constraints. If a range of leisure experiences, including forceful, space-occupying leisure activities and experiences, like climbing, hiking, canoeing, and most sport, is to be a real possibility for conventionally feminine girls and women, it will be necessary for them to accept specific spatial and temporal constraints so that they are enabled to acquire skills required to engage in these activities.

CLOSING COMMENTS

In this chapter, the work of Michel Foucault was used to show that the relationship of constraints to leisure is not a wholly limiting one. Constraints make possible activities and the experiences within them, they enable skill acquisition, and they produce bodily comportment and expectations that may enable or restrict experiences of leisure. By showing that leisure activities and experiences are actually characterized or produced by constraints, it has been emphasized that simply removing constraints is not a solution to improving leisure choices and participation. If constraints that produce leisure experiences are removed without replacing them with other structuring constraints, leisure experiences would simply disappear. If only those constraints that are perceived to be restricting are removed, experiences will be enabled for some but not others. Moreover, in order to engage in leisure activities and experiences, it may be necessary to acquire certain skills. The acquisition of these skills requires subjecting oneself to spatial and temporal constraints that shape movement requirements for an activity. These constraints may also have an impact on how an individual understands his or her identity when subjected to actions not typically associated with the group with which they are identified. Moreover, making it possible for people to actually participate in leisure activities will require that they accept constraints in order to engage in the activity or experience and in order to acquire skills to participate. By opening up the notion of constraints to other characterizations, responsibilities of policy makers and practitioners must include not only removing constraints that restrict participation but introducing those enabling constraints that make participation possible.

NOTES

[1] Constraints that prevent, reduce, or modify participation in an activity have been identified as intervening constraints while constraints that affect the quality of enjoyment of the activity, including time commitment, lack of skills, and interpersonal relationships, have been identified as antecedent constraints (Henderson 1997). Intervening and antecedent constraints can be imposed both externally and internally. Moreover, "despite constraint" (Kay and Jackson 1991), some participants are able to "address, alleviate, or even overcome their constraints; in short, they have negotiated them" (Jackson & Scott 1999).

[2] I would like to thank an anonymous reviewer for pointing to another set of questions that Foucault's understanding of power presents for the leisure constraints literature. As this reviewer indicates, since, according to Foucault, power is not a possession of an authority, exerted in a top-down fashion on those who do not possess power but, instead, circulates and is exercised when individuals act, a valuable study would be to explore how intervening and antecedent constraints function within a network of power relations.

3   Constraints have been differentiated as structural, interpersonal, and intrapersonal (Crawford et al. 1991). Interpersonal constraints are limitations in leisure activity that arise from relationships with others, including family responsibilities, absence of a leisure partner, and a mismatched leisure partner (Samdahl & Jekubovich 1997, pp. 487–438). Intrapersonal constraints are considered to include such things as low self-esteem. Unlike my interpretation here, structural constraints have been limited in the constraints literature to such things as time, money, and health that negatively intervene between someone's interest and actual participation.

REFERENCES

Bartky, S. (1990). *Femininity and domination: Studies in the phenomenology of oppression*. London: Routledge.

Crawford, D.W., Jackson, E.L., & Godbey, G. (1991). A hierarchical model of leisure constraints. *Leisure Sciences 13*, 309–320.

Foucault, M. (1979). *Discipline and punish: The birth of the prison* (trans. by A. Sheridan). New York: Vintage Books.

Foucault, M. (1980a). Two lectures. In C. Gordon (Ed.), *Power/knowledge: Selected interviews and other writings 1972–77* (pp. 78–108). New York: Pantheon Books.

Foucault, M. (1980b). Truth and power. In C. Gordon (Ed.), *Power/knowledge: Selected interviews and other writings 1972–77* (pp. 109–133). New York: Pantheon Books.

Fraser, N. (1989). *Unruly practices: Power, discourse, and gender in contemporary social theory*. Minneapolis: University of Minnesota Press.

Goodale, T.L. & Witt, P.A. (1989). Recreation nonparticipation and barriers to leisure. In E.L. Jackson & T.L. Burton (Eds.), *Understanding leisure and recreation: Mapping the past, charting the future* (pp. 421–449). State College: Venture Publishing, Inc.

Gruneau, R. (1985). Leisure, the state, and freedom. In A. Tomlinson (Ed.), *Leisure, politics, planning, and people*, Volume I Plenary Papers (pp. 120–139). Brighton, UK: Leisure Studies Association.

Henderson, K.A. (1997). A critique of constraints theory: A response. *Journal of Leisure Research 29*, 453–458.

Henderson, K.A.(1996). *Both gains and gaps: Feminist perspectives on women's leisure*. State College: Venture Publishing, Inc.

Jackson, E.L. (1988). Leisure constraints: A survey of past research. *Leisure Sciences 10*, 203–215.

Jackson, E.L. & Scott, D. (1999). Constraints to leisure. In E. Jackson & T. Burton (Eds.), *Leisure studies: Prospects for the 21st century* (pp. 299–321). State College: Venture Press.

Kay, T. & Jackson, E.L. (1991). Leisure despite constraint: The impact of leisure constraints on leisure participation. *Journal of Leisure Research 23*, 301–313.

Samdahl, D.M. & Jekubovich, N.J. (1997). A critique of leisure constraints: Comparative analyses and understandings. *Journal of Leisure Research 29*, 430–452.

Shaw, S.M. (1999). Gender and leisure. In E. Jackson & T. Burton (Eds.), *Leisure studies: Prospects for the 21st century* (pp. 299–321). State College: Venture Press.

Shaw, S.M., Bonen, A., & McCabe, J.F. (1991). Do constraints mean less leisure? Examining the relationship between constraints and participation. *Journal of Leisure Research 23*, 286–300.

Usher, R. & Edwards, R. (1994). *Postmodernism and education*. London: Routledge.

3

THE PARADOX OF SPORT
ACTIVITIES IN THE WILDERNESS

This chapter addresses the possible effects of a shift in emphasis from organized sport programs indoors or in controlled areas outdoors, like soccer pitches, to sport activities in what might be called wilderness areas. In particular, I am interested in ethical responsibilities to spaces, plants, and animals affected by activity that takes place in vulnerable places. As more people are attracted to sport in wilderness areas, they may, paradoxically, contribute to the eventual demise of these areas. Two other paradoxes emerge from this paradox. The first of these is the way in which acting to maximize opportunities in wilderness areas leads to the destruction of both one's own and others' opportunities. The second paradox concerns the relationship of human beings to wilderness areas: human beings are at one and the same time separate and part of wilderness and consequently human culture is paradoxically both the potential destroyer of wilderness and, given present environmental crises, now possibly the only way to preserve them.

WILDERNESS AREAS AS "TRAGIC COMMONS"

In his classic essay, "The Tragedy of the Commons," Garrett Hardin (1968) describes the evolution of an area of land that is open to all to graze their cattle as self-interest dictates. This common area functions without difficulty for many centuries with herders grazing as many cattle as each possibly can. Eventually stability is reached because the "commons" cannot be utilized beyond its fixed "carrying capacity." The herders do not exercise restraint, however, because to do so would be to be eliminated from competing for the now scarce resources of the area held in common. Each herder calculates what the utility of adding one more animal to one's own herd will be. This utility has two components. The positive component is a function of the increment of having another animal in one's herd. The negative component is a function of the overgrazing created by another animal added to the herd. Since, however, the herder will share the effects of the overgrazing with all the others, the herder adds another animal and several more. Each herder does the same because each realizes that to refrain from adding cattle while others do not would be to suffer the effects of more cattle on the land without experiencing any benefits of having more cattle grazing. Each herder adds cattle without limit to an area that has limits on what it can carry. And, of course, therein is the tragedy. The herders are caught in a paradox. In a rational attempt to maximize personal benefits, each is left in a situation that is neither personally beneficial nor beneficial for others.

With an ever-increasing human population, wilderness areas cannot be regarded as "a 'free good' or 'commons' which any person is entitled to use as self-interest dictates" (Lehocky 1979, p. 83). When wilderness areas are recognized as commons with a maximum human carrying capacity, questions arise about the possible impact sport activities in wilderness areas might have on reaching this carrying capacity. Some argue that a wilderness area is wilderness by virtue of having no human inhabitants. Others argue that any notion of wilderness can and should accommodate human beings since humans are also part of the global ecosystem. The latter would have to admit, however, that wilderness areas are distinguishable from, for example, urban or even rural environments and too many people in wilderness areas put these distinguishing features in jeopardy. Too many people, however many that may be, creates a tragedy for wilderness areas.

It might be argued that, although rapidly expanding human population may put some resource systems in jeopardy, there is no real threat to wilderness areas by those who want to be active in these areas since most people will continue to be interested in organized sport in controlled settings. However, even if the proportion of the population interested in wilderness experiences remains constant, total numbers will continue to increase as the population increases. And if leaders and promoters of sports like helicopter and back-country skiing, hiking, white-water rafting, and mountain climbing are successful at what they do, the proportion of people interested in wilderness experiences is likely to increase as well. As more people enjoy wilderness experiences, the maximum human carrying capacity of wilderness areas comes closer to being reached. If the logic of the commons persists, wilderness areas will be tragically and inevitably destroyed just as grazing grounds held in common are inevitably destroyed. Being aware of the detrimental effects of large numbers accessing a wilderness area will likely not be sufficient to stop people from continuing to go these areas. People go back to a wilderness area, even after it is endangered, when they realize that others may not be curtailing their wilderness experiences. This is because they share the negative effects of overuse with others while continuing to enjoy wilderness experiences, at least for a time. If they refrain from having these experiences, they bear the effects of the overuse of wilderness areas while getting no benefits.

SPORT ACTIVITIES IN WILDERNESS AREAS

Despite valuing wilderness areas more than most, leaders and promoters of sport in the wilderness may paradoxically contribute to the creation of wilderness areas as "tragic commons." To be a leader of sport in wilderness areas is to convince others about the value of sport in the outdoors including in remote wilderness areas and to interest at least some to actually have these experiences. As they do their job well, however, wilderness areas are jeopardized. When an enterprise is valuable, it is usually thought to be desirable that this value be shared with others. Someone who enjoys literature, for example, often wants others to see the value of engaging with literature. Paradoxically, it may not be desirable that values associated with engaging in sport in the wilderness areas be shared with others. Unlike the education of literature experiences, where the more who have these experiences, the better, the more people who come to understand the value of wilderness experiences as something in which to engage, the closer we are to wilderness areas as "tragic commons."

Since a central component of outdoor sport programs is that people learn respect for wilderness areas, perhaps outdoor sport programs could be limited to this focus. It is debatable, however, whether someone can come to value and understand wilderness without having at least some wilderness experiences. Moreover, outdoor sport programs without an experiential component may be an oxymoron. If outdoor sport programs require that people have experiences in wilderness areas in order that people come to value wilderness areas and if these programs entail these experiences, these experiences by ever increasing numbers of people will contribute to the overuse of wilderness areas.

An alternative is to be circumspect about sharing the virtues of wilderness experiences by limiting this information to a few. This would solve the problem of wilderness areas as a "commons" because these areas would no longer be a "free good" available to all. This alternative creates other problems. It raises questions, for example, about who are to be the privileged few who are to have these experiences; who will decide this; and how this will be decided. Realizing that the Earth is a commons that cannot carry an infinite number of people does not suggest easy answers about how we are to deal with large numbers of people on the Earth. As Wendell Berry (1987) rightly says, "there is great danger in the perception that 'there are too many people,' whatever truth may be in it, for this is a premise from which it is too likely that somebody, sooner or later, will proceed to a determination of *who* are the surplus" (p. 9).

ALTERNATIVES TO THESE PARADOXES

Garrett Hardin's solution to the "tragedy of the commons" is "mutual coercion, mutually agreed upon." In other words, since the logic of the commons makes it impossible to appeal to people to use constraint because they fear that others will not use constraint, we must agree to legislation that will force us to control our behaviours. Meanwhile, says Hardin, an educational program must be put in place that will allow people to see that they must give up certain freedoms in a world with finite resources. Hardin fails to recognize, however, that unless everyone either accepts the legislation or comes to see the point of relinquishing certain freedoms, some will continue to benefit from short-term gain at the expense of others, including future generations. Being educated to look long term or accepting legislation that forces one to do so, when others ignore legislation and education, is not a remedy for the "tragedy of the commons." This is because those who look short term will continue to gain short-term advantages. It is this kind of dilemma that convinces many that they also must look out for their own short-term interests.

Education about appropriate use of wilderness areas, to be effective, must convince all that they must look long term. It is highly unlikely that all could be educated to do this and consequently legislation with effective penalties is necessary. But more importantly, there must be a fundamental change in all parts of our culture. As Berry writes, "It is not only the number of people inhabiting a landscape that determines its features— it is the way people divide the landscape and use it" (1987, p. 10). "Conservation is going to prove increasingly futile and increasingly meaningless if its proscriptions are not answered positively by an economy that rewards and enforces good use" (Berry 1987, p. 7).

This introduces the third paradox—that human culture and wilderness are different but inseparable. Humanity cannot survive unless the natural world is preserved, but the preservation of the natural world also now depends on human culture. We require nothing less than a radical shift in our thinking about the ways in which human beings can live in harmony with wilderness areas. There needs to be a recognition of the ways in which the lives of people and other living things are interconnected rather than assuming that each of us is a separate, autonomous individual who acts from self-interest and who must contract with one another for protection against the self-interest of others. It is in this latter type of community that tragic commons occur; trust is rare and individuals manoeuvre to take advantage of others before they are taken advantage of. An interconnected community, on the other hand, has the best features of a family or a group of friends in which lives have meaning within the context of the group and in which it would be unthinkable to subvert those who depend on you and on whom you depend. And, as unthinkable, would be the sacrifice of the very physical environment in which the community lives and acts. The boundaries of this community extend to include not only people but the living Earth.

Three paradoxes have been introduced as they relate to real and ongoing threats to wilderness areas. The first of these paradoxes is that, as long as people attempt to optimize personal gain with respect to finite resources, including wilderness areas, the inevitable result is loss of personal gain. The second of the paradoxes is that the very people who value wilderness areas more than most, outdoor sport leaders, may contribute to the demise of these areas. If those they influence live in communities of competing, self-interested individuals, wilderness experiences will proliferate without heed to their eventual effects. The third paradox is that human cultural enterprises, including outdoor sport programs, have both the potential to destroy wilderness areas and to save them. Outdoor sport leaders must be clear about their role in this complex endeavour if they are to protect wilderness areas and not be culpable in their demise.

REFERENCES

Berry, W. (1987). Preserving wilderness. *Resurgence 121,* 7–10.

Hardin, G. (1968). The tragedy of the commons. *Science 16,* 1243–1248.

Lehocky, D. (1979). Review of Garrett Hardin, The limits of altruism: Ecologist's view of survival. *Environmental Ethics 1,* 83.

4 ETHICS FOR STRANGERS IN SPORT

Issues related to fair competition are issues that concern relationships with opponents. Often opponents are not known well because they live in different cities or countries and/or because it is not possible to spend time with them outside of competition. Very often opponents are strangers. In this chapter I am interested in exploring ethical responsibilities to strangers in competition or who are affected by decisions one makes in preparation for competition. Of interest are not only those strangers encountered in sporting contests but also those who are affected by sport policy whom policy makers may never encounter or who are affected by team and league cultures that exclude people because of unacknowledged racism or homophobia. I return to these concerns later in the chapter, but first it is important to consider the question of what ethics for strangers might entail.

AN ETHICS FOR STRANGERS

Is there an ethics to guide our relationships with those who are geographically, culturally, or temporally remote—that is, with most people in the world? Perhaps responsibilities to strangers are, at most, "potential" ethical responsibilities (Card 1990, p. 103) to be actualized only when people are in face-to-face relationships and/or only if they share interests and values. If this is the case, the ethical domain would be very small indeed. We would only need to be concerned about the effects of our actions on those with whom we have daily, personal interactions.

In order to explore later in the chapter what sport ethics for strangers might need to take into account, here I trace how an ethics for strangers might be accommodated within two different approaches to ethics: a justice or fairness approach and a care approach. I pay particular attention to an ethics of care because it is an approach that has gained a significant place within ethical discourse in the last 25 years. I argue that an ethics of care, with its emphasis on engrossment and mutual understanding, cannot appropriately accommodate responsibilities to strangers. However, as Card (1990) indicates, this "leaves the question of what ethical notions *are* relevant to our relationships with strangers, persons whose lives we may significantly affect although we will *never* know them as individuals, [and may] *never* encounter them" (p. 102).

An Ethics of Care and an Ethics of Justice

It is important to sketch a now famous debate that took place in the early 1980s between Carol Gilligan and Lawrence Kohlberg about what constitutes the domain of ethics. Kohlberg's view was that the ethical domain is about what is just or fair. He based this view, in part, on years of empirical work interpreted exclusively, as it turned out, from research with boys and men on their responses to ethical dilemmas. Kohlberg surmised from his research that there are stages of ethical development; the highest stage, which most people do not reach, is based on the ability to reason from universal principles of justice. The experiences of the boys and men in Kohlberg's study were claimed to be experiences of ethics that everyone has. Girls and women tended not to score as well as boys and men on assessments of ethical reasoning designed from the results of Kohlberg's research. Rather than recognize that the assessment procedure might be deficient, the maturity of women's ethical judgment was called into question.

Gilligan (1982) argued that the justice perspective is not the only perspective to take on ethical issues. She contended that a care perspective is an alternate way or a "different voice," which, she said, reflects how girls and women experience ethical problems. The girls and women in Gilligan's studies described their responses to ethical situations not in relation to fairness but as a "network of connection, a web of relationships, that is sustained by a process of communication" (1982, p. 33).

Harding summarized the differences between what appeared to be differences in how women and men contend with moral issues: "men characteristically worry about people interfering with one another's rights … objective unfairness appears immoral to men whether or not it subjectively hurts…. Women worry about not helping others when they could help them, and subjectively a felt hurt appears immoral to women whether or not it is fair" (1982, pp. 237–238).

Many authors have contributed to this debate in the last 20 or more years. As I outline in the introduction to this book, my approach has been to argue that, rather than there being two approaches to every ethical situation, as

Gilligan purports, there are generally two types of ethical situation for which different responses are appropriate: situations involving welfare and situations involving fairness. As I indicated in the introduction, situations involving welfare include those in which others are injured, starved, homeless, distraught, lost, confused, tormented, and the like, or when others do not suffer but there is an opportunity to help them flourish in some way. In this type of ethical situation, welfare is at stake as a result of some predicament or circumstance that requires that someone help. Situations involving fair treatment are those in which there is a conflict between sentient beings or between sentient beings and a standard for which the resolution requires adjudication (see pages 8–9 of the introduction).

When men tend to respond to ethical situations from a justice perspective and women tend to respond from a care perspective, this is not evidence of there being two different perspectives but only that social expectations and experiences of women and men prepare them differently for two fundamentally different ethical tasks. These tasks are to respond fairly when those in an ethical situation require that justice prevail or to respond by helping when welfare of those in an ethical situation is at stake.

Ethics of Care in Relation to Strangers

I have provided this background to this important debate because both justice and care, whether one understands these as perspectives as does Gilligan, or particular responses required of distinct ethical situations as I have argued, are complicated when those in ethical predicaments are strangers. Here I want to say why an ethics of care is inadequate to guide responses in relation to strangers.

There is not unanimity among proponents of an ethics of care about whether its features can be appropriately extended to non-intimates. Noddings (1984) wrote, for example, "Indeed the caring person ... dreads the proximate stranger, for she cannot easily reject the claim he has on her. She would prefer that the stray cat not appear at the back door—or the stray teenager at the front" (p. 47). On the other hand, Diller (1990) argued that care is an appropriate ethic even "once we recognize that we are 'many' that the differences may run deep, and are, as yet, only partially revealed" (p. 5). Like Noddings, my position is that care does not appropriately extend to strangers—whether proximate or remote.

Diller (1990) summarized features of an ethics of care: an acknowledgement that to be human is to be in relation in which the ideal is to improve one's relationships with others; attentiveness in which we attend to and are engrossed in the other; and an insistence on the particularity of each person in her or his context (pp. 4–5). In these times of environmental degradation, it is important that more people recognize that all inhabitants of the Earth are in relation to each other and that we foster an understanding of how these relationships can be improved. However, there are important ways in which relationships of the Earth's inhabitants can and should be differentiated. Human beings can respect relationships with animal and plant life without interacting with this life in the same way as with human life. Midgley (1983) wrote, for example, that "overlooking ... species is a supercilious insult. It is no privilege, but a misfortune, for a gorilla or a chimpanzee to be removed from its forest and its relatives and brought up among humans to be given what those humans regard as an education" (p. 90). An attempt to improve relationships with animal and plant life is an important ideal, yet the likelihood of improving these relationships will depend on being clear about what distinguishes these from relationships with humans. So, too, striving to improve human relationships depends on being clear about the ways in which human relationships may be distinguished from each other. Relationships with intimates and acquaintances are different in important ways from "relationships" with strangers. To regard them as fundamentally the same may be a "supercilious insult" both to intimates and to strangers.

Diller (1990) argued and I agree that moral labour is required to improve relationships. "The question," she says, "is how to do this, what method to use" (p. 3). The method supported by Diller in an ethics of care is a receptive attention "to particular persons in particular situations" (Diller 1990, p. 4). Although important to relationships with intimates and acquaintances, this method is necessarily limited to those relationships characterized by proximity to those to whom one would attend. A method that requires giving receptive attention to a particular person privileges "face-to-face relations" and reflects a "model of social relations that are not mediated by space and time distancing" (Young 1986, p. 18).

> Just as the intimacy of living with a few others in the same household has unique dimensions that are humanly valuable, so existing with others in communities of mutual friendship has specific characteristics of warmth and sharing that are humanly valuable.... Recognizing the specific value of face-to-face relations, however, is quite a different matter from proposing them as the organizing principle of a whole society (Young 1986, p. 18).

A method to improve relationships that require attention to someone in her or his particularity depends upon face-to-face encounters that are possible only with intimates and acquaintances in small groupings of people. It is humanly impossible to become engrossed in everyone. Strangers, by definition, are people who are not attended to, in whom we do not or cannot become engrossed, who are not known.

Attending to the particularities of another in order to understand that person is far more likely to occur in intimate living situations or in communities in which people are already fairly well known. We are likely to find ourselves in these communities and be positioned to understand others in a community because we already do share interests and values. Although many strangers have similar interests and values, and frequent face-to-face encounters may lead to a mutual understanding of these interests and values (strangers would cease to be strangers), many people are strangers to each other because of vastly different interests and values. Diller thinks that it is possible to extend an ethics of care across these differences in a "viable approach to plurality that can still remain true to the precepts of an ethics of care (1990, p. 1). But, as Young (1989) reminds us, when diverse peoples differentiated by social power come together, what will be attended to is what is held in common and what will be held in common will be determined from the perspective of the privileged thus "marginalizing or silencing those of other groups" (p. 257). Attempts to bring strangers together in caring communities, when these strangers exercise power asymmetrically, are based on assumptions that individuals are fundamentally alike or that, by virtue of coming together in pluralist communities, real differences in power will disappear. An ethics for strangers cannot be founded on an extension of an ethics of care to non-intimates in community. By definition, there can be no strangers in a community and we are left with the question: what are our responsibilities to strangers.

Ethics of Justice in Relation to Strangers

I have argued that an ethics of care (when care is understood to entail engrossment and knowing another in his or her particularity) is an ethics for intimates and acquaintances in community and not for strangers. Perhaps, an ethics of fairness or justice with its emphasis on adjudication of rights is a more appropriate ethics to guide responsibilities to strangers.

Aligning care with intimates and justice with strangers falsely separates care and justice, just as does aligning an ethic of care to women and an ethic of justice to men. As I have said, different ethical situations require different ethical responses. Like intimates, strangers find themselves in both types of situation—those requiring help and those requiring adjudication. An ethics of helping and an ethics of adjudication (an ethics of justice) in which it matters to us how things turn out for the particular people involved require that we know those in the ethical predicament. It is not possible to respond to strangers in this way. They are strangers by virtue of the fact that we don't know them.

A SPORT ETHICS FOR STRANGERS

Neither an ethics of care as understood by Diller (an ethics of helping as I have explained it) nor an ethics of justice (an ethics of adjudication from my perspective) can accommodate responsibilities to strangers when care (helping) or adjudication requires that one know something about the person in the ethical situation. It is not that strangers don't get into situations in which they need help or fair adjudication. It is that it is not possible to respond to them in a direct way because they are strangers. Instead, an ethics for strangers relies on recognizing a principle or a duty to unknown others and responding to that duty or principle. Consider this example: I am attempting to beat the rush-hour traffic when I see someone stranded at the side of the road. Because the stranded motorist is a stranger, my desire to help him does not come from being engrossed in this person or knowing anything in particular about him. I believe, however, that generally people should stop to help others in this type of situation. I recognize that I have a duty to stop and I want to do my duty. The focus, then, is not on the person in the predicament but on the principle of helping. Likewise, consider this example: I have the task of adjudicating between two people whom I have never met, both of whom have claimed ownership of a family heirloom. Because these two people are strangers, it is not possible for me to desire that they are treated fairly by virtue of the people they are. It does matter to me, however, that generally people are treated fairly and it is this principle and an acknowledged duty to fulfill this principle that guides my adjudication.

Duty as an impetus for ethical action does not require knowing particulars about another. Nor does it require that one is engrossed in this other person. A duty is usually recognized as owing to all in like circumstances—too broad a sweep to adequately account for the distinctiveness of relationships with intimates but broad enough to account for responsibilities to strangers. Although it is sometimes necessary to rely on some acknowledged duty with intimates, it is almost always necessary to focus on an acknowledged duty if one is to respond to strangers. Strangers are strangers because they do not focus on one another. Therefore some impetus is required if strangers are to be responsive to and responsible for each other's ethical predicaments.

Duty as a Sport Ethics for Strangers

When opponents are friends, they care that each other is treated fairly during the contest and that the friend is not physically harmed. However, opponents are more likely to be strangers than friends. A sport ethics for strangers must, therefore, rely on *principles* of helping and fairness rather than on a direct concern for the welfare and fair treatment of those affected by the ethical situation. It is not possible for it to matter how things turn out for particular individuals when these individuals are strangers. It is possible, however, for it to matter that principles of helping and fair adjudication prevail.

During competition, competitors recognize a duty to treat others in the competition fairly as well as a duty to refrain from injuring them. In preparation for competition, athletes, coaches, and administrators have a duty to notice how decisions they make about training and policy can have an impact on others they may never or seldom meet. A decision to take a performance-enhancing drug when there is a rule proscribing performance enhancers has an effect on immediate competitors and on those strangers throughout competitive sport who want sport to remain drug free. A decision by sport administrators to favour those they know for positions in sport organizations has effects on people they may never meet. An indifference to accounts of racist behaviour in amateur hockey or other leagues or accounts of policing of sexual minorities by team officials has an effect on people one may never encounter. A sport ethics for strangers recognizes a duty to others one does not know but who may be adversely affected by one's decisions.

As with other ethical issues involving strangers, it is an open question about how far a duty to recognize principles of fairness and helping extends. There are some actions that go beyond duty. These supererogatory actions are actions that we praise people for doing but do not blame them if they do not do them. Giving up one's job to go to Uganda to help AIDS victims is an action worthy of praise but not of blame if one does not do it. The action by the Norwegian cross-country official who gave Canadian cross-country skier, Sara Renner, a new ski pole after she broke it, which helped her to win a silver medal at the 2006 Olympics, may be considered to be beyond duty.

Is it a duty to work to make sport a more hospitable place for everyone even if one does not know who, in particular, is excluded or is it an act of supererogation, something we hope that someone will do as an act of supererogation but not expected of all of us? It is a duty to recognize principles of fairness and helping of opponents who are strangers as one competes and, I would argue, it is a duty to be part of a movement in sport that ensures that there is policy in place that anticipates ways in which people might be excluded by virtue of being strangers. While each person does not have to accept the burden of accounting for strangers who are affected by exclusion, it is at least important to support policy change and supportive administrators who are on the front lines of change.

CONCLUDING REMARKS

The ethical relationship between opponents is likened by some to a social contract in which those involved agree to abide by the rules of the contest in order to test skills. In this chapter, I have argued that the ethical relationship between opponents is like that between strangers. Consequently, the ethical relationship between opponents can be understood as a duty to fulfill principles of fair treatment and helping. When ethical responsibility to an opponent is a duty rather than a contract, individuals can respond to others without requiring an agreement that everyone will respond in the same way.

REFERENCES

Card, C. (1990). Caring and evil. *Hypatia: A Journal of Feminist Philosophy* 5(1), 101–108.

Diller, A. (1990). The ethics of care takes on pluralism. Canadian Society for Women in Philosophy. Kingston, ON, Sept. 15.

Gilligan, C. (1982). *In a different voice: Psychological theory and women's development*. Cambridge: Harvard University Press.

Harding, S. (1982). Is gender a variable in conceptions of rationality? A survey of issues. *Dialectica* 36, 225–242.

Midgley, M. (1983). *Animals and why they matter*. New York: Penguin Books.

Noddings, N. (1984). *Caring: A feminine approach to ethics and moral education*. Berkeley: University of California Press.

Young, I. (1986). The ideal of community and the politics of difference. *Social Theory and Practice* 12(1), 1–26.

Young, I. (1989). Polity and group difference: A critique of the ideal of universal citizenship. *Ethics* 99(2), 250–274.

ETHICAL RESPONSIBILITIES
TO TEAM MEMBERS

INTRODUCTION

Sport teams are the site of intense loyalty and camaraderie as well as bitter rivalries and conflicts. As Messner (1992) points out, "individuals on teams are constantly competing against each other—first for a place on the team, then for playing time, recognition, and 'star' status, and eventually, just to stay on the team" (p. 88). While very real antagonisms among teammates are publicly hidden by the rhetoric of "team" and often not properly dealt with within the team context for fear that the team will be exposed as dysfunctional, especially to themselves, my interest is in exploring ethical implications of a constraint on athletes, coaches, and other team personnel that I call the imperative of teamwork. The imperative of teamwork functions to silence those conflicts that can't help but exist when individuals spend significant periods of time with each as well as major conflicts produced by, for example, hazing or sexual harassment, or those silences endured by athletes whose other life experiences are outside the mainstream culture of the team.

Team ethics have not been a focus of sport ethicists. This is in part because there is much that is valuable about a pursuit that requires people to subsume their interests as they strive to achieve something that is of collective value. It is my contention, however, that the imperative of teamwork is ethically problematic when the effect is to overlook abuses that may take place within a team or subsume differences among team members and, in particular, those differences that may constitute them as outsiders or deviants.

TEAMS AS EXEMPLARY FAMILIES

Despite the inevitable conflict that occurs when people interact in an intense environment, teams are often represented as a type of exemplary community or a family whose members are bonded together to achieve the goal of winning games. Team goals are usually stipulated in terms of quantifiable performance outcomes, while means to achieve these goals are understood in relation to unquantifiable notions of teamwork (Larson & LaFasto 1989), team cohesiveness (Carron 1984), or team spirit (Syer 1986) and other social factors such as communication, collaboration, and trust (Larson & LaFasto 1989; Schellenberger 1990; Syer 1986). For example, Syer (1986) indicates that team spirit is the "joy of working toward a shared objective with a group of which I am glad to be a part" (p. 17) and Larson and LaFasto (1989) write that "teamwork succeeds most dramatically when team members are enthusiastically unified in a pursuit of a common objective rather than individual agendas" (p. 84).

Collaboration and achievement of common goals are thought to be possible if there is open communication in which participants are encouraged to not only share their experiences (Brown in Syer 1986, p. 98) but to disclose and share information openly, especially negative information (Larson & LaFasto 1989, p. 84). Trust, in particular, is considered to improve collaboration and promote efficient communication and coordination (Larson & LaFasto 1989, pp. 89, 88). "Trust allows team members to stay problem-focused. The absence of trust diverts the mental concentration and energy of a team away from its performance objective and onto other issues. The team becomes politicized. Communication becomes guarded and distorted.... Conversely, when trust is present, a collaborative climate is more readily fostered—allowing team members to stay focused on their common problem or goal" (Larson & LaFasto 1989, p. 88). Schellenberger (1990) argues that team goals are more easily achieved if teammates are friends and, on the basis of this assumption, he argues that coaches should attempt to encourage athletes to be friends outside practice sessions and competitions.

EXPLORING THE LIMITS OF TEAM

The adage, "What goes on in the family stays in the family" has made it possible for perpetrators of abuse within families to continue their abusive ways. Likewise, the sentiment that disagreements, indiscretions, or power abuses between players or between players and coaches should not be for public consumption makes it possible for abusive practices to continue on teams. In "Racism in Canadian Sport," I explore how racism, both as it occurs on teams and between teams, is a neglected issue in Canadian sport, despite an elaborate sport ethics bureaucracy to contend with racism. In this introduction, I consider three other examples of problems that can occur on teams. I say something about hazing and sexual abuse, and then go on to show, using the example of homophobia, that in each case, an imperative of teamwork allows problems of racism, hazing, sexual abuse, and homophobia to continue unaddressed. Moreover, as I explain, these examples show that there is an inevitable limit to an imperative of teamwork.

Hazing

Hazing is initiation that serves to harass, abuse, or humiliate those who are being admitted to a group. Many perpetrators of hazing rituals claim that hazing helps to produce the cohesiveness that is so important to teams and many of the initiates agree to go along with the rituals because they want to be accepted into the group. Hazing has a long tradition in fraternities and sororities, in many high schools, in the armed forces, and on sport teams. Recent high-profile cases on sport teams in Canada have brought the issue of hazing before the public. The McGill University football team was not allowed to complete its 2005 season after an 18-year-old rookie was sexually assaulted with a broomstick during a hazing ritual. Initially players, including other rookies subjected to the hazing, denied that there was any significant ethical breech. Veteran players reported that the rituals were ones that they had endured in past years and most claimed that it was important for rookie players to participate in initiation rituals in order to show that they would do anything for the team. Later, the provost of McGill indicated that the evidence showed that "the event … involve[d] nudity, degrading positions and behaviours, gagging, touching in inappropriate manners with a broomstick, as well as verbal and physical intimidation of rookies by a large portion of the team" (CBC 2005).

The McGill example is only one of many that have recently gained national and international attention and represents only those instances in which rookies have complained or, in the case of a women's university soccer team in the United States, the attention came after photographs appeared on a Web site, showing members of the team in their underwear, some blindfolded and others bound. (See, for example, the Web site www.stophazing.org for much more information on the extent of this problem and see Johnson & Holman 2004.) My purpose in discussing hazing is not to detail the abuses or overview the extent of the problem. Rather, it is to show how the existence of hazing, like the existence of sexual harassment, racism, and homophobia on teams, undermines the claim that teams are exemplary sites for human interaction. As I explain in the last section of this chapter, the imperative of teamwork makes it possible for these abuses to occur because, as in abusive families, perpetrators can expect silence. Indeed, the rhetoric of "team" demands silence.

Sexual Harassment

In 1993 the Canadian Broadcasting Corporation's (CBC) "Fifth Estate" program aired *Crossing the Line*, a documentary about girl's and women's experiences with sexual harassment and abuse in Canadian sport. Recognizing the extent of the problem, the Canadian Association for the Advancement of Women and Sport and Physical Activity (CAAWS) spearheaded a working group that produced a guide to understanding sexual harassment and abuse in sport, which they called *Harassment in Sport—A Guide to Policies, Procedures, and Resources* (1994). However, it took awareness of the sexual abuse of young men in hockey three years later to bring the issue to the point that national sport-governing bodies were compelled to respond. The profound interest in sexual abuse in sport in Canada was triggered by the charge that junior hockey coach, Graham James, had sexually abused players on teams he coached, including Sheldon Kennedy, who was well known as a National Hockey League (NHL) player. James was later sentenced to three-and-a-half years in prison.

In 1998, the Harassment and Abuse in Sport Collective published the *Speak Out! ... Act Now!* (1998a) handbook. Marg McGregor, then executive director of CAAWS and chair of the Collective, indicated at the release of the handbook that, "Sport organizations have recognized that harassment and abuse occurs in all sport—not just hockey. There is now an increased awareness of the high-risk factors present in sport, and the need to be vigilant to protect the children that have been entrusted to us" (Harassment in Sport Collective 1998b, p. 1). In a related document, a case was made for the importance to sport organizations of having a harassment policy. The argument is a legal argument that connects discourse about sexual abuse to the familiar sport ethics discourse concerning an imperative to abide by rules. According to the Collective, a harassment policy is necessary because it serves as a deterrent; it provides a legal means by which complaints can be handled; it is an organization's best legal defence in the event of a formal complaint; and it is good risk management to minimize liability, control insurance and legal costs, and manage financial and human resources effectively (Harassment in Sport Collective, 1998c, p. 1). Only one rationale talks about interpersonal implications of a harassment policy. According to this rationale, a harassment policy allows an organization to maintain a safe and healthy environment for those engaged in it.

While there have been subsidiary documents produced by individual sport-governing bodies to contend with sexual abuse and harassment in their organizations, the template for these documents is the Harassment and Abuse in Sport Collective's *Speak Out! ... Act Now!* At the time of the publication of *Speak Out! ... Act Now!*, members of the Collective included close to 40 groups, including national sport-governing bodies, Athletes CAN, CAAWS, Sport Canada, and the Canadian Olympic Association. Members of the Canadian Hockey Association played a major role on the writing team for the document. It should come as no surprise, then, that the document is framed in relation to the bureaucratic needs and assumptions of organized sport and that there is little about ethical responsibilities to team members, who, unlike most opponents, are known well.

While there has been a shift in focus from responsibilities to opponents to responsibilities to team members, concern about sexual harassment and abuse in sport has remained firmly within a discourse of ethics as legality, with a few exceptions. In the opening letter introducing *Speak Out! ... Act Now!*, editor-in-chief for the project, Judy Fairholm of the Canadian Red Cross Society, wrote: "I congratulate you on your dedication to understanding this issue and caring enough for your athletes to face discomfort and make difficult decisions. It has often been quoted that 'It takes a village to raise a child.' Your positive response to this material is an example of the sport village coming together to value our greatest resource—Canada's youth!" (Harassment and Abuse in Sport Collective

1998a, p. xiii). This sentiment is repeated in a chapter on "Abuse and Neglect" written by Pam Woodhouse, also of the Red Cross, who indicated that "[a]buse prevention within sport will greatly assist in the development of an attitude where the entire community takes responsibility for the safety of their children and youth" (Harassment and Abuse in Sport Collective 1998a, pp. 1–31). These two statements situate ethical concern within the relationships between people. The bulk of the document, however, is framed in legal language. Indeed the first chapter is written by researchers from the Centre for Sport and the Law, who emphasize that without a harassment and abuse policy, "a sport organization would have difficulty demonstrating that they have satisfied their legal obligation to provide a safe environment for their participants" (Harassment and Abuse in Sport Collective 1998a, pp. 1-2). Within this frame of legal obligations to participants, the guide presents practical guidelines to help sport organizations put mechanisms in place to respond to and prevent harassment and abuse of young people in sport to satisfy legal rather than intrapersonal responsibility.

THE LIMITS EXPOSE THE IMPERATIVE

Open communication and trust, considered central to teamwork, are options only for those athletes and coaches who have no reason to distrust. When the very people one is expected to trust are perpetrating abuse, it is very difficult to communicate disapproval. In the case of hazing, disapproval signals to teammates who do go along with the hazing that the dissenter is not a team player. In the case of sexual abuse, shame and not knowing who can be trusted with the information makes open communication very difficult. When a teammate of Sheldon Kennedy's complained to management about his concern for Kennedy and other players, he was regarded as a troublemaker and later traded.

Open communication and trust are options only for those whose views are already valued. In order to show how teamwork, collaboration, open communication, and trust are limited for those who are expected to remain silent, I use the example of homophobia to deconstruct the limits of these notions. Deconstruction is helpful because it makes apparent that a concept always has a "*beyond* to it, precisely by virtue of what it excludes" (Cornell 1992, p. 1). Cornell has renamed deconstruction the "philosophy of the limit" to refer to a process that attempts to locate what is excluded by "refocuss[ing] attention on the limits constraining philosophical understanding" (1992, p. 1). As Butler (1992) asserts, "[T]o deconstruct is ... to call into question and, perhaps more importantly, to open up a term ... to reusage or redeployment that previously has not been authorized" (p. 15).

There are limits to a call for teamwork in which athletes collaborate on common goals through open communication and trust. An assumption that teamwork will be enhanced through open communication in a context of trust depends upon not noticing that there may be some "open communication" or "negative" disclosure that is outside or beyond what is allowable if team cohesiveness is to be retained. There is a limit to rhetoric about open communication and trust when some athletes or coaches are unable to trust they will not be dismissed from a team or otherwise harmed if some aspect of what is important to them is openly disclosed. In instances of hazing, sexual abuse, racism, and homophobia, team members often remain quiet because of these fears.

Teamwork, with its rhetoric about communication and trust, can be sustained only when there are restrictions on what can be communicated and on information with which athletes and coaches can be entrusted. There are only certain shared experiences that most teams are able to entertain if they are to retain a sense of cohesiveness. For example, there is still an expectation on most teams for gay and lesbian athletes to remain silent about their sexuality. "You did everything you could to hang on to your seat, to make the crew, that you would never jeopardize—you wouldn't even tell the coach you had a cold ... because if there's any perceived weakness, they'll put somebody else in the boat. So to hint that I was gay was to kiss rowing goodbye" (Pronger 1990, p. 147). Likewise, Mark Tewksbury, Olympic gold medallist indicated, "My greatest fear was being found out, and that swimming would be taken away from me" (Nolan 1999, p. 1).

As in other communities and many mainstream families, gays and lesbians can be included only if everyone assumes a "Don't ask, don't tell" policy. If gays and lesbians were to talk about their lives, it would expose the fact that "success" of the community, family, or team depends on these experiences not being communicated. There is a limit, then, to the imperative for teamwork because teamwork is achievable by not noticing that some experiences cannot be told and by not recognizing that it is this very silence that makes possible the rhetoric of "open communication," "trust," and "teamwork." An imperative of teamwork makes it necessary to ignore ethical responsibilities to some even while sustaining the rhetoric of communication and trust.

In "Trusting Paternalism? Trust as a Condition for Paternalistic Decisions," I examine the issue of trust on teams, particularly the trust an athlete might have for a coach. While it is sometimes difficult for an athlete to trust a coach, coaches and athletes do often establish relationships in which there is significant affection, goodwill, and "morally good trust" (Baier 1988).

The fact that some athletes can be targets of abuse on teams is an indication that there is no such thing as a monolithic athlete. There is great diversity among athletes, despite the focused goals of teams to produce homogeneity of skills and values at least as these values relate to the team. The chapter "Hybrid Athletes" details how athletes are differentiated by processes that gender and racialize them. I argue that the discipline of sport, while relentless in its mechanisms to homogenize skill and team values, necessarily is unable to overcome or eliminate the array of interests and values that athletes bring to sport. In other words, if team members are interested in ethical responsibilities to those with whom they spend considerable time, it will be necessary to get to know team members in relation to what makes them different and to risk having this knowledge disrupt a team sensibility. Team members are often different from opponents whom it is often difficult to know very well. It is, however, possible to know "the particularities" of team members (see "Ethics for Strangers in Sport" in the first section of this book) and consequently the responsibilities to team members are often different from responsibilities to opponents. The notion of "sport discipline" to which I refer in "Hybrid Athletes" is a focus of "Disciplinary Technologies of Sport Performance" in the next section. For this reason, I recommend that readers interested in better understanding sport discipline read "Disciplinary Technologies" in relation to "Hybrid Athletes."

The final chapter in this section attempts to understand why racism has not become a prominent ethical issue in Canada. As I explain, Canada has an elaborate bureaucracy to contend with ethical issues in sport. This bureaucracy has been triggered by two high-profile cases, the Ben Johnson steroid case and the incarceration of Graham James for sexually abusing junior hockey players he coached. Despite high-profile cases of racism in sport, and many day-to-day instances, the sport ethics bureaucracy has yet to respond in any systematic way. While racism in sport is an ethical issue that affects both opponents and members of the same team, I have placed this chapter in this section because the case I focus on involving former coach John Vanbiesbrouk and player Trevor Daley occurred within a team, the Sault St. Marie Greyhounds. More importantly, however, I have placed this chapter in this section to be read in relation to "Trusting Paternalism?" and "Hybrid Athletes" to underline that when team is equated with sameness and uniformity of values and interests, it will be impossible to relate to others on a team in anything but the most perfunctory of ways. This in turn makes it very difficult to desire that team members are treated well and fairly because of who they are as individuals.

REFERENCES

Baier, A. (1988). Trust and antitrust. *Ethics 96*, 231–260.

Butler, J. (1992). Contingent foundations: Feminism and the question of "postmodernism." In J. Butler & S. Scott (Eds.), *Feminists theorize the political* (pp. 3–22). New York & London: Routledge.

CAAWS. (1994). *Harassment in sport—A guide to policies, procedures, and resources.* Ottawa: CAAWS.

Carron, A.V. (1984). Cohesion in sport teams. In J.M. Silba & R. Weinberg (Eds.), *Psychological foundations of sport* (pp. 340–351). Champaign: Human Kinetics Publishing, Inc.

CBC (2005). Rookie Night. http://cbc.ca/story/sport/national/2005/10/18/Sport/redmen051018.html Accessed June 27, 2006.

Cornell, D. 1992. *The philosophy of the limit.* New York & London: Routledge.

Harassment and Abuse in Sport Collective. (1998a). *Speak out! ... act now!: A guide to preventing and responding to abuse and harassment for sport clubs and associations.* Ottawa: Hockey Canada.

Harassment and Abuse in Sport Collective. (1998b). Why should sport organizations have a harassment policy? http://harassmentinsport.com/whypol.html 06/25/98: 1–2.

Harassment and Abuse in Sport Collective. (1998c). Collective action to address harassment and abuse in sport. http://www.harassmentinsport.com/collective/index.html.2001-06-07: 1–5.

Johnson, J. & Holman, M. (2004). *Making the team: Inside the world of sport initiations and hazing.* Toronto: Canadian Scholars' Press Inc.

Larson, C.E. & LaFasto, F. (1989). *TeamWork: What must go right/what can go wrong.* Newbury Park: Sage Publications.

Messner, M. (1992). *Power at play: Sport and the problem of masculinity.* Boston: Beacon Press.

Nolan, S. (1999). Gay athletes talk of hardships. http://www.caaws.ca/e/gender_equity/article.cfm?id=105. Accessed June 26, 2006.

Pronger, B. (1990). Gay jocks: A phenomenology of gay men in athletics. In D. Messner and D. Sabo (Eds.), *Sport, men, and the gender order* (pp. 141–152). Champaign: Human Kinetics Publishing, Inc.

Schellenberger, H. (1990). *Psychology of team sport.* Toronto: Sport Books Publishers.

Syer, J. (1986). *Team spirit: The elusive experience.* London: Kingswood Press.

5

TRUSTING PATERNALISM?
TRUST AS A CONDITION FOR
PATERNALISTIC DECISIONS

A number of authors have discussed the problematic issue of the control that coaches have over athletes' lives (e.g., Brown 1980, p. 3, Ravizza & Daruty (1984), Thomas (1988), Thompson (1982), and Zeigler (1988)).[1] For many of these authors, control of athletes occurs at least in part as a result of the power that coaches have to make "paternalistic"[2] decisions on behalf of athletes. Ravizza and Daruty (1984, p. 73), for example, ruled out "paternalism" as morally justified in relationships between coaches and adult athletes because they understood it to entail "compelling the athlete to act or forbear" in situations not involving harm to others. They asked, "does the coach's expertise ... justify applying pressure upon the athlete to do or forbear against his/her will, for his/her own good? In other words, does the expertise of the coach override individual sovereignty and justify paternalism?" (1984, p. 74).

Ravizza and Daruty gave attention to justification for paternalistic interference in the following instances: when an athlete's conduct would impair performance; when an athlete assumes an unreasonable risk; when an athlete has an incomplete understanding of the risk involved; and when an athlete agrees to submit to the wishes of a coach in advance of knowing what these may be. I am interested in this latter set of paternalistic decisions because they demonstrate that paternalistic decisions do not only include those that athletes are compelled to follow.

Athletes often enter into relationships with coaches in order to benefit from decisions that coaches will make on their behalf and, once in the relationship, willingly follow the decisions that coaches do indeed make on their behalf.[3] These decisions are also paternalistic even though athletes may not be forced to forbear. Contrary to Ravizza and Daruty, then, not all decisions a coach makes on an athlete's behalf are enacted by the athlete out of compulsion. Paternalism without compulsion is, nevertheless, often a way of controlling athletes. Indeed, these decisions are effective as a means of control because people so often are willing to be told by those in power what is in their best interests. When our understanding of paternalistic decisions is limited to those involving compulsion, we miss seeing that athletes' behaviour can be controlled in much more subtle ways as well.

In order to come to terms with the fact that coaches often do make legitimate decisions on behalf of athletes, Ravizza and Daruty have opted for a type of contract between coach and athlete in which a coach agrees to a full disclosure of her or his attitude toward coaching, current information about risks and benefits, and recognition that there may be alternative approaches in exchange for "regular ongoing communication" from the athlete (1984, pp. 78, 80).

Missing from Ravizza and Daruty's account is what to expect if either coach or athlete reneges on the agreement. Without an indication of recourse, a contract cannot stop a coach who is inclined to compel, coerce, or control athletes. Yet, even with an indication of recourse, this contract does not do the work Ravizza and Daruty intended for it. Moreover, a contract designed to set the boundaries of an unequal relationship, typical of most relationships between coaches and athletes, cannot even function as a contract because the imbalance in power makes it unlikely that an athlete will have entered the contract with the same control of choices as a coach.4 And, even when symmetry does occur in a particular coach–athlete relationship, a contract is not the best we can do to maintain these relationships. This is because inherent in contracts is an assumption of distrust.

In what follows, I argue that morally decent trust is a more appropriate basis than a contract upon which to form coach–athlete relationships. By doing so, I wish to show that when there is morally decent trust between coach and athlete, and if a context could be achieved in which this trust is not undermined by illegitimate institutional and social power, paternalistic decision-making by coaches is morally justified. In order to do this, I must say more about trust.

TRUST

As Annette Baier noted, moral philosophy has not asked questions such as "Whom should I trust in what way, and why?" even though trust is central to relationships "not only with intimates but with strangers, and even with declared enemies" (1988, pp. 232, 234):

> We do in fact, wisely or stupidly, virtuously or viciously, show trust in
> a great variety of forms, and manifest a great variety of versions of

> trustworthiness, both with intimates and strangers. We trust those we
> encounter in lonely library stacks to be searching for books, not victims.
> We sometimes let ourselves fall asleep on trains or planes, trusting neigh-
> bouring strangers not to take advantage of our defenselessness. We put
> our bodily safety into the hands of pilots, drivers, doctors, with scarcely
> any sense of recklessness. (Baier 1988, p. 234)

What little attention moral philosophy has paid to trust as a morally significant factor in relationships has been with respect to the minimal trust implicit in contracts. This is based on the Hobbesian assumption of "minimally trusting, minimally trustworthy adults who are equally powerful" (Baier 1988, p. 252). Contracts "make explicit just what we count on another person to do, in return for what, and should they not do just that, what damages can be extracted from them" (Baier 1988, p. 250). Although it is unlikely that a contract would be entered into if the parties involved did not have some minimal trust that the terms of the contract would be respected, the explicit punishment associated with breaking a contract signals that contracts are undertaken when there is uncertainty about trustworthiness.

A contract entered into in order to mark out expectations between intimates can actually serve to undermine trust and the relationship.[5] For example, a contract that outlines conditions and damages to govern the breakup of a relationship if one or both parties are disloyal is an indication of distrust in the loyalty of one or both. This example points to at least one difficulty with reducing ethical relationships to contracts, and that is the assumption that people "are social and moral atoms ... actually or potentially in competition and conflict with another" (Whitbeck 1984, p. 79). Relationships between friends and other intimates are not like this. Presumably, a coach–athlete relationship is not intended to be, although in many cases it is a competitive and conflictual relationship.

Contracts attempt to make explicit the boundaries of a relationship between conflicting individuals who exercise *equal* power and therefore miss relationships many of us have—those with people who either exercise less or more power of some kind. As Baier argued, when we ignore relationships between unequals, we miss seeing the ways in which trust is often an important characteristic of these relationships.

Relationships between coaches and athletes are one such set of asymmetrical power relationships in which there is nevertheless a considerable amount of mutual trust. Coaches trust athletes to be serious about

performance goals and not to jeopardize these for the sake of other interests that athletes *claim* to be less important. Athletes trust coaches to be
informed, prepared, provide safe environments, and otherwise make it
possible for them to attain athletic goals. They trust coaches to help
improve athletic skills, and, even when they as athletes are as knowledgeable about skill acquisition and/or game strategies as coaches are,
they often require coaches to observe and provide feedback or suggest
alternative strategies when there are multiple options.[6]

In all trusting relations, whether equal or unequal, the person trusting,
whether more or less powerful, is vulnerable to the person trusted. Trust
entails an "accepted vulnerability to another's possible but not expected ill
will (or lack of good will) toward one" (Baier 1980, p. 235). We make
ourselves vulnerable to others in this way because we need their help.[7]

> Since the things we typically do value include such things as we cannot
> singlehandedly either create or sustain (our own life, health, reputation,
> our offspring and their well-being, as well as intrinsically shared goods
> such as conversation, its written equivalent, theatre and other forms of
> play, chamber music, market exchange, political life, and so on) we must
> allow many other people to get into positions where they can, if they
> choose, injure what we care about, since those are the same positions
> that they must be in in order to help us to take care of what we care
> about. (Baier 1984, p. 236)

When equals are in a relationship of trust, a betrayal of that trust is
often very hurtful to the person betrayed, yet individuals in the relationship are not bound by their lack of power to maintain the relationship
even while betrayed. When in certain contexts some exercise unequal
power relative to others—women to men, children to adults, "people of
colour" to Whites, students to teachers, athletes to coaches—trusting
those who exercise more power not to harm that which is valued may
contribute to powerlessness when there is no other choice but to place
one's trust in this more powerful person. When one's trust is betrayed by
someone who exercises more social power, the betrayal is hurtful to the
person betrayed, the relationship is undermined, and the betrayed person
often has no other choice but to stay in the relationship in some way.
When a coach is not trustworthy, for example, an athlete often must either
stay in the relationship or not compete at least for some time.

Mutual trust in a coach–athlete relationship, then, is not necessarily an indication of the moral decency of the relationship. This is particularly true when trust occurs between unequals, since trust in these instances often sustains present power imbalances. Baier wrote:

> Not all things that thrive when there is trust between people, and which matter, are things that should be encouraged to thrive. Exploitation and conspiracy, as much as justice and fellowship, thrive better in an atmosphere of trust. There are immoral as well as moral trust relationships, and trust-busting can be a morally proper goal. (Baier 1988, pp. 231–232)

Not only do coaches often exercise a type of epistemic power accrued from knowledge about the particular sport and/or from a vantage point not available to an athlete, power that is at least prima facie legitimate,[8] they often exercise power granted by an organization or institution to administer resources, including playing time. The power to control playing time and indeed continued involvement on a team gives a coach power to coerce athletes' behaviour.

Even with this coercive power, however, coaches must also trust athletes and because of this they are also often vulnerable to athletes. Ironically, it is often a coach's coercive power that serves to maintain a relationship of (morally problematic) trust between coach and athlete. A coach may be able to maintain her or his trust in an athlete by counting on the knowledge that athletes are concerned not to jeopardize playing time or a spot on the team. Coaches trust that athletes will not be so foolish as to test this threat. When athletes realize that coaches trust that they (athletes) are regulated by this threat, there is opportunity to take advantage of trust. If this is skilfully done, a coach will maintain trust in the athlete despite her or his untrustworthiness. As Baier wrote,

> Sensible trust could persist, in conditions where truster and trusted suspect each other of willingness to harm the other if they could get away with it, the one by breach of trust, the other by vengeful response to that. The stability of the relationship will depend on the trusted's skill in cover-up activities, or on the truster's evident threat advantage, or a combination of these.... Where the truster relies on his threat advantage to keep the trust relations going, or where the trusted relies on concealment, something is morally rotten in the trust relationship. (Baier 1988, p. 255)

Test of Trust

Since we do trust in aysmmetrical power relations, how are we to know which are morally decent instances of trust and which are not? Baier (1988, p. 259) proposed a moral test for trust relationships: The relationship would "survive awareness by each party ... of *what* the other relies on" in each other "to ensure their continued trustworthiness or trustingness." In the case of an athlete's trust in a coach, the test of trust would be whether this trust would be maintained if the athlete came to understand that the coach relies on the athlete's fear of dismissal from the team or reduced playing time, or on the athlete's stupidity in "not realizing her exploitation, or on her servile devotion ... to keep her more or less trustworthy" (Baier 1988, p. 255).

The test of a coach's trust in an athlete is whether this trust could withstand knowing that the athlete relies on her or his skill in covering up breaches of trust or relies on the coach's assumption that an athlete would do nothing to jeopardize performance. When trust occurs in coach–athlete relationships in these ways—when "either party relies on qualities in the other which would be weakened by the knowledge that the other relies on them" (Baier 1984, p. 256)—trust is morally bad. Morally decent trust between coach and athlete occurs when each party relies on the other's "concern for some common good" and where knowledge of what each other relies on does not "undermine but will more likely strengthen those relied-on features" (Baier 1984, p. 256). As will be discussed later, if morally good trust is to flourish, it is important that coach and athlete specify what is understood by common or shared goods as well as the significance of these relative to other values.[9]

Using the Test of Trust

There is a catch to the test of trust even for those in equal relationships. The catch is that applying the test of trust may ensure some instances of trust failing the test (Baier 1984, p. 260):

> Trust is a fragile plant, which may not endure inspection of its roots, even when they were, before the inspection, quite healthy. So, although some forms of trust would survive a suddenly achieved mutual awareness of them, they may not survive the gradual and possibly painful process by which such awareness actually comes about. It may then be

the better part of wisdom, even when we have an acceptable test for trust, not to use it except where some distrust already exists, better to take nonsuspect trust on trust. (Baier 1984, p. 260)

Baier was right to caution against applying the test of trust to those relations in which one trusts as an equal. Considering whether to test one's trusting relationship with an equal is to suggest that one already suspects there is something problematic about one's trust—much like attempting to secure one's relationship by contract makes the relationship suspect as a trusting relationship. When differences in power are institutionally imposed, however, there should not be the same reservations about using the test of trust—the trustworthiness of these relationships should not be taken on trust. This is because there is always the opportunity for those who exercise more power to use coercion or, if one exercises less power, the opportunity to undermine coercive power.

Power is asymmetrical in coach–athlete relationships largely as a result of institutional power, which allows coaches to be coercive. Trust in these relationships is undermined by this coercive power and should therefore be submitted to the test of trust. The trust between coaches and athletes will often fail the test of trust because of the willingness of many coaches to use coercive power to accomplish team and institutional goals, and the willingness of many athletes to take advantage of a coach's trust that players will not jeopardize standing on the team.

An athlete may find it inappropriate to trust a coach, however, even when trust passes the test of trust, because the institutional context makes the relationship untrustworthy (Ford 1989). The context in which athletes participate is one in which others, including coaches and administrators, have a vested interest in performance outcomes over and above, or often instead of, experiential benefits to the athlete. Where potential benefits for coaches and sport administrators are high when certain performance outcomes are reached, and if coaches' positions are jeopardized when these performance outcomes are not reached, the trust an athlete may have in an otherwise trustworthy coach may be compromised by factors not controlled by either of them. In a context such as this it is often not a simple matter of trusting a coach to make decisions on one's behalf.

There are other ways in which institutions and social contexts can undermine the trust an athlete has in an otherwise trustworthy coach. If an institution is homophobic, for example, a paternalistic decision by a coach to support a gay or lesbian athlete may instead contribute to the vulnerability of this athlete, or the decision may jeopardize the coach's position. The way in which power operates in a coach–athlete relationship will be affected by the particular demands of a specific institutional context, but they will also be affected by race and gender politics. The issue of trust between coach and athlete will not be the same for a woman coaching female athletes as it is for a man coaching female athletes, a White coaching Black players, a Black man coaching White male players, a Black man coaching White female players, and so on. All of these relationships will be confounded by power dynamics quite apart from the athletic context.[10]

Trusting Contracts?

An athlete grants some discretionary powers to a coach in order to have help with what she or he cares about (Baier 1988, p. 237). Because of the opportunity for abuse of discretionary powers, Baier (1988, p. 238) advised that we need to specify just what we understand by "caring for" or "looking after," and we also need to specify what good, including shared good, is in question so that we are able to discern why certain paternalistic decisions "disappoint rather than meet the trust one has in such circumstances."

In some instances, for example, athletes trust coaches to just leave them alone. It is not a coach's responsibility to ensure athletes' long-term security or other values distinct from the athletic context. In these instances a coach is trusted not to interfere. Most often, however, as Baier said, "the most important things we entrust to others are things which take more than noninterference in order to thrive" (1988, p. 238). Because of this, it is important for coach and athlete to specify as much as possible which values are being entrusted and what will be the discretionary powers associated with trust. When a coach exercises coercive power as a result of institutional or other social powers, specification of what values are being entrusted and what discretionary powers will be involved is even more important.

When the differences in power between coach and athlete are differences in epistemic power and not also institutional and coercive power, specification of what values are being entrusted and what discretionary powers will be involved is something like a contract, since such a coach–athlete relationship is one between individuals who are otherwise equal and in which one or both trust the other to provide something that is needed. The specification differs from a contract in that contracts are established on an assumption of untrustworthiness whereas specifying what is valued and what discretionary powers will be involved is done in order to augment morally good trust.

Even if relationships between coaches and athletes could achieve the equal power required to establish a contract, contracts are unsatisfactory for defining relationships between coaches and athletes unless there is reason to suspect that one or both are not trustworthy. When a coach tries to convince an athlete that she or he is trustworthy, all the while expecting the athlete to agree to a contract indicating what recourse is available if or when the trust is betrayed, suspicion is introduced into the relationship. However, if it is discovered that one or both parties cannot be trusted and there is interest or need to carry on the relationship, a contract could set out what to expect if a trust is betrayed again. A contract can be established in these instances only if a coach does not exercise power to coerce an athlete to agree to the contract. This will not often occur since athletes may not be in a position to trust coaches in the first place because of the institutionally enforced asymmetry of the relationship, an asymmetry that makes it a contract in name only.

Trusting Paternalistic Decisions?

Paternalistic decisions by coaches are based on an assumption by both coach and athlete that athletes require coaches' help—that there are certain matters concerning an athlete's performance that an athlete cannot achieve alone. As indicated earlier, not all paternalistic decisions are enacted by compulsion. Often an athlete permits a coach access to what is cared about in the expectation that the coach will help take care of it. Likewise, trusting relationships occur between people because one or both parties must count on the other to care for something that is cared about.

At least some paternalistic decisions occur because the person on whose behalf the decision is made trusts another to make these decisions. In light of this, I would like to consider the following as a moral justification for certain instances of paternalistic decisions: When someone trusts another to help achieve certain specified values, and the person trusted has, without coercion, been granted certain discretionary powers to make decisions to help the truster achieve these values (passes the test of trust), paternalistic decisions are morally justified. A coach, then, is morally justified in making a decision that she or he believes will enhance an athlete's interests (1) when these interests have been specified by the athlete; (2) when, uncoerced, the athlete has granted the coach relevant discretionary powers to attempt to enhance these interests; and (3) when the trust an athlete has in a coach not to abuse these discretionary powers is based on knowledge that they both rely on a common goal and this knowledge strengthens their reliance on each other.

Like trust, paternalistic decisions are morally justified in this instance only if the difference in power between truster and trusted is epistemic and not also or merely a socially created power accrued from the ascription "coach" or an institutionally established power created to prop up or reward a coach's epistemic power. In instances in which other differences in power are conferred by an institution or social role, paternalistic decisions are not morally justified even when the good will of the coach is such that she or he would not take advantage of the inherent coercive power. This is because, regardless of how trustworthy a coach is, paternalistic decisions in these instances are vulnerable to dynamics outside the specific coach–athlete relationship so that a coach's institutional or social power may nevertheless be enhanced and/or an athlete may nevertheless be made vulnerable.

SUMMARY

I have argued that using contracts to define coach–athlete relationships is not a solution to the asymmetrical power that coaches exercise to adversely affect athletes' lives. Putting a contract into place does not make an equal relationship out of one whose asymmetry is institutionally based and enforced. I have also argued that asymmetrical power between coaches and athletes is not created out of paternalistic decisions unless these decisions are made in the context of coercive institutional practices. Paternalistic decisions are not always an indication of the usurpation of athletes' power any more than a decision by an electrician in the interests of a homeowner is a usurpation of the owner's power. It is not possible for an individual to take care of all her or his interests alone. We trust others to make decisions that will help our interests. Yet this trust must not be given indiscriminately since, inasmuch as others are in a position to help, they are also in a position to harm, particularly when they exercise other powers to adversely affect our lives.

When an athlete trusts a coach to help achieve that which is cared about, paternalistic decisions are morally justified if this trust is morally decent (not undermined by coercive power) *and* if this morally decent trust is not undermined by institutional and social powers conferred on the coach. Since the institutionalized nature of coach–athlete relationships does confer much illegitimate power on a coach, trusting paternalism is not yet a real option for athletes. Consequently, we should question whether it is fair to expect athletes to be involved in relationships in which power is automatically conferred on some by virtue of the social group to which they belong.

We might more appropriately work to change these dynamics so that when someone does not have the same epistemic power as someone she or he trusts, there is not also a concomitant lack of institutional and social power. If illegitimate institutional and other social powers are dismantled, athletes would be in a better position to trust that another will make decisions on their behalf, not as an exertion of power but because there is care that these values thrive.

NOTES

1. I am grateful to Gloria Filax for helpful conversations about the role of trust in other asymmetrical power relations and to the three anonymous reveiwers whose comments are reflected in many of these endnotes.

2. I use quote marks around "paternalism" to draw attention to the fact that this word has had a particular historical usage to account for decisions made in what was thought to be a fatherly manner. In this chapter I am interested in those decisions made on behalf of another in what is considered to be that person's best interests by someone, either male or female, who is in a position of authority.

3. However, built into this notion of sport is the presumption that participation requires a coach. Although not coerced into relationships with coaches, athletes may nevertheless be able to participate only if they accept the fact that participation in an activity requires that they are to accept intervention by a coach. I am grateful to Dennis Nighwonger for this observation.

4. There are certain coach–player relationships in which an athlete may have more power than a coach—for example, the coach of a professional tennis player is vulnerable to being fired for unsatisfactory performance. What distinguishes this example from those I consider in this chapter is the absence of an institutional context in which coaches acquire most of their power over athletes.

5. In some instances, however, the creation of a contract may provide the security in which morally good trust might eventually flourish and grow.

6. I am grateful to Maureen Ford for pointing out that helping does not always require that the helper be more knowledgeable. Someone can be helped by a peer who has the advantage of another observation point. Coaches can help by observing from outside; athletes can correct their own performance by reference to a subjective experience of performance—something not available to a coach.

7. It is important to underline the caution advised by Dennis Nighwonger and noted previously. Not all participants go to a sport environment to receive help. Nevertheless, the prevailing sport model is set up so that intervention by a coach is forthcoming whether welcomed or not.

8. Some social groups, of course, do have privileged access to certain knowledges by virtue of perceived membership in that group. As well, certain knowledges are privileged as being more important than others by virtue of being associated with a particular social group.

9 Coach and athlete may agree, for example, on the shared good of improving the athlete's skills, but disagree on the amount of time that should be devoted to acquiring these skills relative to the amount of time the athlete wishes to spend on other activities important to her or him.

10 In personal correspondence to me, Maureen Ford said about this, "Gender politics makes it necessary to consider the implications of entrusting a woman's superior performance to even the most trustworthy male coach. What, for example, are the consequences of associating a woman's success with a man's coaching? When so few women have the opportunity to coach highly successful athletes, this does not seem to be politically neutral."

REFERENCES

Baier, Annette. (1988). Trust and antitrust. *Ethics 96*, 231–260.

Brown, William. (1980). Ethics, drugs, and sport. *Journal of the Philosophy of Sport VII*, 33–35.

Brown, William. (1984). Paternalism, drugs, and the nature of sport. *Journal of the Philosophy of Sport XI*, 14–22.

Ford, Maureen. (1989). Distrusting gender. Unpublished paper.

Ravizza, Kenneth & Daruty, Kathy. (1984). Paternalism and sovereignty in athletics: Limits and justifications of the coach's exercise of authority over the adult athlete. *Journal of the Philosophy of Sport XI*, 71–82.

Thomas, Carolyn. (1988). Criteria for athlete autonomy in paternalistic sport model. In S. Ross & L. Chaquette (Eds.), *Persons, minds, and bodies* (pp. 191–202). North York: University Press of Canada.

Thompson, Paul B. (1982). Privacy and the urinalysis testing of athletes. *Journal of the Philosophy of Sport IX*, 60–65.

Whitbeck, Carolyn. A different reality: Feminist ontology. In Carol Gould (Ed.), *Beyond domination: New perspectives on women and philosophy* (pp. 64–88). Totowa: Rowman & Allanheld.

Zeigler, Earle. (1988). Coach and athlete—in each other's power. In P.J. Galasso (Ed.), *Philosophy of sport and physical activity: Issues and concepts* (pp. 242–251). Toronto: Canadian Scholars' Press Inc.

6 HYBRID ATHLETES

Leaders in organized sports are often involved in aspects of an athlete's life not directly related to skill acquisition, placing restrictions on what athletes eat, when they sleep, other activities in which they are engaged, and with whom they associate. Yet, even with this encroachment into all aspects of athletes' lives, athletes are not homogeneous. The relentlessness of sport discipline, particularly for adult athletes, can never completely eradicate gaps in skill nor completely close the gap between life as an athlete and life outside sport.

Athlete identity is not consumed by sport. Athletes, like other people, participate in a number of overlapping, conflicting disciplines that together produce a distinctive hybrid identity for each person. This hybridity guarantees that there will always be gaps in athletic identity—gaps that can be exploited when it is necessary to refuse the homogenizing impulses of modern sport.

Since the processes of modern sport now occur in a postmodern context of diversity in which athletes are hybrids of gender, sexuality, race, age, and ability, I am interested in looking at implications for modern sport when hybrid athletes are faced with the demands of sport discipline. I am interested in making the case that gender, sexuality, and race are also disciplines with their own set of performances that like sport discipline are also constrained by technologies of docility and correct training.

Establishing gender, sexuality, and race as disciplines is not as straightforward as establishing high-performance sport as a discipline. Sports have acknowledged experts, controlled training sessions, and specific sites for performing and examining skills. Rebounding, for example, is performed and assessed only in the context of a basketball game or practice session. Knowing how to interact with athletes outside an athletic context does not require that athletes be known as athletes because other skills are required for these contexts. Every enclosure, on the other hand, is a site for disciplining bodies by gender, sexuality, and race. If someone does not perform, say, gender skills as a notification of one's sex in all situations, others are baffled or even angered. As philosopher Marilyn Frye writes, "We are socially and communicatively helpless if we do not know the sex of everybody we have anything to do with."[1] The sex of those we encounter is always apparent because each of us performs required skills and behaviours that announce (or lie about) our genitalia.

I realize that by attempting to map disciplinary technologies (see Chapter 9 for a description of disciplinary technologies) onto gender, sexuality, and race, I risk homogenizing them as separate categories. Utilizing the work of Paul Willis, Jean Grimshaw makes it clear that conceptions of masculinity, for example, vary according to class: a conception of masculinity held by working-class boys, for example, included a belief that anything other than manual labour was sissy, including academic or book work.[2] Grimshaw compared Willis's work with that of Hudson's 1966 study of English public schoolboys, which showed that these boys did not have contempt for academic work, although they regarded certain forms of intellectual activity, particularly science, to be more masculine than others.[3] The challenge is to talk about processes that construct identity without privileging, in the case, of gender, a particular racialized, classed, or sexualized version of identity.

By attempting to establish that gender, sexuality, and race are disciplines that may conflict with sport discipline, I also risk reifying the very categories that I want to show are constructed through disciplinary discourses and technologies. To contend with this tension, my focus is on processes that create identities rather than on experiences of those already categorized. As Joan Scott writes, "we need to attend to the historical processes that, through discourse, position subjects and produce their experiences."[4]

This attention to processes that produce experiences of identity is not yet the preferred approach of social scientists of sport. More often, a social scientist of sport starts with a category, say, the category "female athlete," with the goal of describing her experiences. By approaching the question in this way, the social scientist already presumes to know who a female athlete is, thus contributing to the solidification of the category "the female athlete." Finding representatives of this category, and then collecting accounts of experiences that fit this categorization is "the bedrock of evidence upon which explanation is built. Questions about the constructed nature of experience, about how subjects are constituted as different in the first place ... are left aside."[5] An assumption that there are common experiences of "female athletes" posits a standard or normal set of experiences for female athletes, making "other" experiences exceptional accounts. A disabled female athlete, a Black female athlete, or a lesbian athlete are, then, necessarily produced as "other" to the norm of "the female athlete."

Experiences of "female athletes" don't just happen. These experiences are consequences of certain sets of discourses and technologies that make possible these experiences and not others. Tracing discourses and technologies of disciplines that have produced experiences of "athlete," "female," and, say, "White," "able-bodied," or "heterosexual," make it possible to explore how these discourses and technologies differentiate and how they create the fact of different social groups in the first place.

In *Discipline and Punish*, Foucault traced discourses and technologies that produced disciplined imprisoned bodies and the category "prisoner"; those that produced disciplined workplace bodies and the category "worker"; and those that produced disciplined schooled bodies and the category "student." Likewise, in Chapter 9 of Section 3, I show in more detail how disciplined athletic bodies and the category or identity of "athlete" is produced. In this chapter I want to complicate the identity "the athlete" by surfacing other discourses and technologies that differentially produce experiences among athletes and thereby produce variations of "the athlete."

In introducing diversity as a complication for sport discipline, I do not want to lose sight of the fact that each discipline, including gender, sexuality, and race, have standards according to which individuals are assessed and normalized. Even while disciplines overlap and confound each other, it is necessary to be reminded of Foucault's contention that modern disciplines have produced a *"society of normalisation"*[6] in which there is "constant pressure to conform to the same model, so that they might all be ... like one another."[7] In the sections that follow I discuss discourses and technologies that attempt to normalize people into identity categories. I focus on gender, sexuality, and race while touching on class in each of them.

DISCOURSES AND TECHNOLOGIES OF GENDER

In her essay, "Throwing Like a Girl: A Phenomenology of Feminine Body Comportment and Spatiality," first published in 1980, Iris Young cites the 1966 work of Erwin Straus, who commented on the "remarkable difference in the manner of throwing of the two sexes."[8] Straus observed that "girls do not bring their whole bodies into the motion as much as the boys. They do not reach back, twist, move backward, step, and lean forward. Rather, the girls tend to remain relatively immobile except for their arms, and even the arm is not extended as far as it could be."[9]

Boys, as David Whitson points out, "are encouraged to experience their bodies, and therefore themselves, in forceful, space-occupying, even dominating ways ... assertiveness and confidence, as ways of relating to others, become embodied through the development of strength and skill and through prevailing over opponents in competitive situations."[10] "Boys are taught that to endure pain is courageous, to survive pain is manly"[11]; that their bodies are weapons[12]; that "to be an adult male is distinctly to occupy space, to have a physical presence in the world."[13]

Young comments that, "many of the observed differences between men and women in the performance of tasks requiring coordinated strength are due not so much to brute muscular strength, but to the way each sex *uses* the body in approaching tasks."[14] "Not only is there a typical style of throwing like a girl, but there is a more or less typical style of running like a girl, climbing like a girl, swinging like a girl, hitting like a girl. They have in common, first, that the whole body is not put into fluid and directed motion, but rather, in swinging and hitting, for example, the motion is concentrated in one body part; and second, that the woman's motion tends not to reach, extend, lean, stretch, and follow through in the direction of her intention."[15]

These accounts are not of "natural" differences. Indeed, as Michael Messner comments, "throwing 'like a girl' is actually a more anatomically natural motion for the human arm. Throwing 'like a man' is a learned action ... an unnatural act, an act that ... must be learned."[16] Disciplined athletic bodies are not "natural" or "normal," and there is nothing "natural" or "normal" about a body disciplined as feminine or masculine. Femininity and masculinity, like sport skills, are acts or performances that must be learned.

Young acknowledges that many of the differences between females and males in embodied skills are because girls and women have not been exposed to sport discipline. "For the most part, girls and women are not given the opportunity to use their full bodily capacities in free and open engagement with the world, nor are they encouraged as much as boys to develop specifically bodily skills."[17] As important, however, as these differences are the consequences of practising or repeating "feminine" gestures and movements. As Young writes, "the modalities of feminine bodily existence are not merely privative ... and thus their source is not merely in lack of practice, though this is certainly an important element." She goes on to say that, "the girl learns actively to hamper her movements.... In assuming herself as a girl, she takes herself up as fragile.... When I was about 13, I spent hours practising a 'feminine' walk which was stiff, closed, and rotated from side to side."[18]

Children who do not practise appropriate gender skills may be pathologized and sent by parents and teachers to experts for remedial work. Many North American hospitals have gender identity disorder clinics to treat children diagnosed with "gender identity disorder." "Gender identity disorder" is regarded as a "pathology involving the Core Gender Identity ... consistent with one's biological sex."[19] In *Gender Shock*, Phyllis Burke describes the behaviour modification of children who do not conform to expectations for their assigned gender. Seven-year-old Becky, for example, was identified as having "female sexual identity disturbance"[20] because she "liked to stomp around with her pants tucked into her cowboy boots, and she refused to wear dresses. She liked basketball and climbing.... She liked to play with her toy walkie-talkies, rifle, dart game, and marbles. She stood with her hands on her hips, fingers facing forward. She swung her arms, and took big, surefooted strides when she walked."[21] The "cure" for Becky's "gender identity disorder" consisted of 102 sessions of behaviour modification in the clinic and 96 sessions in her bedroom. She was rewarded for playing with "feminine sex-typed" toys and behaviour and rejecting "masculine sex-typed" toys and behaviour.[22]

As Burke indicates, "rather than being 'cured,' Becky's self-esteem was destroyed" by constant monitoring. "Her ... desires and feelings had been worn down, split off from her everyday world, only to become hidden within a secret and shamed place inside her. Becky valiantly strove for acceptance and to do what was necessary in the face of overwhelming odds. She wanted to earn back love, and if that meant choosing the pots and pans over the soft-ball mitt, so be it."[23] A desire to co-operate, a typically "feminine" behaviour, overrode Becky's desire to play with "masculine sex-typed" toys and she was forced or normalized into one of two manifestations of gender.

"Throwing like a girl" is obviously, then, not merely the result of not practising to throw "like a boy." Throwing, walking, sitting, standing, and gesturing like a girl are produced by repetition of techniques that discipline femininity and make femininity feel "natural" and "normal." In "Foucault, Femininity, and the Modernization of Patriarchal Power," Sandra Bartky details some of the disciplinary practices or technologies that go into producing femininity: "practices that produce a body which in gesture and appearance is recognizably feminine."[24] While it is not my intention to itemize these details, practices familiar in North American culture are those that produce particular ways of walking, standing, sitting, getting in and out of vehicles, and that over time produce particular facial expressions. These gestures, movements, and expressions are embodied as a result of daily, disciplined repetition. And, like the embodiment of sport skills, improper or inadequate performance of required feminine skills feels "wrong" or "unnatural" to the performer.

Practising femininity requires an "investment of time, the use of a wide variety of preparations, the mastery of a set of techniques and ... the acquisition of a specialized knowledge."[25] Much of this specialized knowledge is an embodied knowledge about the manipulation of a variety of cosmetic tools, including, "the blow dryer, styling brush, curling iron, hot curlers, wire curlers, eye-liner, lipliner, lipstick brush, eyelash curler, mascara brush."[26] Like disciplined athletes, feminine women are highly skilled.[27] To criticize women for embodying skills of the discipline is to threaten these "women with a certain de-skilling."[28] Feminine women are rewarded for conforming to standards of femininity, but they are also limited because they are often unable to participate in activities that are often standards of competency in a culture, including skills of sport.

An individual's femininity or masculinity is measured or examined against conventional standards, represented in popular media and reinforced by schools, families, religions, medicine, the law, and other institutions. Those whose bodies do not match the standard—that is, the bodies of almost everyone—may turn to expert intervention to remedy their "deficiencies." "How to become healthier, fitter, thinner, and more attractive are recurring themes with variations" in both general women's magazines and in fitness magazines for women.[29] Margaret Duncan argues that the way in which these themes are framed makes them "panoptic mechanisms"—mechanisms that, she says, invite "a continual self-conscious body monitoring in women."[30] Little wonder body altering is a multibillion-dollar business in North America. Dieticians, electrolysists, cosmetic surgeons, fitness instructors, weight trainers, and makeup professionals assist individuals' attempts to achieve the standard or normal gendered body. "All these experts provide services that can be bought; all these experts are perceived as administering and transforming the human body into an increasingly artificial and ever more perfect object."[31]

Notwithstanding or perhaps because of overlapping and often conflicting representations of femininity and masculinity, there is an "everyday stress and anxiety" about how one performs one's gender, which produces bodies habituated to self-monitoring and self-normalization.[32] This internalized panopticon is not only embodied by girls and women. "It isn't only size which provokes anxieties about the body among teenage boys. There is the question of shape. Pubescent, I was quite convinced I was brutally ugly, that my ears stuck out, my face was misshapen, that other people could hardly bear to look at me. There is also the question of clumsiness.... But more important, these anxieties have a great deal to do with the physical definition of oneself as male."[33]

While most girls and women are not formally trained in femininity unless enrolled in, say, "charm" schools or unless, like Becky, they have been sent by parents to a gender identity disorder clinic, organized sport is a central context within which masculine gestures and movements are practised and normalized. According to Whitson, in societies with longer schooling and decline in value attached to other manifestations of physical prowess, "sport has become ... one of the central sites in the social production of masculinity."[34]

Feminine girls and women are ill equipped for sport because they have not practised sport skills *and* because they *have* practised feminine skills. Boys who have practised "conventional masculinity"[35] but who have not practised sport skills will do better than girls who have practised "femininity" and not practised sport skills because to practise masculinity is to practise "forceful, space-occupying" movements—movements that are also important for sport participation. A boy who is not skilled at conventional masculinity may have similar difficulties in a sport environment to those of a feminine girl, while a girl who has practised sport skills and also practised feminine skills is faced with a situation with which a masculine boy in sport is not. She must contend with a conflict between the requisite skills of femininity and the requisite skills of sport.

To say that someone "throws like a girl" is to critique his or her poor throwing technique, while to say that someone (always a girl or woman) "throws like a boy" is intended to compliment her. A girl or woman who "throws like a boy" has properly practised the skill, while a girl or boy, woman or man who "throws like a girl" has not had this practice. "Throwing like a boy" does not, however, only mean that the thrower throws correctly. "Throwing like a boy" also means that the thrower throws in a way that is consistent with bodily comportment and movement disciplined through repetition of masculinity. Since this is the case, a girl in sport must not only practise sport skills, she must practise "masculine" skills. While there is nothing normal about an athletic body for either men or women, male athletic embodiment is an ideal of masculinity, and female athletic embodiment is a contradiction.

Gender and Docility

> If boys simply grew into men and that was that, the efforts described to teach boys how to be men would be redundant. We can suggest, then, that "becoming a man" is something that boys (and especially adolescent boys) work at.[36]

> The disciplinary techniques through which the "docile bodies" of women are constructed aim at a regulation which is perpetual and exhaustive—a regulation of the body's size and contours, its appetite, posture, gestures, and general comportment in space and the appearance of each of its visible parts.[37]

Bartky notes that Foucault paid no attention "to those disciplines that produce a modality of embodiment that is particularly feminine."[38] She goes on to say that, by assuming that "men and women [bear] the same relationship to the characteristic institutions of modern life,"[39] the subject of Foucault's projects is male by default. Technologies of conventional masculinity were not specified by Foucault apart from those that produce the male worker, the male soldier, and the schoolboy. When Bartky provides detail for conventional femininity, we are left with the impression that there are many more disciplinary practices for femininity than masculinity and consequently that feminine women are more docile than masculine men.

While both Whitson and Bartky understand gender to be socially constructed, Whitson attributes this construction to something boys and men work at, while Bartky implies that girls and women are passive recipients of some constructive force. Indeed, Bartky writes that "disciplinary practices ... engender the 'docile bodies' of women ... more docile than the bodies of men."[40]

The superior value attributed to "masculine" skills, even though also acquired by discipline, makes it possible to represent the disciplined docility of femininity, but not of masculinity, as passivity. As Monique

Deveaux writes, "Bartky's use of the docile bodies thesis has the effect of diminishing and delimiting women's subjectivity, at times treating women as robotic receptacles of culture rather than as active agents who are both constituted by, and reflective of, their social and cultural contexts."[41]

DISCOURSES AND TECHNOLOGIES OF SEXUALITY

One of the central projects of North American academic feminism in the 1970s and 1980s was to debunk scientific and social scientific work that linked biology and social position by distinguishing between sex as naturally occurring and gender as culturally acquired.[42] By taking seriously this distinction between sex and gender, it is not possible to attribute "the values or social functions of women [or men] to biological necessity" nor is it possible to "refer to natural or unnatural gendered behaviour."[43] Masculinity and femininity can appear on any body—there is no "natural" home for either.

The persistence of the perception that gender is natural is part of a larger assumption that links together sex, gender, sexual practice, and desire.[44] To disrupt this link requires not only a denaturalization of gender but a denaturalization of sex, sexual practice, and sexual desire as well. Without this, gender, even though conceived as an effect of culture, can still be "inscribed on anatomically differentiated bodies, where those bodies are understood as passive recipients of an inexorable cultural law."[45] "Woman" will continue to be inscribed on a fixed notion of female embodiment and "man" will continue to be inscribed on a fixed notion of male embodiment.

Judith Butler argues that what it means to be sexed as female or male arises from gender performances.[46] What counts as a male or female body is a result of repetitive performances of gendered gestures, movements, and comportment.[47] Even though all human bodies have permeable orifices and appendages that can penetrate these orifices, the openness and forcefulness of masculine comportment suggest a body that is impermeable, forceful, and strong while the closed, passivity of feminine comportment suggests a body that is permeable and penetrable.

Commenting on the photographs of masculine and feminine body posture by photographer Marianne Wex, Sandra Bartky notes the following: "Women sit waiting for trains with arms close to the body, hands folded together in their laps, toes pointing straight ahead and turned inward, and legs pressed together. The women in these photographs make themselves small and narrow, harmless; they seem tense; they take up little space. Men, on the other hand, expand into the available space; they sit with legs far apart and arms flung out at some distance from the body. Most common in these sitting male figures is ... the 'proffering position': the men sit with legs thrown wide apart, crotch visible, feet pointing outward, often with an arm and casually dangling hand resting comfortably on an open, spread thigh."[48]

Gendered performances, then, establish the boundaries of what are regarded as "stable bodily contours"[49] for women and men. These performances produce particular notions of sexed bodies—permeable, penetrable females and impermeable, penetrating males—and notions of what counts as sexual practice linked to these notions of sexed bodies. One is either heterosexually male or female.

Normalized performances of femininity and masculinity produce what counts as sex and sexuality and standardizes a notion of heterosexual culture as "the elemental form of human association, as the very model of inter-gender relations, as the indivisible basis of all community."[50] It is little wonder that those who believe in a binary gender frame in which female and male bodies are complementarily heterosexual are upset when a male body performs femininity. By implication, he is permeable. But, if male bodies can be permeable and female bodies can be impermeable, it is possible to rethink the assumed continuity from gender to sex, sexual practice, and desire.[51]

SPORT DISCIPLINE AND THE PRODUCTION OF GENDER AND SEXUALITY

> It may be suggested that masculinizing and feminizing practices associated with the body are at the heart of the social construction of masculinity and femininity and that this is precisely why sport matters in the total structure of gender relations.[52]

The number of girls vulnerable to diagnosis of "gender identity disorder" has dramatically increased as girls become more assertive and as they engage in "rough-and-tumble play" that, "in psychological terminology, is the hallmark of the male child."[53] Ruckers, Becky's psychiatrist, thinks, for example, that gender identity disorder can be determined by comparing a child with same-sex, same-aged peers in athletic skills such as throwing a ball and percentage of baskets made from the free throw line. As Burke sardonically comments, "I ... hate to think that a child's diagnosis of mental health ... depend[s] on basketball shots made, or not made, from the free throw line."[54] That uncoordinated boys and coordinated girls are vulnerable to a gender identity disorder diagnosis has quite profound implications for ways in which sport programs are administered.

For boys, sports are an important place to try out performances of masculinity since the constitutive skills of most sports are also constitutive of conventional masculinity.[55] Boys who are not interested in sports are as sanctioned as are those girls who are. As Whitson writes, "[D]emonstrating the physical and psychological attributes associated with success in athletic contests has now become an important requirement for status in most adolescent and preadolescent male peer groups."[56] Commenting about the attraction of combative sport for men, Whitson writes that "body contact sport are now one of the few areas of public life in which force and intimidation are still allowed to triumph, where men who love to hit can still enjoy doing so, and others will celebrate their toughness and their willingness to pay the price."[57] While Whitson emphasizes that male bodies are masculinized in sport, it is also important to notice that sports are a site in which what counts as a male body is reinforced through repetition of movements that suggest impermeability, forcefulness, and strength.

If one takes seriously the assumptions that link gender, sex, sexual desire, and sexual practice, sports for girls have the potential to increase "gender deviance."[58] Conventional notions of masculinity and femininity and male and female bodies are troubled when girls and women are present in sport. Even "feminine" sports such as figure skating and synchronized swimming accommodate female bodies uneasily. Performance of skills constitutive of both "femininity" and "feminine" sport—skills such as grace, ease, and charm—invoke the binary gender frame of femininity and masculinity, but do so tenuously because strength and speed, even though masked, are necessary for "feminine" sports as well.

I am looking at photographs by Annie Leibovitz of U.S. Olympic athletes published in *Vanity Fair*.[59] One of the photographs is of a grouping of highly muscular individuals, one of whom is supporting the shoulders and the other the legs of someone in a horizontal position. This person, in turn, is supporting the weight of another who is standing in a crouched position on the stomach and thighs of the person in the horizontal position. When I first looked at this photograph, I thought I was seeing an elaborate pose by male body builders. I was only aware that this was a photograph of women when

I focused on the fact that the athletes were wearing women's bathing suits. I had to read the caption beside the photograph to realize that the athletes were female synchronized swimmers in an underwater manoeuvre.

The tremendous strength represented in this photograph is the necessary prelude to above-water display of flexibility, grace, and expression. Literally kept under water is the strength, skill, and stamina required to set up this feminine pose. Synchronized swimmers are the quintessential female athlete but, unlike other female athletes, they keep their strength and skill under water, subterranean, hidden. Synchronized swimming requires this subterfuge and, therefore, is a metaphor for femininity itself.

The fear of "gender deviance" has meant that female participation in sport has been strictly policed and monitored.[60] In the early part of the 20th century in North America, medical doctors and female physical educators advised against vigorous exercise and "unhealthy," "unnatural" competition that, they cautioned, would tax female bodies to the point of hysteria, damage female reproductive systems, and contribute to "mannishness." Media still portray female athletes as novelties, beauty queens, or "mannish" freaks and there is ongoing fear-mongering from media, administrators, coaches, and the sporting public about the "'mannish' athlete and the lesbian threat."[61] An effect of these measures has been to convey the message that, if women wish to participate in sport, they must do so in ways that are minimally disruptive of sport as a process contributing to a two-gender, two-sex system, or else be punished.

One of the more striking ways in which sports work to reinforce gender categories is through "gender verification" or "sex testing." Sex testing entails scraping tissue from the inside of the athlete's cheek and then analyzing this tissue for X and Y chromatin. Jennifer Hargreaves comments that, "'sex testing' ... was introduced in order to prevent males from competing in women's events, and so it also symbolizes the idea of male athletic superiority."[62] Since strength, skill, and aggression are considered to be masculine performances and these performances solidify notions of maleness, someone who excels at these performances is presumed to be male. Even females in mixed competitions such as equestrian events must undergo sex testing[63] because sex testing "is the most potent symbol of the concern to prove that there is an absolute distinction between the sexes."[64]

In 1966 female athletes were visually inspected to verify their "femininity" at the European Championships in Budapest and in 1968 the International Olympic Committee (IOC) instituted mandatory chromosomal testing of women athletes.[65] The IOC persisted with "sex testing" despite evidence that chromosomes are not neatly packaged as XX or XY and that sex assignment based on chromosomal readings is often related to assumptions about genitalia. Medical doctors have declared individuals to be male who have XX chromosomes ("normal" for females) because of the presence of external genitalia. John Hood-Williams comments that, "they were assigned as men, we have to presume ... because of the appearance of external genitalia. But, of course, in some circumstances physicians decide that the external genitalia should be surgically 'corrected' since they do not match the chromosomal sex."[66] Part of the difficulty with attempting to line up chromosomes with genitalia and these, in turn, with an assignment of biological sex is that there are not only two sexes into which all bodies fit. Medical science is aware of the existence of at least five sexes—what Anne Fausto-Sterling refers to as male, intersexed male, true intersexed male, intersexed female, and female.[67] Despite this knowledge, those whose bodies do not match the normal standard for femaleness or maleness are "normalized" through surgical alteration.

Anti-drug campaigns in high-performance sport are also based on an assumption that sexual dimorphism is a natural fact that steroids undermine. These campaigns have often relied on scare tactics that send the message that by taking steroids, one's sex will be changed.[68] Davis and Delano argue that anti-drug campaigns assume a dichotomization of "physical gender" that "conceal[s] the physical realities of many people ... and label[s] such people as ugly, freakish, and disgusting."[69]

The norm in high-performance sport is masculine and heterosexual. Repetition of sport skills in men's sport materializes notions of a male body as forceful and impermeable and invokes the gendered binary frame—a masculine body as heterosexually complementary to a necessarily absent female body or a female body cheering on the sidelines. Women and "effeminate" gay men in sport disrupt this masculine, heterosexual norm for athletic bodies. Women do so by undermining an assumption that there is a coherence between gendered performance and sexed bodies. When bodies identified as female perform masculine skills, questions emerge about presumed softness, passivity, and permeability of female bodies.

A stereotypical gay man in sport calls into question the assumed immutability of conventional masculinity. As Brian Pronger indicates, "being both athletic and gay presents a seeming contradiction."[70] For the most part, however, gay men are invisible in sport. Whereas lesbians are assumed to predominate in women's sport, gay men are assumed to be absent. Locker room talk ensures that everyone understands that gays are outsiders to sport because they are not masculine, more like girls and women, and hence certainly not athletes. Teasing and ridiculing other boys and men about being a "fag" is the most common way that both athletes and coaches police sexuality in sport.[71]

Recently, figure skating has purportedly become more masculine because many skaters are performing more athletic and less artistic movements and are wearing fewer sequins and more leather. According to some sport journalists, a new "macho" look has made men's figure skating more interesting.[72] "Macho," "cowboy," and "daring dirt-bike look" are coded as heterosexual, even though these images have cultural meaning in gay male culture as well.[73] If we have any doubts about the sexuality of at least some of the skaters, mainstream sport journalists are willing to help us out: "[H]e's on the ice at 8 a.m. Two hours later, he's at work. He has skating bills and a family to look after, a one-year old and a seven-year-old stepdaughter."[74]

Lesbians in sport are perhaps less disruptive of an assumed coherence among sex, gender, and sexual practice to the extent that performances by lesbians in sport match stereotypical notions of the masculine lesbian. Yet there is an ongoing policing of lesbianism in sport that affects all women. As Cahn indicates, "women can compete, even excel, in sport as long as they demonstrate that they are sexually interested in and accessible to men."[75] Those who do not make their heterosexuality apparent are targets of anti-lesbian harassment. An extreme but common example is Rene Portland who, as coach of the Pennsylvania State women's basketball team, dismissed players when she uncovered that they were lesbians.[76] "Portland's anti-lesbian bias even translated into fear for straight players. Rene told us when we came on the team that she didn't go for the lesbian lifestyle, that she didn't want it on her team—wouldn't tolerate it.... I'm not a lesbian, but when I played for her, I was afraid she might think I was and take away my scholarship. I started changing the way I dressed, started going out with a guy I didn't like—just to stay on the team. It meant my academic career, that scholarship."[77]

Female athletes who worry about their femininity and sexuality find a number of ways to work out the incongruity between their female bodies and their "masculine" performances. I recall happily quoting my grade 11 basketball coach that, "we play like boys on the court and behave like ladies off the court." While many women stay away from sport altogether for fear of the lesbian label, others perform a hyper-femininity when not training or competing. Female athletes often attempt to reconcile their beliefs about female embodiment and sexuality with the "masculine" gestures and movements they perform in competition by an exaggeration of feminine comportment, dress, and makeup, particularly immediately after competition.

Despite the fact that discourses and technologies of sport discipline reinforce conventional sexuality, sports are often a site of identity formation for lesbians and gay men. Many men, including gay men, are attracted to sport as a way to prove their maleness and, for some, to divert attention from their homosexuality. Olympian Tom Waddell, who was also the founder of the Gay Games, indicated that he became involved in sports because "I wanted to be viewed as a male.... I wanted the male, macho image of an athlete."[78]

As Cahn indicates, "the paradox of women's sport history" is that simultaneous with homophobic fear of the mannish lesbian in sport, there are lesbians in sport who struggle "to create new ways of being female in a society profoundly afraid of women's sexual autonomy and collective power."[79] Sport provides a context within which women who are unsure about or coming to terms with their sexual identity can "explore different social and sexual possibilities."[80] Indeed, even committed heterosexual women experience in sport what it is like to cross-dress and perform conventional masculine skills.

DISCOURSES AND TECHNOLOGIES OF RACE

I have argued that what counts as a sexed body is interpreted through cultural lenses. The same can be said about what counts as embodiment for other identity categories. In a convincing essay, "The Suit and the Photograph," John Berger[81] argues, for example, that there is a recognizable working-class embodiment produced by physical work. Berger writes that even though there are many variations and exceptions, it is possible to note a "characteristic physical rhythm which most peasants, both women and men, acquire," which is directly related to the amount of work that is performed each day.[82] When peasants or working-class people wear clothes that were designed for those who are sedentary, they are, says Berger, "condemned ... within the system of those standards, to being always, and recognizably to the classes above them, second-rate, clumsy, uncouth, defensive."[83]

Even though both sex and gender are cultural, a distinction between sex as biological and gender as cultural *has* been helpful as a way to undermine arguments that behaviour is biological. Unfortunately, there has not been comparable differentiation in understanding race and, consequently, race is still understood by many as entirely biological. Marilyn Frye goes some way in exposing the social underpinnings of race by distinguishing between what she calls being "whitely" and having white skin.[84] Frye writes: "being whitely (like being masculine) I conceive as a deeply ingrained way of being in the world. Following the analogy with masculinity, I assume that the connection between whiteliness and light-coloured skin is a *contingent* connection: this character could be manifested by persons who are *not* 'white'; it can be absent in persons who *are*."[85]

In distinguishing "whiteliness" as behaviour from white skin as a feature of bodies, Frye does not consider, however, that what counts as characteristics of whiteness are interpreted through and solidified by performances of "whiteliness." I want to propose that, just as performances of masculinity solidify what counts as a male body, "whitely" performances solidify the notion of what counts as a white body. This is not a denial of the physicality or materiality of skin colour and other features. Rather, it is to contend that, like sexed bodies, what counts as the boundaries or limits of a "raced" body is constructed within expectations of what these bodies do or should perform.

Variations in skin colour and facial features have been reduced to three categories—that is, into three races. Anthropologist Alan Goodman comments that, "race as a way of organizing [what we know about variation] is incredibly simplified and bastardized.... There is no organizing principle by which you could put 5 billion people into so few categories in a way that would tell you anything important about humankind's diversity."[86] Yet cultural performances of "raced" behaviour continue to solidify the notion that human variation in skin colour and facial features can be reduced to three categories.

Culturally dominant notions of white bodies are, in part, the consequence of "whitely" bodily comportment that operates within confined spatial constraints. The "whitely" comportment of the Aryan Nazi soldier is the epitome of "whitely" gesture and movement, designed to represent "whiteness" as clean, pure, contained, orderly, controlled, restrained, and disciplined.[87] Likewise, culturally acquired "blackly"[88] gestures, comportment, and movement produce or materialize what is perceived to be the physical dimensions of a black body. The boundaries or limits of these gestures, comportment, and movement are often expansive and solidify the bodily contours of blackness as "strong, athletic" or as "potent ... savage, animal."[89] In this culture, "contained, orderly, restrained, disciplined" people are those in positions of authority—those who judge or help others[90]—and "strong," "potent" people are often athletes.

Whiteliness or blackliness have much different meanings on male or female bodies and, as a result, materialize what counts as whiteness and blackness in much different ways. Black males are often thought by Whites to have superior athletic abilities, abilities also linked to masculinity. Black males may take up this stereotype and cultivate what Richard Majors calls the "cool pose"[91]—"a construction of unique, expressive, and conspicuous styles of demeanour, speech, gesture, clothing, hairstyle, walk, stance, and handshake ... as a means to show the dominant culture (and the black male's peers) that the black male is strong and proud and can survive."[92] These performances are solidified into a bodily "hyper masculinity" and "hyper(hetero)sexuality" in contrast to the norm of conventional White masculinity.

In a racist culture, light skin defines a male as rational and a female as beautiful. A performance of conventional femininity by a dark-skinned female is, then, at odds with conventional beauty. Because "dark skin is stereotypically coded ... as masculine,"[93] someone who is dark skinned is never quite able to perform conventional femininity even with cosmetic assistance. Moreover, the history of black women in North America as "slaves, tenant farmers, domestics, and wageworkers disqualifie[s] them from standards of femininity defined around the frail or inactive female body."[94] The racist association of masculinity with dark skin in this culture makes it possible, then, to more readily associate sport with black womanhood than with white womanhood. As Susan Cahn writes: "The assertion that sport made women physically unattractive and sexually unappealing found its corollary in view of black women as less attractive and desirable than white women. The correspondence between stereotyped depictions of black womanhood and athletic females was nearly exact, and thus doubly resonant in the case of African-American women athletes."[95]

Nevertheless, most black women's lives defy and exceed the stereotypes. A study by Mimi Nichter indicates, for example, that there is "growing evidence that black and white girls view their bodies in dramatically different ways."[96] Said one black girl, "in our culture, women are the power. Often the woman is the sole parent, who holds down two jobs, takes care of the house, raises the children, works in the church. And power means being large in every way. Big is healthy, strong."[97]

SPORT DISCIPLINE AND
THE PRODUCTION OF RACE

> There right in front of the student union, was a statute entitled *The Student Body*. It was a collection of cast bronze figures, slightly smaller than life-size. One was of an apparently white, Mr. Chips-style figure with a satchel of books on his back, pursuing his way. Another was of a young woman of ambiguous racial cast, white or maybe Asian, carrying a violin and some books and earnestly pursuing her way. A third figure was of a young white woman struggling with a load of books stretching from below her waist up to her chin.... In the centre of this arrangement was a depiction of an obviously black young man. He was dressed in gym shorts and balanced a basketball on one finger. The last figure was of a solemn-faced young black woman; she walked along, a solitary book balanced on her head.[98]

I have argued that what counts as identifiable features of a white or black body are established through bodily comportment—white as orderly and contained; black as powerful and strong—as well as through expectations of what "roles" these bodies can rightfully assume in a culture. Not only is whiteness associated with certain qualities such as "personal drive, responsibility, integrity, and success,"[99] when someone who is black displays these qualities, his or her blackness may be overlooked. In "The Facts of Michael Jordan's Blackness: Excavating a Floating Racial Signifier," David Andrews shows how Chicago Bulls' superstar Michael Jordan's blackness fades when Jordan is represented as successful and responsible. Instead of breaking down the stereotype of "the responsible white" and "the irresponsible black," Michael Jordan is represented *as* white because, in this culture, to be responsible and a success "mean[s] *white*."[100]

High-performance sports contribute to the demarcation of racial identities by reinforcing another stereotype: White athletes are successful in sport because of their intelligence and hard work and black athletes succeed because of their "natural" athleticism. The publication of *The Bell Curve: Intelligence and Class Structure in American Life*[101] keeps this racist myth alive by claiming to have found a genetically based deficiency in blacks on IQ tests. The authors argue that blacks should become more involved in activities that will develop pride in black communities instead of receiving special educational opportunities. As C. Roger Rees comments, "In other words, to paraphrase Marie Antoinette, 'Let them play basketball.'"[102]

When blacks do play basketball and dominate in the sport, this dominance is taken as evidence for genetic differences between blacks and whites. Black athletes are caught in a double bind. When exhibiting superb skill in sport, they reinforce the stereotype of blacks as "naturally" stronger and tied to their physicality. Their accomplishments in sport are not attributed to skill and knowledge.[103] Yet, if blacks do not engage in sport, they are cut off from one of the few means available for at least some black people in North America to gain public recognition and, in the case of black men, financial reward for their abilities. For many black males, sports are one of the few contexts within which they can perform conventional masculinity. As Majors comments, "many black males have accepted the definitions, standards, and norms of dominant social definitions of masculinity ... but access to the legitimate means to achieve these goals has been largely denied [them]."[104]

In an article written over 10 years ago, Susan Birrell critiqued the way in which sport sociologists take up racial relations in sport. She argued that, by focusing on black male athletes, sport sociologists equate "'race' ... with black, obscuring other racial identities."[105] It should also be emphasized that, when "race" is equated with black, there need not be any attempt to understand ways in which sports contribute to the construction of whiteness. For many "white" scholars, it is still the case that to be concerned with "race" is to study people of colour (just as for some, to be concerned about gender is to study women). As Catherine Hall comments, "it is only relatively recently that white people have begun to address explicitly the historical specificity of their own 'racial' and ethnic identities, to explore the ways in which whiteness has been constructed as a vital element in power relations, to specify the gendered nature of that whiteness and the inadequacy of a homogeneous notion of white."[106]

The problematic of "race" in sport requires much more than providing equal time for experiences of other racial identities, although this may be a necessary first step. Also required is a tracing of the mechanisms or technologies of sport that contribute to the reification of racial boundaries. These will be studies of "racial relations," but they will likely not focus on ways in which those of different "races" get along with each other. Rather, these "racial relations studies" will seek to describe and reveal processes by which experiences are differentially constructed in sport according to assumptions about race and, as importantly, how these differences, in turn, serve to demarcate the cultural boundaries of whiteness as "the standard."

A good illustration of how racial categories can become reified even as there is an attempt to expose "the myth of race" is John Hoberman's *Darwin's Athletes: How Sport Has Damaged Black America and Preserved the Myth of Race*. Hoberman ably shows the racist implications of athleticizing black identity, but he also argues that racial categories can be scientifically significant categories, in part, "because they are useful in organizing data."[107] This begs the question about why one would organize data in this way in the first place. It also misses that, by starting with these categories, a researcher must predetermine or "operationalize" what characteristics make up the categories. Hoberman states, for example, that "separate hemoglobin norms for whites and blacks are widely accepted, if still controversial."[108] But "What Colour Is Black?"[109] At what shade of black would someone no longer be considered to be black for the purposes of measuring hemoglobin? Setting categories and stipulating at least some of the characteristics of these categories in advance limit what can be learned about variations in hemoglobin or, for example, sport skills across human beings.

CONCLUDING REMARKS

Sport discipline at the millennium is still relentless in its preparation of skilled athletes but the diversity and hybridity of athletes make it impossible for modern sport to produce homogeneous athletes. Demands from other parts of an athlete's identity do not always coincide with demands from high-performance sport, resulting in "necessary failures."[110] These failures open up gaps in which it is possible for athletes to make some decisions about how they will participate in high-performance sport. However, the assortment of interests and values athletes bring to sport often tests how and whether those on the same team respond ethically to the differences among them. A measure of how seriously teams take ethical responsibilities to team members is whether the hybridity of atheletes is sacrificed to the imperative that everyone has the same values and interests in order to achieve team goals.

NOTES

1 Frye, *The politics of reality*, 22.
2 Grimshaw, *Philosophy and feminist thinking*.
3 Ibid., 62.

4   Scott, "Experience," 25.
5   Ibid.
6   Foucault, "Two Lectures," 107, emphasis in original.
7   Foucault, *Discipline and punish*, 182.
8   Young, "Throwing like a girl: A phenomenology of feminine body comportment," 137.
9   Ibid., 142.
10 Whitson, "Sport in the social construction of masculinity," 23.
11 Sabo, "The politics of homophobia in sport," 86.
12 Messner, *Power at play: Sport and the problem of masculinity*, 64.
13 Connell, *Which way is up?: Essays on class, sex, and culture*, 19.
14 Young, "Throwing like a girl," 142.
15 Ibid., 143.
16 Messner, "Ah, ya throw like a girl!," 30.
17 Young, "Throwing like a girl," 152.
18 Ibid., 153.
19 Sedgwick, *Tendencies*, 158.
20 Burke, *Gender shock: Exploding the myths of male and female*, 5.
21 Ibid.
22 Ibid., 19. These interventions are recommended to doctors in Ruckers's *Handbook of child and adolescent sexual problems*, published in 1995.
23 Ibid.
24 Bartky, "Foucault, femininity, and the modernization of patriarchal power," 65.
25 Ibid., 71.
26 Ibid.
27 Feminine "men" are also highly skilled in the discipline of femininity. Drag queens and transsexuals require these skills in order to perform their femininity.
28 Bartky, "Foucault, femininity, and the modernization of patriarchal power," 77.
29 Duncan, "The politics of women's body images and practices: Foucault, the panopticon, and *Shape* magazine," 51.
30 Ibid., 49.
31 Morgan, "Women and the knife: Cosmetic surgery and the colonization of women's bodies," 31.
32 Bordo, "Reading the slender body," 85.
33 Connell, *Which way is up?*, 20.
34 Whitson, "Sport in the social construction of masculinity," 19.
35 Connell, *Which way is up?*
36 Whitson, "Sport in the social construction of masculinity," 22.
37 Bartky, "Foucault, femininity, and the modernization of patriarchal power," 80.
38 Ibid., 65.
39 Ibid., 65.
40 Ibid.
41 Deveux, "Feminism and empowerment: A critical reading of Foucault," 227.
42 Bleier, *Science and gender: A critique of biology and its theories on women*, vii. Some scientists and social scientists still are in the business of devising ways to measure, demonstrate, and establish two discrete sexes in order to establish biological bases for differences in social, economic, and political positions. There are also research programs to establish biological bases to explain and politically differentiate sexuality and race.
43 Butler, "Sex and gender in Simone de Beauvoir's *Second sex*," 35.
44 Butler, *Gender trouble: Feminism and the subversion of identity*, 17.
45 Ibid., 8.
46 Butler, *Gender trouble*.
47 Ibid.
48 Bartky, "Foucault, femininity, and the modernization of patriarchal power," 68.
49 Butler, *Gender trouble*, 32.
50 Warner, *Fear of a queer planet*, xxi.

51 See Brian Pronger's discussion of "receptive men" in *The arena of masculinity: Sport, homosexuality, and the meaning of sex*, 136–141.

52 Whitson, "Sport in the social construction of masculinity," 23.

53 Burke, *Gender shock: Exploding the myths of male & female*, 5.

54 Ibid., 205.

55 See Kidd, "Sport and masculinity"; Messner, *Power at play*; Messner & Sabo, *Sex, violence & power in sport*; Pronger, "Gay jocks: A phenomenology of gay men in athletics"; Whitson, "Sport in the social construction of masculinity," "The embodiment of gender: Discipline, domination, and empowerment."

56 Whitson, "Sport in the social construction of masculinity," 19.

57 Whitson, "The embodiment of gender," 359.

58 Burke, *Gender shock*, 204.

59 Leibovitz, "An Olympic portfolio," 152.

60 See, for example, Cahn, *Coming on strong*; Creedon, *Women, media, and sport: Interdisciplinary perspectives*; Hargreaves, *Sporting females: Critical issues in the history and sociology of women's sport*; Lenskyj, *Out of bounds: Women, sport, and sexuality*.

61 Cahn, *Coming on strong*.

62 Hargreaves, *Sporting females*, 222.

63 Daniels, "Gender (body) verification (building)," 375.

64 Hargreaves, *Sporting females*, 222.

65 Daniels. "Gender (body) verification (building)," 374.

66 Hood-Williams, "Sexing the athletes," 301.

67 Fausto-Sterling, *Myths of gender*.

68 Davis & Delano, "Fixing the boundaries of physical gender: Side effects of anti-drug campaigns in athletics," 90.

69 Ibid., 11.

70 Pronger, "Gay jocks," 149.

71 Sabo, "The politics of homophobia in sport," 103–104.

72 Cole, "Men making moves in a new arena," A1.

73 Adams, "Real men don't wear sequins: Sex, gender and figure skating."

74 Cole, "Men making moves in a new arena," A12.

75 Cahn, *Coming on strong*, 268.

76 Brownworth, "The competitive closet," 79.

77 Ibid.

78 Messner, "Gay athletes and the gay games: An interview with Tom Waddell," 116.

79 Cahn, *Coming on strong*, 206.

80 Ibid., 190.

81 Berger, "The suit and the photograph."

82 Ibid., 428.

83 Ibid., 431.

84 Frye, "White woman feminist 1983–1992."

85 Ibid., 151–52; emphasis in original.

86 Quoted in Begley, "Three is not enough: Surprising new lessons from the controversial science of race," 67.

87 Haug, *Female sexualization*, 173.

88 For purposes of illustration, I focus on "blackliness" and blackness, while acknowledging that other "races" materialize from expected performances.

89 Fanon, *Black skin white masks*, 166. It is important to emphasize that the culturally dominant materialization of "blackness" is what appears in the "White imagination." See hooks, "Representing whiteness in the Black imagination" for an "ethnographic account" of the ways in which Black people conceptualize whiteness.

90 See Marilyn Frye's discussion of White people as judgers, preachers, and peacekeepers in "White woman feminist: 1983–1992," 153–157.

91 Majors, "Cool pose: Black masculinity and sport."

92   Ibid., 111.
93   hooks, *Outlaw culture: Resisting representations*, 180.
94   Cahn, *Coming on strong*, 127.
95   Ibid., 127–128.
96   Nickson, "She's not heavy, she's my sister," D3.
97   Reported by Nickson in ibid., D3.
98   Williams, *The rooster's egg: On the persistence of prejudice*, 37–38.
99   Andrews, "The facts of Michael Jordan's blackness: Excavating a floating racial signifier," 138.
100 Ibid., 137.
101 Hernstein & Murray, *The bell curve: Intelligence and class structure in American life.*
102 Rees, "Race and sport in global perspective: Lessons from post-apartheid South Africa," 22.
103 Cahn, *Coming on strong*, 128.
104 Majors, "Cool pose: Black masculinity and sport," 110.
105 Birrell, "Racial relations theories and sport: Suggestions for a more critical analysis," 213.
106 Hall, "White identities," 114.
107 Hoberman, *Darwin's athletes: How sport has damaged Black America and preserved the myth of race*, 223.
108 Ibid., 224.
109 This was the question posed on the cover of *Newsweek* (February 13, 1995).
110 Butler, *Gender trouble*, 145.

REFERENCES

Adams, Mary Louise. (1995). Real men don't wear sequins: Sex, gender, and figure skating. Presented to the Canadian Lesbian and Gay Studies Association. Montreal, June 3.

Andrews, David L. (1996). The facts of Michael Jordan's blackness: Excavating a floating racial signifier. *Sociology of Sport Journal 13*, 125–158.

Bartky, Sandra. (1990). Foucault, femininity, and the modernization of patriarchal power. In S. Bartky (Ed.), *Femininity and domination: Studies in the phenomenology of oppression* (pp. 63–82). New York & London: Routledge.

Begley, Sharon. (1995). Three is not enough: Surprising new lessons from the controversial science of race. *Newsweek* (February 13), 67–69.

Berger, John. (1991). The suit and the photograph. In Chandra Meurji & Michael Schudson (Eds.), *Rethinking popular culture: Contemporary perspectives in cultural studies* (pp. 424–431). Berkeley, Los Angeles & Oxford: University of California Press.

Birrell, Susan. (1989). Racial relations theories and sport: Suggestions for a more critical analysis. *Sociology of Sport Journal 6*, 212–227.

Bleier, Ruth. (1984). *Science and gender: A critique of biology and its theories on women.* New York, Oxford, Toronto, Sydney, Paris & Frankfurt: Pergamon Press.

Bordo, Susan. (1990). Reading the slender body. In M. Jacobus, E. Fox Keller & S. Shuttleworth (Eds.), *Body/politics: Women and the discourses of science* (pp. 83–112). New York & London: Routledge.

Bordo, Susan. (1991). Docile bodies, rebellious bodies: Foucauldian perspectives on female psychopathology. In H.J. Silverman (Ed.), *Writing the politics of difference* (pp. 203–215). Albany: State University of New York Press.

Brownworth, Victoria. (1994). The competitive closet. In Susan Fox Rogers (Ed.), *Sportdykes* (pp. 75–86). New York: St. Martin's Press.

Burke, Phyllis. (1996). *Gender shock: Exploding the myths of male & female*. New York, London, Sydney & Auckland: Anchor Books.

Butler, Judith. (1986). Sex and gender in Simone de Beauvoir's *Second Sex*. In Helene Vivienne Wenzel (Ed.), *Simone de Beauvoir: Witness to a century* (pp. 35–49).

Butler, Judith. (1990). *Gender trouble: Feminism and the subversion of identity*. New York & London: Routledge.

Cahn, Susan K. (1994). *Coming on strong: Gender and sexuality in twentieth-century women's sport*. Cambridge & London: Harvard University Press.

Canadian Centre for Drug-Free Sport. (n.d.). *Guide to drug-free sport*. Gloucester: The Canadian Centre of Drug-Free Sport.

Cole, Cam. (1996). Men making moves in a new arena. *Edmonton Journal* (February 14), A1, A12.

Connell, R.W. (1983). *Which way is up?: Essays on class, sex, and culture*. Sydney, London & Boston: George Allen & Unwin.

Connell, R.W. (1990). An iron man: The body and some contradictions of hegemonic masculinity. In M.A. Messner & D.F. Sabo (Eds.), *Sport, men, and the gender order: Critical feminist perspectives* (pp. 83–95). Champaign: Human Kinetics Books.

Creedon, Pamela J. (Ed.). (1994). *Women, media and sport: Challenging gender values*. Thousand Oaks, New Delhi & London: Sage Publications.

Daniels, Dayna. (1992). Gender (body) verification (building). *Play & Culture 5*, 370–377.

Davies, C. & Lonsbrough, A. (1995). Lost chance to halt the rapist coach. *The Daily Telegraph* (September 28), 3.

Davis, Laurel. (1990). The articulation of difference: White preoccupation with the question of racially linked genetic differences among athletes. *Sociology of Sport Journal 7*, 179–187.

Davis, Laurel & Delan, Linda. (1992). Fixing the boundaries of physical gender: Side effects of anti-drug campaigns in athletics. *Sociology of Sport Journal 9*, 1–19.

Deveaux, Monique. (1994). Feminism and empowerment: A critical reading of Foucault. *Feminist Studies 20*(2), 223–247.

Duncan, Margaret C. (1994). The politics of women's body images and practices: Foucault, the panopticon, and shape magazine. *Journal of Sport and Social Issues 18*(1), 48–65.

Fanon, F. (1967). *Black skin white masks*. New York: Grove Weidenfeld.

Fausto-Sterling, Anne. (1992). *Myths of gender*. New York: Basic Books.

Foucault, Michel. (1979). *Discipline and punish: The birth of the prison*. Trans. by A. Sheridan. New York: Vintage Books.

Foucault, Michel. (1980). Two lectures. In Colin Gordon (Ed.), *Power/knowledge: Selected interviews and other writings 1972–1977* (pp. 78–108). New York: Pantheon Books.

Frye, Marilyn. (1983). *The politics of reality: Essays in feminist theory*. Trumansburg: The Crossing Press.

Frye, Marilyn. (1992). White woman feminist 1983–1992. In M. Frye (Ed.), *Willful virgin: Essays in feminism* (pp. 147–169). Freedom: The Crossing Press.

Grimshaw, Jean. (1986). *Philosophy and feminist thinking*. Minneapolis: University of Minnesota Press.

Grimshaw, Jean. (1990). *The taming of chance.* Cambridge: Cambridge University Press.

Hall, Catherine. (1992). White identities. *New Left Review* (May/June), 114–119.

Hargreaves, Jennifer. (1994). *Sporting females: Critical issues in the history and sociology of women's sport.* London & New York: Routledge.

Harvard Lampoon. (1975). *Women in sport: Hit or ms?* Boston: Harvard Lampoon.

Haug, Frigga. (Ed.). (1987). *Female sexualization.* London: Verso.

Herrnstein, R. & Murray, C. (1994). *The bell curve: Intelligence and class structure in American life.* New York: Free Press.

Hoberman, John. (1997). *Darwin's athletes: How sport has damaged Black America and preserved the myth of race.* Boston & New York: Houghton Mifflin Company.

Hood-Williams, John. (1995). Sexing the athletes. *Sociology of Sport Journal 12,* 290–305.

hooks, bell. (1992). Representing whiteness in the Black imagination. In Lawrence Grossberg, Cary Nelson & Paula Treichler (Eds.), *Cultural studies* (pp. 338–346). New York & London: Routledge.

hooks, bell . (1994). *Outlaw culture: Resisting representations.* New York & London: Routledge.

Kidd, Bruce. (1987). Sport and masculinity. In M. Kaufman (Ed.), *Beyond patriarchy: Essays by men on pleasure, power, and change* (pp. 250–265). Toronto & New York: Oxford University Press.

Kissling, Elizabeth A. (1991). One size does not fit all, or how I learned to stop dieting and love the body. *Quest 43,* 135–147.

Kleinman, Seymour. (1979). The significance of human movement: A phenomenological approach. In Ellen Gerber & William Morgan (Eds.), *Sport and the body: A philosophical symposium* (pp. 177–180). Philadelphia: Lea & Febiger.

Leibovitz, Anne. (1996). An Olympic portfolio. Photographs in *Vanity Fair 429* (May 1996), 125–159.

Lenskyj, Helen. (1986). *Out of bounds: Women, sport, and sexuality.* Toronto: The Women's Press.

Lenskyj, Helen. (1994). Sexuality and femininity in sport contexts: Issues and alternatives. *Sport and Social Issues 18*(4), 356–376.

Majors, Richard. (1990). Cool pose: Black masculinity and sport. *Sport, men, and the gender order: Critical feminist perspectives* (pp. 109–114). Champaign: Human Kinetics Books.

Marshall, James. (1989). Foucault and education. *Australia Journal of Education 33*(2), 99–113.

Messner, Michael A. (1992). *Power at play: Sport and the problem of masculinity.* Boston: Beacon Press.

Messner, Michael A. (1994). Ah, ya throw like a girl! In M.A. Messner & D.F. Sabo (Eds.), *Sex, violence & power in sport* (pp. 28–32). Freedom: The Crossing Press.

Messner, Michael A. (1994). Gay athletes and the gay games: An interview with Tom Waddell. In M.A. Messner & D.F. Sabo (Eds.), *Sex, violence & power in sport* (pp. 113–119). Freedom: The Crossing Press.

Messner, Michael A. & Sabo, Don F. (Eds.).(1994). *Sex, violence & power in sport.* Freedom: The Crossing Press.

Morgan, Kathryn. (1991). Women and the knife: Cosmetic surgery and the colonization of women's bodies. *Hypatia: A Journal of Feminist Philosophy* 6(3), 23–53.

Newsweek. (1995). What colour is black?: Science, politics, and racial identity (February 13), front cover.

Nickson, Liz. (1996). She's not heavy, she's my sister. *The Globe & Mail* (April 13), D3.

Painter, N.R. (1992). Hill, Thomas, and the use of racial stereotype. In Toni Morrison (Ed.), *Race-ing justice, en-gendering power: Essays on Anita Hill, Clarence Thomas, and the construction of social reality* (pp. 200–214). New York: Pantheon Books.

Pronger, Brian. (1990). Gay jocks: A phenomenology of gay men in athletics. In D. Messner and D. Sabo (Eds.), *Sport, men, and the gender order: Critical feminist perspectives* (pp. 141–152).Champaign: Human Kinetics Books.

Pronger, Brian. (1992). *The arena of masculinity: Sport, homosexuality, and the meaning of sex.* Toronto: University of Toronto Press.

Rees, C. Roger. (1996). Race and sport in global perspective: Lessons from post-apartheid South Africa. *Journal of Sport and Social Issues* 20(1), 22–32.

Sabo, Don. (1994). The politics of homophobia in sport. *Sex, violence & power in sport.* Freedom: The Crossing Press.

Scott, J. (1992). Experience. In J. Butler & J. Scott (Eds.), *Feminists theorize the political* (pp. 22–40). New York & London: Routledge.

Sedgwick, Eve Kosofsky. (1993). *Tendencies.* Durham: Duke University Press.

Warner, Michael. (1994). Introduction. In Michael Warner (Ed.), *Fear of a queer planet* (pp. vii–xxxi). Minneapolis & London: University of Minnesota Press.

Whitson, David. (1990). Sport in the social construction of masculinity. In M.A. Messner & D.F. Sabo (Eds.), *Sport, men, and the gender order: Critical feminist perspectives* (pp. 19–29). Champaign: Human Kinetics Books.

Whitson, David. (1994). The embodiment of gender: Discipline, domination, and empowerment. In S. Birrell & C. Cole (Eds.), *Women, sport, and culture* (pp. 353–372). Champaign: Human Kinetics Press.

Williams, Patricia. (1995). *The rooster's egg: On the persistence of prejudice.* Cambridge: Harvard University Press.

Willis, P. (1977). *Learning to labour: How working-class kids get working-class jobs.* Farnborough: Saxon House.

Young, Iris M. (1980). Throwing like a girl: A phenomenology of feminine body comportment, motility, and spatiality. *Human Studies* 3(137), 137–156.

7 RACISM IN CANADIAN SPORT

INTRODUCTION

In the 1970s and early 1980s, sport ethics was of interest to only a few academics in Canadian universities and rarely taken up by government officials, sport administrators, and coaches or by the sport media. All that changed in the early 1980s as official agencies and media became more aware of the use of performance-enhancing drugs by athletes. When Ben Johnson tested positive for steroids at the 1988 Seoul Olympics, interest in sport ethics increased in Canadian government documents at all levels as well as in the popular press. Proliferation of documents, policy, editorials, conferences, associations, and centres devoted to the study and policing of ethics in sport in Canada over the last 15 years has been nothing short of astounding (Shogan 1999; Shogan & Ford 2000). No other country has gone to the lengths that Canada has to prescribe and organize behaviours of its sporting participants. Issues of ethical concern in sport are now not only a daily occurrence in the Canadian sport media, sport ethics has become institutionalized with its own set of legitimated ethical issues and acknowledged experts. This has been possible because of an elaborate system for distribution of information, and mechanisms for sanctions through the Canadian sport-delivery system.

High-profile scandals were catalysts for the sport bureaucracy to respond with initiatives that identified performance-enhancing drugs and sexual harassment and abuse as ethical issues in Canadian sport. The Ben Johnson scandal in 1988 and Graham James's incarceration for sexual abuse of hockey players in 1997 mobilized the sport bureaucracy, which, in turn, produced more policies, procedures, experts, and policing mechanisms to deal with these two issues. Not all high-profile scandals have provided the impetus to mobilize this bureaucracy, however. In March 2003, coach and general manager of the Sault St. Marie Greyhounds, former NHL player John Vanbiesbrouck, was fined and banned from the

Ontario Hockey League for his racial slur directed at team captain of the Greyhounds, Trevor Daley. Vanbiesbrouck was fired and there was a flurry of editorials in the daily papers. Yet, the incident did not spark the intense public and institutional reaction that the Johnson and James scandals did. Unlike the response to Johnson and James, there has been no public inquiry into racism in sport in Canada, no systematic policies, no attempts at widespread education, and little response from the sport ethics bureaucracy. In this paper I explore why, despite bureaucratic mechanisms to contend with racism in sport, this has not happened.

One possibility is that racism is not a pervasive ethical problem in Canadian sport, or it may be that, while there are mechanisms in place to contend with ethical issues within the Canadian sport-delivery system, there isn't the "right" kind of bureaucratic organization to champion this issue. Another consideration is that the dominant understanding of what counts as genuine harm to a person does not include racial slurs or harassment. In the Vanbiesbrouck incident and other incidents in boys' and men's sport, it is likely also the case that what counts as harm is complicated by dominant discourses of masculinity that shape understandings of what can or should harm boys and men irrespective of perceived racial background. Moreover, stories about Canadian multiculturalism and Canada as a nation of "nice" people may influence how and whether racism in sport can be taken up. Arguably these stories and others impact the emergence of a systematic conversation about racism in sport in Canada. In order to better understand the claim that racism in sport has not been taken up as an ethical issue despite a sport bureaucracy that is more than capable of addressing racism, it is important to get a better sense of Canada's sport-delivery system.

SPORT ETHICS IN THE CONTEXT OF CANADA'S SPORT-DELIVERY SYSTEM

The most influential condition for the institutionalization of sport ethics in Canada is the highly rationalized and bureaucratized Canadian sport-delivery system. Without this bureaucracy to organize and rationalize sport in Canada, sport ethics in Canadian sport would not have gained the currency it now has, even with high-profile cases. There is an established system for distribution of information through the formal structures of sport in Canada as well as mechanisms for sanctions.

The place of sport in Canadian culture was profoundly different prior to government involvement in the organization and promotion of sport when, as the often-quoted phrase indicates, Canadian sport was a "kitchen table" operation in which sports were organized and sustained by part-time volunteers (Canada 1969). Bill C-131, *The Fitness and Amateur Sport Act* of 1961 marked the formal involvement of the federal government in the promotion and support of sport. While Bill C-131 was to support fitness and sport for all Canadians, the effect of Bill C-131 was to put in place administrative support mechanisms to create what we now understand as high-performance sport in Canada.

Bill C-131 set the stage for the first administrative grants by the government to sport-governing bodies in 1966 and the first Canada Games followed this in 1967, sponsored and supported by the federal government (Hall et al. 1992, p. 91). Recommendations from the *Report of the Task Force on Sport for Canadians* in 1969 led to *A Proposed Sport Policy for Canadians* (1970), which justified federal government involvement in high-performance sport. This resulted in the creation of Sport Canada, a centre in Ottawa for the housing of national sports organizations, and the creation of the Coaching Association of Canada (CAC), which eventually established a sophisticated coaching certification program. Other government programs since the early 1970s have served to further formalize the federal government's role in sport. McIntosh and Whitson (1990) indicate that this formal structure occurs at five levels: the federal government, specifically through the minister in charge of sport; the federal sport bureaucracy, which includes sport consultants; the sport bureaucracy of the national centre that houses the sport-governing bodies; the national sport-governing bodies and other associations like the Canadian Olympic Association, and including volunteer members; and key actors that influence each of these levels, including sport participants and members of provincial organizations (McIntosh & Whitson 1990, pp. 5–6).

As sports have become more organized, rationalized, and institutionalized in Canada, so too have the vehicles to convey information about the perceived value of sport as well as legitimate ethical issues in sport. There is a ready-made system for distribution of information through each of the formal structures of sport in Canada as well as mechanisms for sanctions. For example, the minister of state established the Commission for Fair Play in 1986 for Fitness and Amateur Sport in response to concerns about violence in sport. Documentation from what became Fair Play

Canada indicates that, "from the outset, Fair Play Canada has sought to promote ethics and fair play by working within the existing sport system at all levels, from community programs to national teams" (Fair Play Resource Folder n.d., n.p.). Fair Play Canada relied on partnerships with Sport Canada and the Coaching Association of Canada and other groups, and later with the Canadian Centre for Drug-Free Sport to disseminate materials such as "Fair Play for Kids" and a "Code of Ethics for Athletes."[1]

The Commission of Inquiry into the Use of Drugs and Banned Practices Intended to Increase Athletic Performance, also known as the Dubin Inquiry, was a state-sponsored response to Ben Johnson's disqualification at the 1988 Olympics. The Honourable Charles Dubin was "directed to inquire into and report on the facts and circumstances surrounding the use of ... drugs and banned practices by Canadian athletes and to make recommendations regarding the issues related to their use in sport" (Dubin 1990, p. xviii). Commentators have been pessimistic about the impact of the Dubin Inquiry on cheating in sport because Dubin did not address the demands and structures of the sport-delivery system that make abuses possible (Hall et al. 1991, p. 225). What is important to note, however, is that the commission produced other agencies and other commissions that promoted discourse about the connection between rules, obligations to others, and fair play. *Values and Ethics in Amateur Sport: Morality, Leadership, and Education*, published in 1991, was the federal government's commissioned response to the "moral crisis in sport" identified by the Dubin Inquiry. *Sport: The Way Ahead*, a minister's task force of 1992, recommended that the Commission for Fair Play as well as Sport Canada examine the ethics of rules and conventions by initiating a discussion among athletes, coaches, and officials. This was followed in 1996 by *Power and Ethics in Coaching*, produced by the National Coaching Certification Program (Tomlinson & Strachan 1996).

In the Graham James case, almost all of the documents and associations produced to contend with sexual harassment and abuse in sport were created in conjunction with already existing sport organizations. For example, the *Speak Out! ... Act Now!* document was produced out of the collective efforts of Sport Canada, National Sport Organizations, the Canadian Association for the Advancement of Women in Sport (CAAWS), and CCES. Endorsement and circulation of materials about sexual harassment and abuse would not have been possible without the intricate infrastructure of the Canadian sport-delivery system. Not only was the sport bureaucracy a condition for the proliferation of materials about sexual harassment and abuse, these materials reflect an approach to sexual harassment and abuse that reinforces the values and infra-structures of bureaucracy: a codified, rationalized approach to intraper-sonal relationships. *Speak Out! ... Act Now!* makes sense as a document only in relation to already existing governing sport organizations, which are in a position to develop policies and procedures to contend with sexual harassment and abuse.

RACISM AS AN ETHICAL ISSUE IN SPORT

The sport harassment and abuse literature takes up issues of respect and allows for a response to harassment beyond sexual contexts, including harassment that is racially motivated. Both Fair Play Canada and the CCES have addressed racism in sport and there is a unique initiative from Sask Sport in Saskatchewan coordinated by the Committee for the Elimination of Racism in Sport and Recreation, called Working, Living, and Playing Together. As well the Aboriginal Sport Circle was founded in 1995 as a response to the need for sport and recreation for Aboriginal peoples that is accessible and equitable. Nevertheless, there is no compre-hensive conversation in Canadian sport about racism, despite impressive bureaucratic mechanisms to take up this issue, and despite some very high-profile incidents of racism in Canadian sport and many everyday occurrences of racism at every level of sport. Neither high-profile nor everyday occurrences have been enough to spark the intense public and institutional reaction that the Johnson and James scandals did.

Like racism, sexual harassment and abuse was once also off the radar screen of what count as ethical issues in Canadian sport. And again, this was despite a sport-delivery system that was very capable of taking up this issue. The event that first brought sexual harassment and abuse into the public eye in Canada was the showing of *Crossing the Line*, a television production about the sexual harassment of female athletes, and while this production was the impetus for the CAAWS (1994) initiated publication *Harassment in Sport: A Guide to Policies, Procedures, and Resources*, there was little formal follow-up by Canada's sport-delivery system. There was no impetus to have this guide integrated into the sport system. As Robinson indicates, "although we had been exposing the systemic sexual abuse of female athletes since 1992, the problem [was] virtually ... ignored"

(2002, pp. 105, 106). Sexual harassment and abuse did not catch on as an ethical issue until the Graham James scandal. It took the abuse of male athletes to propel this issue into the national limelight.

It took a high-profile case involving boys to make talk about sexual harassment and abuse part of the sport ethics conversation. Well-documented incidents of harassment of girls in sport were not enough to propel sexual harassment and abuse into the public domain, despite existing mechanisms to include sexual harassment and abuse as a central part of the talk about sport ethics. Likewise, the periodic newspaper reports of difficulties faced by Aboriginal athletes in sport and by Black players in the NHL have not been adequate conditions to invoke widespread public and institutional response to racism in sport. Not even a high-profile case involving a former NHL player (Vanbiesbrouck) and junior hockey players (conditions crucial to the response to the James case) has been sufficient to trigger the response of the sport ethics bureaucracy.

Sport journalists have been more interested in racism in sport than have scholars and sport organizers. The scholarly works about racism in sport in Canada are few (Abdel-Shehid 1999, 2000, 2003; Carnegie 1997; Cosentino 1986; Howell 1995; Parachack 1985, 1991, 1997; Vertinsky et al. 1996; Wilson 1997) and there are no associations comparable to CAAWS or the Canadian Centre for Drug-Free Sport to champion this issue. It is curious why racism in sport has not been an issue worthy of systematic investigation for scholars of sport studies or by sport organizations since racism in sport is a central ethical issue in both Europe and the United States. For example, Football against Racism in Europe (FARE) is a major initiative that aims to rid football (soccer) of racism by combining the resources of football organizations throughout Europe. There are also significant numbers of U.S. scholars of sport who document and write about racism in sport (Bloom 2002; Edwards 1970; Hoberman 1997; King & Springwood 2001; Lapchick 2001).

My contention is that racism has not emerged as a significant issue in Canadian sport because there are other ways of understanding sport, harm, and Canada that override a systematic response to racism. I can only suggest some possibilities here. As indicated earlier, it may be that the dominant discourse of what counts as genuine harm to a person does not include racial slurs or harassment. For example, comments on a TSN chat line shortly after the sanctions against Vanbiesbrouck were announced reflected the following sentiments: "This punishment is overkill ..."; "way too harsh—sure he made a mistake"; "This has all been blown out of proportion ..."; "I do believe the OHL had to act on this matter but ..."; "Man, I agree that racism has no place in society but ..." (TSN 2003, pp. 2, 3). In the Vanbiesbrouck incident, what counts as harm also may be complicated by dominant discourses of masculinity, which shape understandings of what can or should harm boys and men irrespective of perceived racial background. In competitive sport, where often there is an expectation, especially for men, to play through physical pain, verbal taunts might seem inconsequential to some. As well, it may be that racism is regarded as a problem of individuals and this overrides understandings of racism as systemic (James 2003) and part of, in this case, hockey culture (Todd 2003). Certainly in the Vanbiesbrouck incident, much of the media commentary located the responsibility for the incident solely with John Vanbiesbrouck and not with hockey culture or the larger Canadian culture.

Also contributing to the foregrounding of racism as an ethical issue—not just in sport but in Canadian society—is a particular story Canadians tell about Canadian identity. Stories about Canadians as a people who play fair and who are forthright in competition have many similarities to stories about Canada as a peacekeeper in the world. Canada has a long tradition of both being and being viewed as a good international citizen (Roche 2003, p. 358). According to Roche, "Canada's interests were framed in ethical terms, it felt an obligation to honour its membership in international society and to work multilaterally, and it often achieved its morally defined objectives by leading others" (2003, p. 368).

These stories about the fairness of Canada and its people have some grounding in the role Canada has assumed in international affairs, including removal of its armed forces from Europe after the end of the Cold War, playing a leading role in the indefinite extension of the Nuclear Non-Proliferation Treaty in 1995, spearheading the Anti-Personnel Mines Convention of 1997, and rallying international denunciation of South African apartheid (Roche 2003, p. 366).[2]

What launched Canadians' preoccupation with the image of themselves as a peace-loving and fair people was the awarding of the Nobel Peace Prize in 1957 to Lester Pearson, then secretary of state for External Affairs and later, from 1963–1968, prime minister of Canada, for his role in the Suez crisis. Pearson's award created tremendous support for peacekeeping by Canadians and became a way in which Canadians have marked out a national identity (Jockel 1994, pp. 16–18).

Peacekeeping became a role for Canada in world affairs and the "Canadian people demanded the right to play it. The national self-image required it" (Granatstein 1993, p. 280). Canada's "tenacity" for peacekeeping is part of what Canadians believe to be their national character (Legault 1999, p. 72). An indication of the seriousness with which Canadians take the image of Canada standing for peace and fairness is reflected on the Canadian $10 bill. What looks to be a peace arch is actually the War Memorial in Ottawa. The warriors have been blotted out and a Canadian peacekeeper is represented instead, standing in front of a partial globe with the inscription, "Au Service de la Paix/In the Service of Peace."

Canada has gained considerable status on the international scene as a peace-loving country that is concerned about fairness for people worldwide. This concern to be perceived as a country with values associated with peace, honesty, and fairness has also extended to the realm of sport. As Chief Justice Dubin indicated, "government funding of sport has become a means for promoting the national, international, and social policies of the country ... sport is relied on to give Canada a high international profile as a modern, thriving, healthy, and prosperous nation that values the ideals of fairness and honesty" (Dubin 1990, pp. 4–5). Indeed, the national media was concerned to show how Canada was represented internationally after Johnson was stripped of his gold medal (Jackson 1998, p. 231). These international headlines included, "Fastest junkie on earth," "Drugs turn Johnson's medal into a piece of fool's gold," "CHEAT!," and "The fastest man in the world— a doping sinner" (Jackson 1998, p. 231). The national media reported the following responses by Canadians to the blow to the "international reputation of Canada" (Boudreau & Konzak in Jackson 1998, p. 232): shock and disbelief, humiliation, despair, mourning, and tragedy (Jackson 1998, p. 232). These reactions are not unlike the concern expressed by some that Canada has "endangered its reputation as a good international citizen" (Roche 2003, p. 359) by participating in the Persian Gulf War of 1991, the Kosovo bombing in 1999, and the bombing of Afghanistan in 2001.

My claim is that a long-standing concern by the Canadian government—as well as by many Canadians to maintain Canada's international image as a country that values peace, honesty, and fairness—was a condition that made possible the intense government and sport bureaucracy response to Ben Johnson's disqualification. However, it is also this image of ourselves as honest and fair that interferes with us taking seriously that there is systemic racism in this country, including in sport.

In Chapter 4, "Ethics for Strangers in Sport," I argued that opponents are often strangers and therefore require a different ethical approach than is possible with friends. Being on the same team, however, is no guarantee that someone is a friend or that he or she will be treated well and fairly. Despite frequent contact and common goals, members of the same team may otherwise be strangers to one another when interpersonal relationships are affected by racism. In these instances, team members who are thought to be less worthy because of their ethnic and racial backgrounds are not seen as complex and interesting people. Rather, they are regarded as John Vanbiesbrouck regarded Trevor Daley—as a stereotype who could be maligned but not harmed by racial slurs.

NOTES

1   In 1995 Fair Play Canada amalgamated with the Canadian Centre for Drug-Free Sport to form the Canadian Centre for Ethics in Sport (CCES).
2   Canadian businesses do, however, play a significant role in the international arms trade just as some Canadian athletes continue to find ways to cheat.

REFERENCES

Abdel-Shehid, G. (1999). Can't forget Ben: Representational ambiguities and Canadian nationalism. In M. Reif-Hulser (Ed.), *Borderlands, spaces in-between: Negotiating boundaries in post-colonial writing* (ASNEL 3). Amsterdam: Rodopi.

Abdel-Shehid, G. (2000). Writing hockey thru race: Rethinking Black hockey in Canada. In R. Walcott (Ed.), *Rude: Contemporary Black Canadian criticism* (pp. 69–86). Toronto: Insomniac Press.

Abdel-Shehid, G. (2003). In place of race, space: Basketball in Canada and the absence of racism. In R. Wilcox et al. (Eds.), *Sporting dystopias: The making and meanings of urban sport cultures* (pp. 247–264). Binghamton: SUNY Press.

Blackhurst, M., Schneider, A. & Strachan, D. (1991). *Values and ethics in amateur sport: Morality, leadership, education.* London: Fitness and Amateur Sport.

Bloom, J. (Ed). (2002). *Sport matters: Race, recreation, and culture.* New York: New York University Press.

CAAWS. (1994). *Harassment in sport: A guide to policies, procedures, and resources.* Ottawa: Canadian Association for Women Sport and Physical Activity.

Canada. (1969). *Report of the task force on sport for Canadians.* Ottawa: Queen's Printer.

Carnegie, H. (1997). *A fly in a pail of milk.* Oakville: Mosaic Press.

Cosentino, F. (1986). *Afros, Aboriginals, and amateur sport in pre-World War One Canada.* Ottawa: The Canadian Historical Society.

Dubin, C.L. (1990). *Commission of Inquiry into the Use of Drugs and Banned Practices Intended to Increase Athletic Performance.* Ottawa: Supply and Services Canada.

Edwards, H. (1970). *The revolt of the Black athlete*. New York: The Free Press.

Fair Play Resource Folder. (n.d.). Gloucester: Fair Play Canada.

Granatstein, J. (1993). Canada and peacekeeping: Image and reality. In J.L. Granatstein (Ed.), *Canadian foreign policy, historical readings*, revised edition. Toronto: Copp Clark Pitman.

Hall, Ann, Slack, T., Smith, G. & Whitson, D. (1991). *Sport in Canadian society*. Toronto: McClelland & Stewart Inc.

Harassment and Abuse in Sport Collective. (1998a). *Speak out! ... act now!: A guide to preventing and responding to abuse and harassment for sport clubs and associations*. Ottawa: Hockey Canada.

Hoberman, J. (1997). *Darwin's athletes: How sport has damaged Black America and preserved the myth of race*. Boston & New York: Houghton Mifflin Company.

Howell, C. (1995). *Northern sandlots: A social history of maritime baseball*. Toronto: University of Toronto Press.

Jackson, S. (1998). Life in the (mediated) Faust lane: Ben Johnson, national effect, and the 1988 crisis of Canadian identity. *International Review for the Sociology of Sport 33*(3), 227–228.

James, C.E. (2003). *Seeing ourselves: Exploring race, ethnicity, and culture*, 3rd ed. Toronto: Thompson Educational Publishing Inc.

Jockel, J.T. (1994). *Canada & international peacekeeping*. Toronto: Canadian Institute for Strategic Studies.

King, C. & Springwood, C. (2001). *Beyond the cheers: Race as spectacle in college sport*. Albany: SUNY Press.

Lapchick, R. (2001). *Smashing barriers: Race and sport in the new millennium*. Lanham: Madison Books.

Legault, A. (1999). *Canada and peacekeeping: Three major debates*. Toronto: The Canadian Peacekeeping Press.

Macintosh, D. & Whitson, D. (1990). *The game planners: Transforming Canada's sport system*. Montreal & Kingston, London, Buffalo: McGill-Queen's University Press.

Parachack, V. (1985). Racial accommodation in sport: A case study of Native Canadians. In *Proceedings of the HISPA International Congress* (pp. 189–192). Glasgow.

Parachack, V. (1991). Sport festivals and race relations in the Northwest Territories of Canada. In G. Jarvie (Ed.), *Sport, racism, and ethnicity* (pp. 74–93). London: Falmer.

Parachack, V. (1997). Variations in race relations: Sporting events for Native peoples in Canada. *Sociology of Sport Journal, 14*, 1–21.

Reisman, C.F. (1993). *Narrative analysis*. Newbury Park: Sage.

Robinson, L. (2002). *Black tights: Women, sport, and sexuality*. Toronto: HarperCollins.

Roche, D. (2003). Canadian security for a new era: Principles and pragmatics. In J. Brodie & L. Trimble (Eds.), *Reinventing Canada: Politics of the 21st century* (pp. 358–374). Toronto: Prentice-Hall.

Shogan, D. (1999). *The making of high-performance athletes: Discipline, diversity, and ethics*. Toronto: University of Toronto Press.

Shogan, D. & Ford, M. (2000). A new sport ethics. *International Review for the Sociology of Sport, 35,* 49–58.

Task Force Report. (1992). *Sport the way ahead: Minister's task force on federal sport policy.* Ottawa: Government of Canada.

Todd, J. (2003). Ex-NHL star's conduct clearly unacceptable. *Edmonton Journal* (March 13), D3.

Tomlinson, P. & Strachan, D. (1996). *Power and ethics in coaching.* Ottawa: Coaching Association of Canada.

TSN.ca Canada's Sport Leader. (2003). Your call. http://tsn.ca/news-stories/34213.html, 3/21/98:2–3.

Vertinsky, P., Batth, I. & Naidu, M. (1996). Racism in motion: Sport, physical activity, and the Indo-Canadian female. *Avante* 2(3), 1–23.

Wilson, B. (1997). "Good Blacks and bad Blacks": Media constructions of African-American athletes in Canadian basketball. *International Review for the Sociology of Sport, 32*(2), 177–189.

A NEW SPORT ETHICS

INTRODUCTION

By now it should be apparent that sport ethics cannot be limited to obligations to maintain game rules or even to obligations to opponents. In Section 2 I made the case for including responsibilities to team members within the ethical domain of sport ethics. In this final section I argue that sport ethics must be expanded in three additional ways. First, sport ethics must find ways for sport participants to be more actively involved in questioning the commonly held expectations of sport and to refuse these expectations when necessary. Second, as I also argued in "Racism as an Ethical Issue in Sport" from Section 2, sport ethics must include issues that sport ethicists have typically ignored, including racism, able-ism, and homophobia in sport. Third, as I hope to demonstrate in the chapters in this section, an understanding of the domain of ethics requires an interdisciplinary approach and cannot be limited to philosophical ethics.

The first chapter in this section, "A New Sport Ethics: Taking König Seriously" outlines pedagogical, political, and scholarly implications that arise from a "new ethics" for sport. This new sport ethics encourages noticing, questioning, and refusing when necessary the norms and demands of sport. One of the demands of high-performance sport is that difference in skill and often in values is eradicated in the quest for superior performance. In "Disciplinary Technologies of Sport Performance" and "The Social Construction of Disability in a Society of Normalization," I show how interventionist technologies are developed by disciplines, including sport discipline, to alter those who are "abnormal" so that they are as close to "the normal" population as possible.

REFUSING "THE NORMAL"

Biomechanical adjustments, repetitive skill exercises, and resistance training are necessary if skill in physical activity is to improve to meet the standards for the activity. These interventions are commonly regarded as "natural" performance enhancers and those who use them are regarded as "natural" participants in contrast to "unnatural" technological interventions such as performance-enhancing drugs and the "unnatural" participants who use them. This contrast between "natural" and "unnatural" technologies and participants is also used to distinguish between participants with disabilities and able-bodied participants. I say something more in this introduction about the dichotomy between the "natural" and the "unnatural" as additional context for both "Disciplinary Technologies of Sport Performance" and "The Social Construction of Disability in a Society of Normalization."

When technologies are utilized by people with disabilities to "adjust" to participation in "normal" physical activity, the use of these technologies constructs this person as "unnatural" in contrast to a "natural" able-bodied participant even though both able-bodied and disabled participants utilize technologies in order to participate. When it is assumed that some technologies like resistance training are "natural," that other technologies like wheelchairs and prostheses are "unnatural," and still others like steroids are unethical *because* they are "unnatural," this category confusion makes it possible to argue that those who use "unnatural" technologies should not participate with or compete against those who only utilize "natural" technologies. In competitive sport this requires that "natural" able-bodied athletes be separated from "unnatural" athletes with disabilities. When, however, it is recognized that all participants rely on technological intervention as they aim to meet or surpass the standards or norms for their activities, not only is the dichotomy between the "natural" able-bodied participant and the "unnatural" disabled participant called into question, there is potential to disrupt the specious link that is sometimes made between technological intervention and ethical impropriety. Some technologies such as performance-enhancing drugs are arguably ethically problematic, but linking technology to the "unnatural" and then to the unethical not only commits the "naturalistic fallacy," which "take[s] disputed values and make[s] them seem innate, essential, eternal, nonnegotiable" (Cronon 1995, p. 36), it undermines physical activity for people with disabilities who rely on technology.

It is often necessary to categorize participants in order to achieve fair competition, but separation of disabled and able-bodied participants is not legitimate when this separation is based on assumptions about "natural" abilities. Until the late 1970s, athletes with disabilities competed in their disability classification based on medical diagnosis of potential (Valandewijck & Chappel 1996, p. 70). For the most part athletes are now grouped according to a functional classification system that assesses ability related to strength, range of motion, motor coordination, and balance. Functional classification makes possible integrated competitions in which athletes are assessed and compete across disability classifications.

Competition between those with, say, amputations and those with cerebral palsy is not to deny the physicality of differences between them. What these competitions avoid is the assumption that it is possible to know in advance what each individual can do. Claims to be able to assess potential performance based on impairment are claims to be able to distinguish the natural from the social. There is, of course, a limit on what any human body can do. We can neither fly nor stay underwater for long periods of time unassisted, and while there surely are limits on how fast, how high, and how far human beings can go, it is not clear what these limits are for male or female athletes with or without disabilities. Yet, when female athletes surpass the predictions or expectations for performance, this has not called into question the predictions of potential. Rather, it has called into question their status as female. Female athletes who have surpassed predictions of potential are considered to be genetically suspect—they are considered to be men.

Some worry that an emphasis on ability rather than on disability will take attention away from adaptation/modification of activities and make it more likely that the more severely impaired will be eliminated from athletic competition (Depauw & Gavron 1995, p. 204). Hans Lindstrom comments that, "just as a person with a short stature would not choose high jumping or basketball for his sport (and a person with fine motor coordination would not choose a sport which tests minimal fine motor coordination), so a disabled person should not choose a sport that does not suit his or her functional ability" (Lindstrom 1986, p. 134). Lindstrom argues that there should not be swimming events in the International Games for the Disabled that permit the use of floating devices or allow a coach to swim beside the competitor. My argument, on the other hand, is that all types of participation should be enabled. Rather than ruling out those who require floating devices or a coach's assistance, those who don't require these techniques should be ruled out of this particular competition.

Interestingly, those who argue for functional classification within sport for disabled athletes do not question separate men's and women's competitions. Lindstrom argues, for example, that muscle mass is a reason to separate men and women in competition (Lindstrom 1986, p. 132). This not only assumes that muscle mass equates with athletic ability, it takes for granted that men "naturally" have muscle mass, that women cannot acquire muscle mass, and, of course, it undermines an argument for functional classification in sport for people with disabilities. That a move to a functional system of classification has not broken down a male–female division in sport for people with disabilities is an indication that notions of "natural" male and female abilities have a very strong hold.

A CULTURAL STUDIES APPROACH TO SPORT ETHICS

A new sport ethics is situated within philosophical ethics, but it also learns from sociology, literary theory, social and political theory, media theory, history, and cultural anthropology. It learns as well from cultural studies, which is a combination of these approaches as they pertain to the meaning and practices of everyday life. A cultural studies approach to sport ethics understands ethical issues in sport to be a product of contemporary culture and consequently focuses on the social, political, and personal contexts within which these issues occur. The final chapter in this section, "Queering Pervert City," is an example of how attempting to better understand what is at stake in an ethical issue requires that one explore the issue—or what may turn out to be more than one issue—in a variety of ways, including situating oneself within the issue. This chapter is by far the most personal because I write about my mother, someone who, while conventional in many ways, was willing to help her daughter refuse convention. Moreover, by situating myself in the chapter, I was able to complicate how the Graham James sexual abuse case was represented in the media. Not all scholarly writing needs to take this personal approach, but from my perspective, much more writing in ethics, and particularly sport ethics, can and should be concerned with everyday life.

REFERENCES

Cronon, W. (Ed.). (1995). *Uncommon ground: Toward reinventing nature*. New York & London: W.W. Norton and Co.

Depauw, K. & Gavron, J. (1995). *Disability and sport*. Champaign: Human Kinetics Publishers Inc.

Lindstrom, H. (1986). Sport classification for locomotor disabilities: Integrated versus diagnostic systems. In Claudine Sherril (Ed.), *Sport and disabled athletes: The 1984 scientific congress proceedings* (pp. 131–136). Champaign: Human Kinetics Publishers Inc.

Valandewijck, Y.C. & Chappel, R.J. (1996). Integration and classification issues in competitive sports for athletes with disabilities. *Sport Science Review 5*(1), 65–88.

8

A NEW SPORT ETHICS:
TAKING KÖNIG SERIOUSLY

with Maureen Ford

In a scathing critique of what he sees as the hypocrisy of sport technologists, scientists, and particularly sport ethicists, Eugen König (1995) argued that there is no pure, natural, or authentic sport to be defended against doping. Doping is consistent with other practices and technologies that push human limits of performance but that have been arbitrarily included as part of "pure," "natural," and "authentic" sport, but only because they are not against the rules. What has made a practice worthy of ethical consideration is whether it is related to an agreement to comply with rules. Consequently, only those practices that can be understood in relation to an agreement to comply with rules have been considered to be ethical issues. Concerns about the health or well-being of competitors have been limited to consequences of drugs or limited to injuries that occur as a result of breaking rules against fighting.

Health problems that are effects of training practices or injuries that are incurred from performing prescribed rules of contact sport such as boxing, football, or hockey are accepted as legitimate effects of attempting to meet either the rules or demands of one's sport and are seldom seen as ethical problems. These health effects are considered part of "natural" competition because they are established by the rules and, as a consequence, are thought to be ethically neutral or, at best, ethically trivial. Still other practices are ignored altogether. Drug taking, the "good" foul, violence, and cheating are prominent ethical issues in sport ethics while racism and, until very recently, harassment of athletes, for example, are not.

König argued that doping exposes sport as an enterprise that is inherently exploitative: "the compulsory and unlimited exploitation of oneself and others is a constituent factor of sport itself" (1995, p. 251). The constitutive *demand* of sport discipline that athletes "push on until the limits of human performance capacity are reached" (König 1995, p. 253) creates the desire for technologies that make this possible, including technologies like doping, which are against the rules. What has come to be identified as ethical issues in high-performance sport, then, are actually produced by the *demands* of competitive sport. By circumscribing what is to count as ethical inquiry in sport within a discussion of obligations in relation to proscriptive rules, sport ethicists cannot avoid complicity in supporting a sport culture that is often harmful to athletes. As König so poignantly asked,

> [D]o we hear of an unmistakable accusation of those irreversible damages, not caused by doping but by "classical" training of numerous former high-performance athletes? Who takes care of the army of nameless ones, who ruined their bodies for the rest of their lives by using "normal" technological aids in sport? (1995, p. 250)

König went on to say that, "ethical philosophy on sport is not able to dedicate the appropriate amount of reflections to these phenomena as it tends to marginalize these daily catastrophes as merely ephemeral ones" (1995, p. 250). When sport ethicists criticize drug taking, while ignoring the constitutive *demands* of high-performance sport, observed König, the ethics of sport is condemned "to remain but a bad idealism with an antiquated knowledge value" (1995, p. 257) and "actually prevents what it pretends to intend" (1995, p. 256). König charged that a sport ethics that concerns itself only with questions that emanate from rule breakage "does not deserve the name of ethical criticism" and is "a powerless protest against sport" (1995, p. 256).

We take König's critique of sport ethics seriously and, through our commentary, we hope to initiate a discussion about a new sport ethics that would have quite different pedagogical, political, and scholarly tasks. In order to get this work started, we situate our discussion in the ethics of French intellectual Michel Foucault.

FOUCAULT'S ETHICS

According to Foucault, every morality consists of codes of behaviour as well as ways in which individuals subject themselves to these codes. Some moral systems emphasize the code and "the ethical subject refers his conduct to a law, or set of laws, to which he must submit at the risk of committing offences that may make him liable to punishment" (Foucault 1985, pp. 29–30). This is a fair description of the way in which sport ethics has been conceived as well as the way in which participants govern themselves in sport. As we explain in the next section, sport ethics has almost exclusively been interested in the conduct of participants in relation to the proscribed rules of a contest. For Foucault, however, relation of one's conduct to rules qualifies as moral but not ethical conduct. Moralities are ethical only when they emphasize "the manner in which one ought to form oneself as an ethical subject acting in reference to the ... code" (1985, p. 26). Rather than conformity to rules, the law, or standards, the emphasis in ethics is on the relationship of the self to the code and on the methods and techniques through which this relationship is worked out.

Foucault outlined four ways in which someone might embrace or reject a code each of which is related to aspects of the constitution of the self as a moral subject. First, one must ask what part of one's behaviour is concerned with moral conduct. Is one faithful, to use Foucault's example, because of resolve to follow the rule, feelings for one's partner, or the mastery of desires (Foucault 1985, p. 26)? Second, one must ask about the source of moral obligations. Is the source external or is it a response to some internal desire? Third, one must ask how one can change in order to become an ethical subject. The final inquiry is to question what kind of being one aspires to be when one behaves in a moral way (Foucault 1985, pp. 27–28). These four questions can be directed at any rules, codes, or standards that shape action or behaviour. For example, athletes can question how their participation as athletes is shaped by their relationship to the codified rules of their sport and they can ask how they are shaped by the demands of sport that have become standardized expectations for athletes.

Ethics problematizes "the events that have led us to constitute ourselves and to recognize ourselves as subjects of what we are doing, thinking, saying" (Foucault 1984, p. 46) so that "we [can] refuse what we are" (Foucault 1983, p. 216). Ethics, then, involves an investigation not only of one's relationship to moral codes but a tracing of those standards or norms that shape one's actions and behaviour. This tracing provides information from which one can refuse uninformed or passive acceptance of what is "given to us as universal, necessary, and obligatory" (Foucault 1984, p. 45). By taking up an exploration of how rules and standards shape the kind of people they are, athletes might notice, for example, that what appear to be necessary and obligatory demands of sport ("push on until the limits of human performance capacity are reached") actually create the necessity to break some of the codified rules of sport.

Refusing to just passively accept rules, codes, and standards allows one to meet what Foucault believed to be an obligation to face the endless task of reinventing oneself. When someone refuses codified or standardized expectations after an investigation of the effects of these expectations on the formation of self, the limits of these expectations can be pushed and new experiences of participation can be created.

If Foucault's approach to ethics was taken as a model for sport ethics, sport ethics would be more concerned with how each participant understands how rules and demands of sport shape them as people. Sport ethics would also be concerned with how each person makes decisions to comply with or refuse certain rules and demands of sport. This approach has pedagogical, political, and scholarly implications for a new sport ethics.

PEDAGOGICAL IMPLICATIONS FOR A NEW SPORT ETHICS

As König argues, sport ethics has been preoccupied with identifying codes of behaviour for participating in sport and these codes have been circumscribed by what the rules of a contest establish as "natural" competition irrespective of the effects on athletes' bodies and lives. When concerned at all with individuals' relations to these codes (what Foucault calls ethics), the focus has been on the second of Foucault's questions: the source of moral obligation for sport participants. The source of moral obligation for most sport ethicists has been located in the logic of rules. Suits captures this concern in this way: "If the rules are broken the original end becomes impossible of attainment, since one cannot (really) play the game unless one obeys the rules of the game" (Suits 1978, p. 24). On this argument, there is a tacit agreement by participants to abide by the rules of a game in order to test who is the better competitor.

Sport ethics, as a scholarly field, has not been interested in differentiating the reasons why participants may or may not meet obligations. That participants may abide by rules because coerced, to maintain an image as a "good" competitor, for expedience, or because of a desire to honour a perceived agreement with competitors does not centre in discussions. This lack of attention to motivations participants have for engaging in particular behaviours can, in part, be explained by the prevailing assumption that if participants can be helped to understand the logic of rules (one can't win a game as constituted by its rules unless one plays by the rules), they will act to comply with rules.

There is no work in sport ethics of which we are aware that encourages participants to explore their relationship to the rules and demands of their sport. This is because, as König implies, sports in all of their manifestations, are considered to be a good thing. Taking the lead from Foucault, we suggest a new pedagogical role for sport ethics that encourages an active and ongoing questioning by participants about the ways in which both the rules and the demands of sport normalize certain practices that would otherwise be considered harmful and that produce athletes capable of and willing to engage in these practices.

By asking questions about the rules of sport, participants may become aware of the ways in which certain prescriptive rules of sport (i.e., rules that prescribe blows to human bodies such as rules that prescribe body checking in hockey) permit actions that in other contexts are proscribed by rules (i.e., blows from fighting in hockey). By asking questions about how the demands of sport have come to have a hold on one's engagement in sport, it is possible for participants to become aware of how these demands of sport have implicated them in certain practices. For example, an athlete may come to see how a demand to push the limits of human performance has affected other parts of life that are important to him or her such as interpersonal relationships, honesty, or health. Once aware of how both rules and demands shape engagement with sport, it may then be possible for participants to consent only to those rules and demands that affirm one's values while refusing the others. In those instances in which an athlete refuses, an opportunity may be opened to create other ways of understanding the rules and demands of high-performance sport and perhaps other ways of participating. It should be kept in mind that a refusal of rules of a sport would commit an athlete to not participating in the activity. For example, when someone refuses the prescriptive rules of boxing, he or she refuses to box. Moreover, if an athlete refuses certain proscriptive rules, say, those that rule out doping, this refusal must be done not as a deception, but as an open action in which the person is prepared to make explicit how this rule is problematic in relationship to an understanding one has of oneself.

Questioning rules and demands that are taken for granted is not an easy task for sport ethicists to get started. There is no motivation for someone who values high-performance sport to notice and then question how some rules and demands may implicate him or her in practices that are harmful. Sport ethicists might encourage questioning by drawing to the attention of participants other practices to which they are committed that have standards that are in conflict with certain rules or demands of sport. For example, for female athletes, the demands of conventional femininity such as nurturing and caring are often at odds with the demands of competitive sport such as aggressiveness and taking advantage of others. By making these conflicting demands explicit, it may be possible for female athletes, in this case, to begin to question demands of both sport and femininity.

It is unlikely that questioning will be taken seriously, even with the pedagogical prompting of a sport ethicist, unless participants do experience and then notice some dissonance from the demands of other commitments and interests. Fortunately, sport participants do experience this dissonance since even the most dedicated participants are engaged in other enterprises and categories in their culture, the demands of which don't always coincide with the demands of sport. When noticing that one has failed to achieve the demands from a variety of commitments and interests, participants might begin to question how each set of demands shape their lives. They may then give assent to those features with which they agree, and refuse to conform to those demands with which they disagree. A new sport ethics may then make it possible to open up questions about other demands in an athlete's life that are driven by norms, standards, or codes, including demands of gender, sexuality, class, race, and ability categories.

Developing skills so that participants can read and interpret representations from popular culture as well as those produced by experts in their sport might be part of a pedagogical project of a new sport ethics. Becoming a skilled "reader" of popular culture and expert texts would help participants understand the relation of rules and standards in their own lives if they could critically assess other participants' negotiation of the rules and demands of their sport. How, for example, might Ben Johnson's refusal of the rule against steroids be understood or Dennis Rodman's refusal of the demands of a professional basketball player? Developing these skills will require that sport ethics move out of the strict disciplinary boundaries that have contained sport ethics and into multi- and interdisciplinary ways of noticing and questioning the rules and demands that shape people's lives.

Questioning and refusal are central to ethics for Foucault, but he was also interested in creating something new. This "something new" is "not something that the individual invents by himself. They are patterns that he finds in his culture" (Foucault 1994, p. 11), but these "patterns" can be extended to their limit, played with, reconfigured, and redeployed (Butler 1990, p. 145). According to Foucault biographer James Miller, Foucault attempted to create something new in his own living by seeking out potentially transformative "limit-experiences ... deliberately pushing his mind and body to the breaking point ... thus starkly revealing how distinctions central to the play of true and false are pliable, uncertain, contingent" (Miller 1993, p. 30).

A new pedagogical approach to sport ethics can encourage noticing, questioning, and affirming or refusing normative demands of sport, but it is more difficult to assist participants in creating new ways of participating in high-performance sport. Pushing limits of identity has been open to only a few athletes, for example, members of the Beehives, a women's hockey team with "big hair"(Roxxie 1993, p. 14), who parody both "feminine" and "masculine" sport by representing themselves as hyper-feminine in appearance while performing a sport that requires skills of conventional masculinity. As one player reported, "the big hair thing flies in the face of how hockey players usually define themselves—macho, virile, all of that. Beehives are a contradiction in terms: we are ... women with a femmy icon who can REALLY play hockey" (Roxxie 1993, p. 15). Most athletes of conventional teams, however, must comply with demands of their sport or not be regarded as good teammates. As we suggest in the next section, encouraging diversity may then be the most effective way a new sport ethics has to intervene in sport to create new ways of participating.

POLITICAL IMPLICATIONS OF A NEW SPORT ETHICS

It is our contention that if participants are to notice, question, and perhaps refuse certain rules and demands of sport, they must have experienced a range of cultural experiences in addition to sport. Commitments to families and friends and interest in, say, music, politics, or community will provide an antidote to the demands of sport. Having diverse cultural experiences and being exposed to the different cultural experiences of others presents alternatives to participants that may provoke questions about the demands of sport.

By noticing that conflicting demands from other commitments and interests do disrupt the demands of sport and then questioning and refusing passive compliance with these demands, participants are in a position to make decisions about how they wish to participate in sport. There are many ways that participants may contend with the dissonance they feel as a result of failure to meet the conflicting demands of their diverse commitments and interests. Some may be willing to live with ambiguities that arise when the demands of each cannot be met. Others may understand that these demands shape the way in which they are involved in an activity, agree with these, and see no point in refusing these identities. Still others may value what the demands require, but wish to question and actively alter ways in which sport and other enterprises are controlled by experts. Questioning may lead still others to a refusal of the ways in which these demands are constructed, represented, and imposed by sport. When a participant questions the demands of sport and refuses those with which he or she cannot comply, a new configuration of sport participation is created for that participant.

We have argued that possibilities for a new sport ethics emerge from the disruptions that occur when competing commitments and interests of participants come up against the demands of sport. If sport ethicists are to accomplish the pedagogical task of making it possible for participants to notice disruptions, to question and refuse demands of sport, it may also be necessary for sport ethicists to assume the political task of promoting a diverse population of participants with hybrid interests. For example, sport ethicists could have more to say about the channelling of children into competitive sport at the expense of other childhood activities and they could encourage teams to include participants from diverse backgrounds with an array of interests and commitments.

Some will see the potential for disruption of the demands of sport as an argument for reducing rather than increasing diversity among athletes and for recruiting and supporting athletes with few commitments and interests outside sport. Like political struggles over diversity in workplaces, legislatures, courts of law, and communities, diversity will not be welcomed by those who want participants to be homogeneous since goals are often more readily achievable when values, interests, and desires of participants are the same. We have argued, however, that if the pedagogical work of a new sport ethics is to be possible, another important task of a new sport ethics will be to upset this homogeneity by promoting diversity among athletes and encouraging each participant to cultivate interests outside sport.

SCHOLARLY IMPLICATIONS
FOR A NEW SPORT ETHICS

Foucault's focus on questioning ways in which behaviour is shaped by demands of a discipline suggests still other tasks for a new sport ethics; tasks that focus on how sport ethics, including its values and experts, came to be produced and legitimated in the way that they have. While work that focuses on justification of behaviour in sport will still be important to sport ethics, a new scholarly project for sport ethicists will make apparent how the scholarly field of sport ethics has had its own set of demands that have produced, legitimated, and institutionalized certain kinds of talk about ethics and not others. This new scholarly project shifts the terrain from an inquiry into the (apparently innocent) meaning of ethics or the value of particular actions in high-performance sport to an inquiry that locates ethical discourse historically and socially in order to notice the political work it accomplishes.

Sport ethics exists in its present form because sport ethicists have had an opportunity to provide expert understanding of the implications of issues such as cheating, violence, and drug taking produced by high-performance sport. If the demands of sport did not produce rule breakage, sport ethicists would not have been able to provide expert advice about obligations to keep rules. An example follows of what we mean by this.

It is our contention that sport ethics has become a legitimate part of the discursive field of high-performance sport in Canada, the country in which we reside, and that legitimate speakers of this discourse of sport ethics include sport ethicists, sport journalists, and spokespeople for associations like the Professional Coaches' Association, the Canadian Centre for the Study of Ethics in Sport, and members of the Harassment and Abuse in Sport Collective. Proliferation of documents, policy, editorials, conferences, associations, and centres devoted to the study of and policing of ethics in high-performance sport in Canada over the last 10 to 12 years has been nothing short of astounding. In the 1970s and early 1980s, sport ethics was a discourse of only a few academics and rarely taken up by government officials, sport administrators, and coaches in Canada or by the sport media. In the late 1990s, issues of ethical concern in sport are not only a daily occurrence in the Canadian sport media, sport ethics has become institutionalized in Canada with its own set of legitimized social practices and acknowledged experts. Examples of agencies, associations, commissions, and projects, some government related and others not, that are both effects of and productive of the increased discourse about sport ethics in Canada include the Commission of Inquiry into the Use of Drugs and Banned Practices Intended to Increase Athletic Performance also known as the Dubin Inquiry, the Commission for Fair Play, The Professional Coaches' Association, Fair Play Canada, and the Canadian Centre for Drug-Free Sport now amalgamated to form the Canadian Centre for Ethics in Sport (CCES), the Harassment and Abuse in Sport Collective, and former NHL player Sheldon Kennedy's skateathon to raise money for sexually abused children.

Included among the numerous federal government- and government agency-commissioned studies and reports that feature discussions about sport ethics in the last 10 years are *Fair Play: Integrity, Fairness, and Respect* issued by the Commission for Fair Play in 1988; *Values and Ethics in Amateur Sport: Morality, Leadership, and Education*, published in 1991 as a response to the "moral crisis in sport" identified by the *Dubin Report*; *Sport: The Way Ahead*, the Minister's Task Force of 1992 that recommended that the Commission for Fair Play and Sport Canada examine the ethics of rules and conventions by initiating a discussion among athletes, coaches, and officials; the 1994 Sport Canada *Harassment in Sport—A Guide to Policies, Procedures, and Resources*; the National Coaching Certification Program's *Power and Ethics in Coaching* published in 1996; and *Speak Out! ... Act Now Handbook* produced by Sport Canada in 1998 in conjunction with the Harassment and Abuse in Sport Collective and the Canadian Hockey Association.

A new scholarly approach to sport ethics is interested in asking how sport ethics became an important part of the discursive field of Canadian high-performance sport (Shogan & Ford, 1998). Attempts to address this question would draw the sport ethicist to two major events within Canadian high-performance sport: Ben Johnson's disqualification at the 1988 Seoul Olympics for steroid use and Graham James's incarceration in 1996 for sexually abusing junior hockey players coached by him. The inquiry would not, however, be limited to these. Instead, an inquiry into the production and legitimation of sport ethics in Canada would pay attention to conditions that made possible the emergence of discourses about sport ethics without which the events themselves would likely not have precipitated. This approach does not aim to trace causal influences among events but to show how what Edward Said refers to as adjacent events (in Bové 1995, p. 55) "can ... transform entire domains of knowledge production" (Bové 1995, p. 60)—in this case the production of what counts as sport ethics in Canadian high-performance sport. This approach to sport ethics may find, for example, that the bureaucratization, rationalization, and scientization of high-performance sport in Canada is one "condition of possibility" (Foucault 1970, p. xxii) for the emergence and proliferation of a sport ethics discourse, and that federal bureaucratic support for sport made possible proliferation of discourse in relation to performance-enhancing drugs or doping in Canada, but not in relation to, say, anorexia nervosa and bulimia in female gymnasts. This approach may also show how adjacent discourses of race and gender, for example, created conditions of possibility for a sport ethics discourse based on cheating rather than health, and how adjacent discourses of gender and sexuality created conditions for the burgeoning of discourse about sexual assault and harassment of male athletes, but ruled out taking up the pervasive sexual harassment and abuse of female athletes prior to the Graham James's case.

This scholarly project in sport ethics is not an empirical analysis of causal relations that might promise to get the "real" story of why sport ethics in Canada has become an academic growth industry. Rather than telling a truth about sport ethics, this new approach focuses on how discourses of sport ethics work strategically (Halperin 1995, p. 30). This approach to the scholarly field of sport ethics does not attempt to improve ethics or show that sport ethics in Canada is "progressing." Instead, it attempts to notice what legitimately can be said about sport ethics in Canada now. A project like this refuses to engage with the questions of legitimation produced by the normative demands of traditional sport ethics. We need "to stop playing long enough to stand back from the game [in this case, the game of sport ethics], to look at all its rules in their totality, and to examine our strategic situation: how the game has been set up, on what terms most favourable to whom, with what consequences to which of its players" (Halperin 1995, p. 38).

CONCLUDING REMARKS

In this chapter we have attempted to find ways that a new sport ethics might challenge, rather than be complicit with, the demands of sport. Since rule breakage is often a consequence of the demands of sport, and traditional sport ethics has focused on rule breakage, we agree with König that a challenge to the demands of sport must include a critique of how sport ethics has been conducted. We have suggested that Michel Foucault's understanding of ethics is one way that we can begin to think about ethics differently. If ethics is less about compliance with codes and more about how we explore the ways in which these codes shape our lives, it is possible for people to become more directly involved in understanding and changing their own conduct. A new sport ethics is interested in creating the conditions to make possible the investigation of rules, codes, and norms in the lives of sport participants. This will require that sport ethicists not only concern themselves with the pedagogy of facilitating this examination, but that they engage in political work to encourage diversity of experience among participants. Important as well will be a scholarly task in which sport ethicists challenge the demands of "sport ethics as usual" so that sport ethics can serve as a powerful "protest against sport."

REFERENCES

Bové, P.A. (1995). Discourse. In F. Lentricchia & T. McLaughlin (Eds.), *Critical terms for literary study*, 2nd ed. Chicago & London: University of Chicago Press.

Butler, J. (1990). *Gender trouble: Feminism and the subversion of identity*. New York & London: Routledge.

Foucault, M. (1970). *The order of things: An archaeology of the human sciences*. Translated by A. Sheridan. New York: Pantheon.

Foucault, M. (1983). The subject and power. In H.L. Dreyfus & P. Rabinow (Eds.), *Michel Foucault: Beyond structuralism and hermeneutics*. Chicago: University of Chicago Press.

Foucault, M. (1984). What is enlightenment? In P. Rabinow (Ed.), *The Foucault reader*. New York: Pantheon Books.

Foucault, M. (1985). *The use of pleasure: The history of sexuality*, vol. two. Translated by R. Hurley. New York: Vintage Books.

Foucault, M. (1994). The ethic of care for the self as a practice of freedom. In J. Bernauer & D. Rasmussen (Eds.), *The final Foucault*. London & Cambridge: The MIT Press.

Halperin, D. (1995). *Saint Foucault: Towards a gay hagiography*. New York & Oxford: Oxford University Press.

König, E. (1995). Criticism of doping: The nihilistic side of technological sport and the antiquated view of sport ethics. *International Review for the Sociology of Sport* 30(3/4), 247–261.

Miller, J. (1993). *The passion of Michel Foucault*. New York: Anchor Books.

Roxxie. (1993). Hockey action: Beehives! *Girljock* 9, 14–15.

Suits, B. (1978). *The grasshopper: Games, life, and utopia*. Toronto: University of Toronto Press.

Shogan, D. (1999). *The making of high-performance athletes: Discipline, diversity, and ethics*. Toronto: University of Toronto Press.

Shogan, D. & Ford, M. (1998). Ethics and sport in Canadian high-performance sport: An analysis of the proliferation of discourse. Presented to the North American Society for the Sociology of Sport, Las Vegas, November.

9 DISCIPLINARY TECHNOLOGIES
OF SPORT PERFORMANCE

In a prescient essay published in 1988, *Omni* magazine ventured an account of the Olympics as they might look in 2088. The essay described Olympic athletes who are products of elaborate genetic engineering. These athletes have bionic parts and utilize chemical aids that are not harmful. "As they compete, [they] are enhanced by a multitude of sensors studding their skin. Measuring everything from heartbeats to muscle contractions to brain waves, the sensors radio information to a nearby computer station manned by each athlete's coaching staff. The coaching staff radios physiological as well as cognitive-pattern updates and strategy suggestions back to the athlete via a tiny speaker in his or her ear" (Weintraub & Teich 1988, pp. 35–36). The authors ask rhetorically, "how could any of these enhancements be immoral when the net result is improvement of performance and safety?" (Weintraub & Teich 1988, p. 36).

Many, of course, do find offensive sport performances that are augmented by these types of technological interventions (Herman 1975; Simon 1988; Fraleigh 1985; Hoberman 1988; Fairchild 1989; Gardner 1989). Arguments against technological interventions include appeals to preserve "natural" sport for "natural" performers because the substance or practice is unnatural and/or because the effects of the substances or practices are dehumanizing or unnatural (Butcher & Schneider 1993). For example, Gardner argues that "any procedures that might change or control 'the nature of our species' or that allow for 'mechanical' influencing of the human organism ... undermine the standard ethical touchstones of 'human nature,' 'humanity,' and 'rationality'" (1989, p. 198). Others worry that drug-enhanced performance creates a competition among drug companies rather than competition among (natural) humans (Simon 1988; Fraleigh 1985; Fairchild 1989). As I show in this chapter, however, sport performance is wholly the result of technological intervention. Performance in sport could not be achieved without organized, systematic, expert application of techniques, mechanisms, or practices that are designed to produce change.

Technology in sport includes both macro- and micro-interventions. Macro-technological interventions are those that involve equipment, external or internal alterations of joints, or ingestion of substances. Micro-interventions are those practices that make possible acquisition of sport skills and include such things as biomechanical adjustments and repetitive skill exercises. Micro-technological interventions are often regarded as "natural" performance enhancers and those who rely only on these to improve performance are considered to be "natural" participants. Macro-technologies like wheelchairs, prostheses, and artificial joints and those who use them are considered by some to be "unnatural." Still others, like steroids and their users, are considered to be unethical *because* they are "unnatural."

While macro-technological interventions—drugs, equipment, artificial joints, microchips—will continue to dramatically alter sport performance, in this chapter I am more interested in how micro-interventions or what might be called disciplinary technologies are constitutive of sport performance. It is through these technologies that skill is acquired. In order to establish that micro or disciplinary technologies are constitutive of sport performance, I utilize the map set out by Foucault in "Docile Bodies" and "Correct Training" from *Discipline and Punish*. Foucault presents three kinds of micro-technological interventions: technologies of docility, technologies of normalization, and technologies of subjectivation. I take up each of these disciplinary technologies to underline that sport performance is wholly the effect of technological intervention. I then briefly turn to Foucault's work on confessional technology from *The History of Sexuality, Volume I* to explore technologies that make it possible for participants to know themselves as subjects of sport while at the same time being subjected to its technologies.

TECHNOLOGIES OF DOCILITY

Technologies of docility are those technologies that control time, space, and modality of movement. Foucault showed how large numbers of people could be controlled in factories, schools, workplaces, armies, hospitals, and prisons by technologies that organized the time and space within which people performed designated tasks. It is through technologies that control time, space, and movement that skilled performance is produced.

The ordering of *space* was a central part of the change from pre-modern to modern institutions. According to Foucault, "the organization of serial space was one of the great technical mutations of elementary education" (1979, p. 147). From a traditional system of education in which each student worked with a teacher for a few minutes while the rest of the students were unattended and idle, there was a transition to a modern education in which space was organized so that each student had his or her own place, making possible supervision of everyone and the engagement of everyone in work. This organization of space "made the educational space function like a learning machine, but also as a machine for supervising, hierarchizing, rewarding" (Foucault 1979, p. 147).

Like other disciplined performances, the achievement of skilled sport performance relies on the organization of space or what Foucault referred to as an "art of distributions." The technologies that make up "the art of distribution"—technologies that organize enclosure, partitioning, function, and rank—make it possible for athletes to learn and use skills continuously and without interruption. Coaches must not only organize training spaces to create optimal possibilities for movement, they must understand ways in which boundary lines, target dimensions, and equipment constrain the use of space and consequently how skills are then enabled and limited by these constraints. Skills for defending against an advancing pass are different in basketball than they are in American football because of the length of the playing field and are further circumscribed by the distance an offensive player is from the ball. Offensive skills are different in racquetball than in squash because of the shape of the racquet in each, the size and resiliency of the ball, and because of what is constituted as "playable space." Ceilings are in-bounds in racquetball but out-of-bounds in squash.

Employment of particular defensive or offensive alignments in team sport can only be taken up in relation to the set boundaries of the playing field. Organization of defensive pressure in the game of basketball, for example, is only possible in relation to the spatial constraints of the basketball court—sidelines, end lines, mid-court lines. To strategically manipulate space during competition, technologies that organize space must be taken up during practice sessions in order that athletes always know where they are in relation to opponents, teammates, implements, targets, and boundaries. In order for athletes to acquire a bodily understanding of where they are, coaches must eliminate distractions by ensuring, whenever possible, that practice space is separated from those not engaged in the training session. For discipline to do its work, it is important to enclose space and in so doing specify it as different from other space to "derive the maximum advantages and to neutralize the inconveniences" (Foucault 1979, p. 142).

In order for participants to acquire skills, they are enclosed in a practice space that itself is often subdivided, particularly when skills are acquired with others on a team. Subdivision into smaller groups prevents idleness and makes it possible to ensure that everyone is engaged in the assigned task. By confining athletes' movements to a space, coaches are able to see everyone practising skills required in games.

Partitioning eliminates "the uncontrolled disappearance of individuals, their diffuse circulation, their unusable and dangerous coagulation" (Foucault 1979, p. 143). While these are less likely to be concerns in a practice session of high-performance athletes, they are often concerns in instructional sessions in schools where it is possible for individuals to slip out of teaching sessions when congregated in large groups, or where it is possible that any discontent with the instructor can grow in the large group. The advantages of partitioning, as Foucault describes it, are that it aims to: "establish presences and absences, to know where and how to locate individuals, to set up useful communications, to interrupt others, to be able at each moment to supervise the conduct of each individual, to assess it, judge it, calculate its qualities of merits. It was a procedure, therefore, aimed at knowing, mastering, and using" (Foucault 1979, p. 143).

Partitioning of players into spaces within the larger enclosure "eliminated the effects of imprecise distributions" (Foucault 1979, p. 143). Instances are avoided in which athletes watch some few others perform. As well, movements that are extraneous to the skill are eliminated. When practising shooting at the basket in basketball, for example, participants are stationed close to baskets, thus eliminating the necessity of moving to the basket in order to shoot or shooting from a distance that would not likely occur in a competition.

Enclosures within the larger enclosure are *functional sites*. They create useful spaces (Foucault 1979, p. 144). If skill acquisition is to have any function in a competition, organization of space during practice sessions must replicate competition as much as possible. Each player is partitioned on the floor according to his or her function on the team or according to a particular sequence of possibilities. Although the distribution of players on a playing field is not as predictable, say, as students in a classroom or workers in a workplace, there are limits on where a player may go and these limits are related to their function within the space. In American football, for example, each player assumes an assigned position in relation to teammates and relevant to the function to be served in the next play sequence. There are certain skills that can only be performed when players are situated in particular places on the playing field.

Partitioning players in practices and competitions makes it possible for a coach to make an assessment of the differences in skill acquisition among players that enables further partitioning of players according to their level of skill. Distribution of players into designated spaces for skill acquisition allows coaches to *rank* players. For example, in a weight-training room, the particular exercise sites remain fixed and athletes move as they acquire skill or need remedial work on skill. Coaches have in their heads, or at least on paper, a series of grids and charts with information about what activities athletes are capable of performing. They have at their disposal what Foucault called a *tableaux vivants*—a living table—that provides a means to both organize and control the activities that are to be performed by any individual when he or she occupies a particular space or role. As Foucault indicated, "supervision and intelligibility ... are inextricably bound up" (Foucault 1979, p. 148).

Coaches must not only introduce micro-technologies of space within which athletes learn skills, they must control movement through technological intervention that manipulates *time*. In most sport there is a specified amount of time for the contest as well as other temporal constraints. In basketball, for example, there are temporal constraints in relation to the time to advance the basketball from the back-court to the front-court; time to shoot the basketball at the basket once in possession of the ball; time to inbound the ball or shoot the ball during a foul shot; and time spent in the key area in front of the basket.

Coaches must not only be able to organize practice sessions so that athletes understand the temporal dimensions of their sport, they must intervene so that timing of movement is embodied. This includes manipulation of tempo. Embodiment of a tempo at which skills are to be performed and the tempo of team manoeuvres are affected by the intensity at which skills are practised. Tempo in a game like basketball can be affected in the transition from offence to defence (by putting pressure on the ball at the point on the floor at which advance of the ball begins) and defence to offence (by an organized movement of the basketball up the floor with ball possession).

Understanding spatial constraints of an activity is necessary if players are to become disciplined in their movements, but this discipline will remain discrete with no relation to other activities unless it is possible to specify how activities should be coordinated (Townley 1994, p. 52). Activities are coordinated by what Foucault referred to as "timetables," "temporal elaboration of the act," "correlation of the body and the gesture," "body-object articulation," and "exhaustive use."

THE TIMETABLE

> 8.45 entrance of the monitor, 8.52 the monitor's summons, 8.56 entrance of the children and prayer, 9.00 the children go to their benches, 9.04 first slate, 9.08 end of dictation, 9.12 second slate, etc. (Tronchot in Foucault 1979, p. 150)

The minute organization of time in elementary schools in the early 19th century may not be as prevalent in schools in the early part of the 21st century, but it is still very prevalent in sport. For one thing, coaches are intolerant of those who arrive late at practice.

> When [players show up late for practice], the best way to handle it is to have a standard rule that players arriving late go ahead and dress out, do stretching or limbering up exercises on the sidelines until the next shooting drill or water break, and then report to the head coach to discuss the reason for their tardiness. If their excuse is valid, they can join practice; if not, they are dismissed for the day (and possibly the next day as well). But in all cases the problem should be dealt with quickly, quietly, and forcefully. (Warren & Chapman 1992, pp. 124–125)

In order to ensure efficient use of time, coaches must be masters of the timetable. The timetable makes it possible for coaches to rule out unnecessary actions and concentrate effort on activities designed to improve skill. Preparing high-performance athletes requires "totally useful time ... a time of good quality, throughout which the body is constantly applied to its exercise" (Foucault 1979, pp. 150, 151). It is common in practice sessions to spend no more than five or 10 minutes on a drill with very little transition time from drill to drill. Many coaches use the game clock to indicate the time for each drill and run the clock during the drill so that everyone can see how much time is remaining. When the buzzer sounds, players move to the next drill and an assistant puts up the next designated time. The sequence of drills and the time for each are preplanned according to a timetable that designates how each minute of the practice is to be spent.

A coach must not only have time organized for daily practices, he or she must have a timetable to establish a rhythmic training schedule that follows the seasons—the post-season and pre-season—and time scheduled for conditioning, psychological preparation, skill development, team work, and strategy. Without timetables, coaches would be unable to establish training cycles or the rhythms of specific activities. Nor would they be able to regulate cycles of repetition. Repetition of skills under competition conditions is a technology of time that produces disciplined performance.

THE TEMPORAL ELABORATION OF THE ACT

> The length of the short step will be a foot, that of the ordinary step, the double step and the marching step will be two feet, the whole measured from one heel to the next; as for the duration, that of the ordinary step and the marching step will last one second, during which two double steps would be performed; the duration of the marching step will be a little longer than one second. (Ordonnance in Foucault 1979, p. 151)

The lay-up shot in basketball is one of many skills that require coordination of the components of the skill as well as a direction, a sequential order, and a duration for each of the movements (Foucault 1979, p. 152). The lay-up shot consists of one-and-a-half steps while carrying the ball. This shot involves a rhythm—a temporal sequencing—the elaboration of which a player must incorporate if the shot is to be performed correctly. To assist a player in acquiring the rhythm for the lay-up, coaches intervene by focusing on footwork first—"one, two-up; one, two-up; one, two-up" over and over with the emphasis on an elongated first step and short, propulsive second step. This intervention makes it possible for time to penetrate the body (Foucault 1979, p. 152).

CORRELATION OF THE BODY AND THE GESTURE

> Good handwriting ... presupposes a gymnastics—a whole routine whose rigorous code invests the body in its entirety, from the points of the feet to the tip of the index finger. (Foucault 1979, p. 152)

Time is used correctly only if movement is efficient—if "everything is called upon to form the support of the act required" (Foucault 1979, p. 152). Shooting a basketball, for example, is not merely a matter of performing a "series of particular gestures." If one is to be a skilled shooter, one must achieve "the best relation between a gesture and the overall position of the body, which is its condition of efficiency and speed" (Foucault 1979, p. 152). Coaches intervene with technologies that make a correct use of time so that nothing "remain[s] idle or useless: everything [is] called upon to form the support of the act required" (Foucault 1979, p. 152). Good shooters and good coaches of good shooters know that if the feet, ankles, knees, hips, head, and eyes are not supporting the shoulders, arms, wrist, and hands, any ball that goes through the basketball hoop arrived there accidentally.

THE BODY–OBJECT ARTICULATION

> Bring the weapon forward. In three stages. Raise the rifle with the right hand, bringing it close to the body so as to hold it perpendicular with the right knee, the end of the barrel at eye level.... At the second stage, bring the rifle in front of you with the left hand, the barrel in the middle between the two eyes.... At the third stage, let go of the rifle with the left hand, which falls along the thigh, raising the rifle with the right hand, the lock outwards and opposite the chest.... (Ordonnance in Foucault 1979, p. 153)

Most sports involve the articulation of the body with one or more objects or implements. Baseball players articulate with the baseball, their gloves, and the bat; rowers with their boats and oars; synchronized swimmers with the water and their props; even distance runners must articulate with the track. Some sports require a more sophisticated breakdown of the movements of a skill in relation to the object.

For a player to become skilled in relation to the object to be manipulated, coaches intervene with micro-technologies to break down the total gesture into two parallel series: the parts of the body to be used and the object to be manipulated. Once each of these is mastered, technologies are introduced to correlate them together "according to a number of simple gestures" and in a "canonical succession in which each of these correlations occupies a particular place" (Foucault 1979, p. 153). The reverse dribble in basketball, for example, is a skill that is performed in specific circumstances when attempting to change direction when closely defended. The reverse dribble consists of a particular type of footwork while manipulating the basketball. In order to acquire this skill, players must master the footwork and ball-handling techniques separately before putting the two together.

Foucault wrote that "over the whole surface of contact between the body and the object it handles, power is introduced, fastening them to one another" (Foucault 1979, p. 153). The articulation of bodies and objects is a technological intervention that enables skilled athletes to perform a range of manipulations of the object. Without this intervention, unskilled players are encumbered by having to manoeuvre not only their own bodies but their bodies in relation to the object.

EXHAUSTIVE USE

Practice sessions are organized to teach "speed as a virtue" and also to "extract ... from time, ever more available moments and, from each moment, ever more useful forces" (Foucault 1979, p. 154). The timetable of daily practice is controlled to the extent that it ensures that athletes practise at the tempo expected in competition. Players must come to feel a bodily discomfort or feel "unnatural" when they have not followed the temporal sequence and intensity for a particular skill and when skills and team play are not executed at the expected tempo. In order for players to achieve bodily discomfort as a consequence of improper sequencing or intensity, interventions are made to "intensify the use of the slightest moment, as if time, in its very fragmentation, were inexhaustible or as if ... one could tend toward an ideal point at which one maintained maximum speed and efficiency" (Foucault 1979, p. 154).

Technologies designed to control space and time also control *movement*, which enables athletes to perform skills not otherwise possible. What Foucault refers to as "*the organization of geneses*" involves the gradual progression and acquisition of knowledge in segments, building on each other and making possible coordination with others. Through repetitive, different, and graduated exercise, tasks are imposed on the body. These technologies comprise a "machinery for adding up and capitalizing time" (Foucault 1979, p. 157).

According to Foucault, there are four technologies that "capitalize the time of individuals ... in a way that is susceptible to use and control" (Foucault 1979, p. 157) and which together produce "a matrix ... of activity through time, upon which a population and individuals within it may be located" (Townley 1994, p. 74). The four technologics include the following:

(1) *Divide duration into successive or parallel segments, each of which must end at a specific time.*

This technique separates the learning of a skill from its practice. "Teach in turn posture, marching, the handling of weapons, shooting, and do not pass to another activity until the first has been completely mastered" (Foucault 1979, p. 158). For example, in order to perform a reverse dribble in basketball, it is necessary to master reverse footwork before moving onto the manipulation of the basketball. Progressive building of a team offence in basketball, for example, include first footwork and ball-handling skills followed by manoeuvre of one offensive player against one defensive player and then "elementary team play": two against two, three against three, and four against four. Each of these stages also includes progressively more intense defence.

Central to the organization of geneses in disciplines such as the army and apprenticeships is the separation of new recruits from the exercise of veterans. Coaches also take advantage of homogeneous groupings if there is a wide gap in skill level among athletes. Seldom, however, is the skill difference between "recruits" and veterans on teams so marked that separation of these two groups is required.

(2) *Organize these threads according to an analytical plan—a succession of elements as simple as possible, combining according to increasing complexity.*

Consider this adaptation of this technique from a basketball coaching text (Warren & Chapman 1992, pp. 139–144):

> We recommend a nine-step approach to installing an offensive system:
> (1) Teach your players the basic pattern or movement sequences by walking them through it until everyone is thoroughly familiar with it.
> (2) Drill the players in isolated segments of the basic pattern.
> (3) Add defence to the drill sequences.
> (4) Introduce options to the pattern one at a time in walk-through fashion.
> (5) Break down the options into drill segments.

(6) Add passive defence to the options drill segments.

(7) Practise the basic pattern, option, and automatics, first in breakdown drills and then in team form.

(8) Add full-scale defence to the breakdown drills and team run-throughs.

(9) Whenever you encounter problems, go back to the breakdown drills in practice.

Possibilities for team play become embodied in athletes as a result of progressing with teammates from the elementary to the complex. This also arranges and correlates a hierarchy of knowledge in terms of complexity in relation to time.

(3) *Finalize these temporal segments, decide on how long each will last, and conclude it with an examination.*

During team tryouts, coaches introduce selected skills over a period of designated time while determining which players have satisfactorily met the standard necessary for continued participation. Setting the time for tryouts, fixing those segments on which potential players will be assessed, and examining them on these has "the triple function of showing whether the subject has reached the level required, of guaranteeing that each subject undergoes the same apprenticeship and of differentiating the abilities of each individual" (Foucault 1979, p. 158).

Athletes on teams may gain or lose opportunity to compete as a result of how they are assessed by coaches in practice sessions. Regularly scheduled competitions are also a form of examination that establishes periods of time within which players are to gain competency in certain skills. How well an athlete performs in competition determines whether he or she will be permitted other competitive opportunities.

(4) *Draw up series of series.*

[L]ay down for each individual, according to his level, his seniority, his rank, the exercises that are suited to him; common exercises have a differing role and each difference involves specific exercises. At the end of each series, others begin, branch off and subdivide in turn. Thus each individual is caught up in a temporal series which specifically defines his level or his rank. It is a disciplinary polyphony of exercises. (Foucault 1979, pp. 158–159)

Preparation of athletes for a team sport like American football, in which there are separate offensive and defensive squads, each with a number of highly specialized positions, requires an organization of activities for each practice session that both discipline an athlete in his requisite skills and identify him as occupying a particular position on the team in terms of his playing position and rank on the team. Thus, defensive teams, offensive teams, and special teams are engaged in skills specific to those teams. Quarterbacks, running backs, receivers, and linesmen are each engaged in specific exercises and within each of these groups less-skilled athletes are engaged in activities to improve skill.

In team sports, skills of individual players must be combined into an efficient unit "whose effect [is] superior to the sum of [abilities] that compose ... it ..." (Foucault 1979, p. 163). A group of skilled individuals who are unable to integrate their skills with others will not constitute a successful team. According to Foucault, the composition of forces is achieved in the following ways:

(1) *The individual body becomes an element that may be placed, moved, or articulated on others.*

Foucault quotes an "Ordonnance," which describes the training of soldiers first:

> one by one, then two by two, then in greater numbers.... For the handling of weapons, one will ascertain that, when the soldiers have been separately instructed, they will carry it out two by two, and then change places alternately, so that the one on the left may learn to adapt himself to the one on the right. (Ordonnance in Foucault 1979, p. 164)

Embodying the progressions of team offence is not just a matter of learning skills in sequence. Players must be able to take any position in the sequence. In a sequence called the "give and go," for example, basketball players must be able to pass and cut to the basket, but they must also be able to receive a pass and be able to pass it back to the cutting player. Technological interventions are introduced by coaches so that players can adapt to a number of circumstances.

(2) The various chronological series that discipline must combine to form a composite time are also pieces of machinery.

A skilled player knows how fast or quickly to move in a particular situation and still be in control. If a player cannot travel from one point to another and still be in control of his or her body and the basketball, for example, then speed must be adjusted accordingly. In a team sport, players move in relation to teammates and so they must incorporate an understanding of how quickly each player can move and stay in control. There is no advantage to being able to move very quickly, passing and cutting at great speed, if a teammate has not managed to catch the ball thrown at this speed. Coaches introduce interventions so that athletes know how to adjust their speed in relation to others "in such a way that the maximum quantity of forces may be extracted from each and combined with optimum result" (Foucault 1979, p. 165).

(3) This carefully measured combination of forces requires a precise system of command.

> All the activity of the disciplined individual must be punctuated and sustained by injunctions whose efficacy rests on brevity and clarity; the order does not need to be explained or formulated; it must trigger off the required behaviour and that is enough. (Foucault 1979, p. 166)

Once skills and team combinations are embodied, coaches rely on brief cues to signal that attention needs to be paid to some aspect of the team play or, during practice sessions, to move the team or segments of the team from drill to drill. A verbal cue signals a drill with which players are familiar and that they can begin without an explanation of what is involved in the drill; another cue during a game or practice signals that players must pay attention to the details of a particular skill; still another signals a change in strategy. It is not necessary that players understand why the injunction to do a particular skill or perform a particular strategy is to occur when it does; only that they "perceive the signal and react ... to it immediately" (Foucault 1979, p. 166).

The effect of these technologies of docility-technologies of space, time, and movement is to produce skilled performers of a discipline. Without these technologies, there would be no skill.

TECHNOLOGIES OF NORMALIZATION

Technologies of docility make it possible to identify and control positions or roles in relation to each other, but they do not make it possible to identify details about an individual other than that he or she is someone who is able to perform the skills associated with a position. What activities are to be performed by any individual in a particular space can be specified, but who is performing the activity in the particular space cannot be specified through these technologies. Information about who individuals are is provided by the technologies of correct training, an art of "strict discipline" using "simple instruments; hierarchal observation, normalizing judgment and their combination in a procedure that is specific to it, the examination" (Foucault 1979, p. 170).

It is not enough for coaches to introduce technologies to distribute individuals in time and space, say, in an offensive system or to utilize technologies developmentally to produce athletic bodies to fit these roles. A coach must also know who is most skilled for a particular competition or situation. A central responsibility of coaches is the assessment of athletic ability in order that the most skilled athletes compete when appropriate. Information about which athlete is most suitable for what position or situation is determined through examinations in which coaches observe athletes in relation to other athletes on the team and in relation to standards of performance for the sport. Through observation, the gaps between an athlete's performance and the standards for the activity are judged and noted. Precision and detail are central to the examination since it is only through close attention to detail that appropriate differentiations between people can be made. Through the compilation of dossiers the examination makes each individual into a case to be known (Dreyfus & Rabinow 1983, p. 159).

Comprehensive records of athletes' performances make it possible for coaches to intervene to improve skill. The effect of observation is not merely that athletes are seen. Observation makes it possible "to know them; to alter them" (Foucault 1979, p. 172). With examinations coaches are able to assess how much work needs to be done to achieve a "good" performance and to intervene with even more exacting technologies of docility to close the gap between an athlete's present performance and the desired performance. For example, if an athlete is assessed as deficient in his ability to run at top speed while dribbling a basketball, the coach can intervene with technologies that constrain time, space, and movement in such a way that performance improves.

Through a "normalizing judgment," a coach assesses which athletes are better at which skills and rewards better players with playing opportunities. Athletes are as concerned as coaches to "norm the non-standard" (Davis 1995) because of the lure of being rewarded by more competitive opportunities and perhaps by fame of some kind. "Conformity is rewarded with applause and fame; neglect is punished with poor test results, the shame of defeat, and extra training sessions" (Heikkala 1993, p. 400). There are, then, other effects of the examination of athletes in addition to knowledge of individual athletes. Normalization and homogenization are a consequence of the "constant pressure [for athletes] to conform to the same model, so that they might all be ... like one another" (Foucault 1979, p. 182). As Heikkala indicates, "normalization ... means conformity to the rationale of both training and competing according to the plans made (by the coach) and conformity to the institutional forms, customs, and rules of sport" (1993, p. 400).

Observation and judgment are technologies of normalization because they implicate examined individuals in the project of closing the gap between their present performance and the "norm" or standard for performance. Conformity takes hold of an athlete, in part, because he or she is visible. Realizing that they can be seen by coaches, athletes come to monitor their own behaviour and shape it according to the expectations of the sport. In effect, the watchful eye of the coach and the normalizing standards of the sport become embodied by the athlete. Foucault refers to this embodiment of the gaze of authority as "panopticism"—"a generalizable model of functioning; a way of defining power relations in terms of the everyday life of men" (Foucault 1979, p. 205).

The notion of panopticism was derived by Foucault from the Panopticon, an architectural design for a prison produced by the philosopher and prison reformer, Jeremy Bentham. Bentham's Panopticon was an architectural figure consisting of a tower at its centre with windows looking out at a building divided into cells. Each individual in these cells is seen by the supervisor in the tower and prevented from seeing either the supervisor or those in the other cells. "He is seen, but he does not see" (Foucault 1979, p. 200). Because of the structure of the tower, the prisoner is unable to tell whether he is watched and consequently has a feeling of constant surveillance. The awareness that one may be watched leads to an internalization of the gaze and a policing of one's own behaviour. The inmate becomes his own guard.

In sport, training sessions are organized so that all athletes in the session can be seen by a coach or coaches and so that athletes are constantly engaged in activity. Athletes are unaware of when they are actually watched, yet know that this is always possible. Since less than intense participation in practice sessions often leads to some kind of punishment, the worst of which would be fewer or no opportunities for competition, athletes come to understand that it is in their best interest to train with intensity. The effects of panopticism are visceral. When athletes perform skills incorrectly or without intensity, the movement feels wrong or unnatural. Self-policing the intensity of personal training is not only done to avoid punishment. Athletes police their own behaviours because they have incorporated the technologies of docility and the technologies of correct training and their value.

TECHNOLOGIES OF SUBJECTIFICATION

The examination produces documented information about individuals and the differences between them. Another way knowledge about individuals is produced in relation to standards occurs when participants in a discipline are required to talk about their experiences. In what Foucault refers to as the confessional, participants tell or perhaps write their experiences to an authority, who records the information along with his or her expert interpretation of the information. This is followed by an intervention "in order to judge, punish, forgive, console, and reconcile ... and [to] ... produce ... intrinsic modifications in the person who articulate[d] it" (Foucault 1980, pp. 61–62). Coaches often utilize confessionals through technologies introduced by sport psychology. In paper-and-pencil tests, for example, athletes indicate (confess) their responses to a variety of possibly stressful situations.

> By your answering a number of questions about how you have functioned in the past, it's possible for us to conclude to some degree of accuracy what your attentional strengths and weaknesses are.... If ... you indicate that you make mistakes because you concentrate on one player and forget about what other players are doing, I know that you can narrow attention, but are unable to broaden it, and when a broad focus is demanded,

you have difficulty. With this kind of information, plus additional knowledge about your level of anxiety, I can suggest procedures for you to use to learn to broaden your attention. (Nideffer 1980, p. 281)

This "attention-control training" relies on expert interpretation of these questionnaires, followed by remedial techniques. These techniques include exercises to control focus of attention, so that athletes can achieve and surpass expectations for attention that have been produced as normal for a particular situation. By using confessional technology in this circumstance, it is possible to "discover" players' attentional abilities and then interpret this information to make decisions about what technologies of docility to impose. For example, if a player has a narrow focus of attention, training sessions can be organized so that situations that require attention are emphasized and repeated. Interpretation of athletes' "confessions" produces another set of coaching imperatives and more interventions to change players. Confessional technology, then, is used to validate more interventionist technology.

Fiske notes that the more examinations we pass, the more normal we become (1993, p. 75). Likewise, the more we confess, the more normal we become because, like the examination, the confessional entails interventions by experts to change individuals so that they meet the standards of a discipline. When the interventions are successful, normalization is a consequence. Normalization is an effect of the "constant pressure to conform to the same model, so that they might all be ... like one another" (Foucault 1979, p. 18).

Implicit in the confession is the assumption that individuals attain self-knowledge by confessing to experts who interpret the confession for them. The confessional is a technology of subjectification because it both produces the confessor as the subject of the discipline while subjecting the confessor to it. In the case of attentional control confessionals, athletes come to know themselves and be known by others through the following labels: confident, hesitant, aggressive, "choker." Those who confess their experiences of not being able to meet the standards of normalized tasks or activities are labelled by experts as awkward, clumsy, unskilled, incompetent, or disabled.

CONCLUDING REMARKS

A skilled athlete is able to perform prescribed skills with minimum error and maximum intensity in dynamic and often stressful circumstances. In order to achieve skilled performance, individuals must be subjected to detailed control of time, space, and modality of movement as well as technologies that normalize them into subjects who are invested in their own conformity. Foucault used the phrase "docile bodies" to describe effects of techniques and strategies of disciplinary technology but "docility" for Foucault was not passive. Docile bodies are productive bodies—bodies that are able to carry out precise and often rarified skills. Nevertheless, there remains an ambiguity about using "docility" to describe disciplined, skilled bodies. While disciplines produce performers who are superbly skilled, both the mechanical training to achieve skills and the automatic way in which skills are performed supports a concern that while athletes are active with respect to movement, they are often passive in making decisions about the acquisition of movement skills and in reflecting on their continued involvement with technologies that produce these skills. Disciplinary technology may produce bodies that can perform amazing skills but, during the acquisition and performance of skills, athletes seem to have little or no agency. Paradoxically, the dynamism of athletes on the playing field may be evidence of their conformity.

Disciplinary technologies that produce skilled athletic performers are arguably not more controlling than, say, disciplinary technologies that produce skilled surgeons, skilled pianists, or skilled machinists. Like these other skilled performers, a disciplined athlete is someone "who submits him or herself to the power of a particular way of knowing/behaving in order to participate in that power, to become more effective in applying it and thus to gain satisfaction and rewards that it offers" (Fiske 1993, p. 64).

Consequently, there can be no argument against technology in sport without advocating the end of sport itself. Technology, in particular what I have referred to as micro or disciplinary technology, is constitutive of sport performance because without these interventions, there would be no sport performance.

REFERENCES

Butcher, R. & Schneider, A. (1993). *Doping in sport: An analysis of the justification for bans and the ethical rationale for drug-free sport.* Canadian Centre for Drug-Free Sport.

Davis, L. (1995). *Enforcing normalcy: Disability, deafness, and the body.* London & New York: Verso.

Dreyfus, H.L. & Rabinow, P. (1983). *Michel Foucault: Beyond structuralism and hermeneutics.* Chicago: University of Chicago Press.

Fairchild, D. (1989). Sport abjection: Steroids and the uglification of the athlete. *Journal of the Philosophy of Sport 16,* 74–88.

Fiske, J. (1993). *Power plays power works.* London & New York: Verso.

Foucault, M. (1979). *Discipline and punish: The birth of the prison.* Translated by A. Sheridan. New York: Vintage Books.

Foucault, M. (1980). *The history of sexuality, Vol. 1: An introduction.* Translated by R. Hurley. New York: Vintage Books.

Fraleigh, W. (1985). Performance-enhancing drugs in sport: The ethical issue. *Journal of the Philosophy of Sport 11,* 23–29.

Gardner, R. (1989). On performance-enhancing substances and the unfair advantage argument. *Journal of the Philosophy of Sport 16,* 59–73.

Heikkala, J. (1993). Discipline and excel: Techniques of the self and body and the logic of competing. *Sociology of Sport Journal 10,* 397–412.

Herman, D. (1975). Mechanism and the athlete. *Journal of the Philosophy of Sport 2,* 102–110.

Hoberman, J. (1988). Sport and the technological image of man. In W.J. Morgan & K.V. Meier (Eds.), *Philosophic inquiry in sport* (pp. 319–327). Champaign: Human Kinetics Press.

Nideffer, R. (1980). Attentional focus-self assessment. In R. Sunin (Ed.), *Psychology in sport: Methods and applications* (pp. 281–290). Minneapolis: Burgess Pub. Co.

Shogan, D. (1999). *The making of high-performance athletes: Discipline, diversity, and ethics.* Toronto: University of Toronto Press.

Simon, R.L. (1988). Good competition and drug-enhanced performance. In W.J. Morgan & K.V. Meier (Eds.), *Philosophic inquiry in sport* (pp. 289–296). Champaign: Human Kinetics Publishers.

Townley, B. (1994). *Reframing human resource management: Power, ethics, and the subject at work.* Thousand Oaks: Sage Publications.

Warren, W.E. & Chapman, L.F. (1992). *Basketball coach's survival guide: Practical techniques and materials for building an effective program and a winning team.* West Nyack: Parker Publishing Co.

Weintraub, P. & Teich, M. (1988). Body and Seoul. *Omni 10*(12), 34–39, 86–88.

10

THE SOCIAL CONSTRUCTION OF DISABILITY IN A SOCIETY OF NORMALIZATION

INTRODUCTION

To understand disability in relation to socially established standards for socially created tasks is to provide a social constructionist account of disability. This account does not deny the physicality of discomfort, pain, and impairment. Instead, it recognizes that notions such as success and failure, good and bad performance, ability and disability acquire meaning in relation to what has been established as normal within a social context, including what are considered to be normal tasks and the skills necessary for these tasks. A social constructionist account recognizes that those who do not achieve the standards established for the tasks of a discipline are labelled as, among other things, "deficient," "lacking," or "disabled" and that they become the focus of expert interventions designed to change them so they can participate in these tasks.

A SOCIETY OF NORMALIZATION

> An essential component of technologies of normalization is the key role they play in the systematic creation, classification, and control of anomalies in the social body ... certain technologies serve to isolate anomalies.... [O]ne can then normalize anomalies through corrective or therapeutic procedures, determined by other related technologies. In both cases, the technologies of normalization are purportedly impartial techniques for dealing with dangerous social deviations. (Rabinow 1984, p. 21)

Foucault was interested in the emergence of modern institutions and how they placed constraints on ways of participating in modern life. Modern institutions began to emerge in the 17th and 18th centuries as a way to contend with the efficient management of growing populations. Control of large numbers of people in factories, schools, workplaces, armies, hospitals, and prisons was made possible through disciplines that organized the time and space within which people performed designated tasks.

We commonly understand the notion of discipline in two ways. One is in reference to a body of knowledge; for example, the knowledge that is produced by researchers and practitioners in psychology, medicine, or adapted physical activity. Discipline also refers to the control or management of people; for example, the discipline of students by a teacher, or athletes by a coach. For Foucault, discipline simultaneously entails both of these meanings. Foucault's work documented how practices of controlling people develop as the subject matter or knowledge base of a discipline develops. In the discipline of sport performance, for example, coaches utilize knowledge generated by sport performance and translate this information into ever more exacting technologies of intervention to produce disciplined athletes (Shogan 1999, p. 39). By monitoring and examining the consequences of these disciplinary interventions, more knowledge (discipline) is produced, which, in turn, makes control (discipline) even more meticulous.

How does a discipline produce knowledge about people, and what are the procedures by which this knowledge comes to socially control? Disciplines establish standards of achievement, behaviour, or performance for specified tasks in relation to the physical and social spaces within which these can occur. Everyone engaged in or by a discipline is measured in relation to these standards and ranked in relation to each other.

Abilities or behaviours are assessed by experts who observe and judge participants in relation to the standards established for the discipline. Observation and judgment by experts are part of an examination process that produces information about an individual's placement in relation to the standards of the discipline and in relation to others. This information makes it possible to isolate individuals so that their weaknesses can be corrected. Participants are subjected to interventions designed by experts in order to close the gap between the deficient skill or behaviour and that imposed by the standard. As Foucault (1979) indicated, examinations make it possible "to know them; to alter them" (p. 172). As deviations from the standard are corrected and an individual's behaviour or skills come closer to the standard, she or he becomes more like others, both in terms of the tasks in which they all engage and their abilities to perform these tasks. Through repeated interventions, everyone is moved closer to the standard, although it is also true that standards "climb slowly up the scale to accommodate a shifting mean of performance" (Ransom 1997, p. 50).

Schooling at all levels is a good example of the way in which discipline works. Education is conceived as a series of tasks to engage in and behaviours and skills to attain in relation to these tasks. Attainment of behaviours and skills is measured in relation to standards established by the discipline and assessed by teachers or professors whose job it is to gain detailed information about each individual's abilities so that strategies of correction can be introduced. A successful classroom, school, or school district is one in which students are engaged in "normal" tasks and meet the standards of these tasks. To the extent that students meet the standards of tasks in which they all engage, they become more alike. Not all students meet or surpass the standards. Those who do not are subject to ever more exact interventions to attempt to close the gap between the deficiency and the standards.

Another effect of the examination is the production of information about how participants behave or perform in relation to standards and how they respond to corrective measures. This information contributes to the body of knowledge of the discipline and serves to reposition what counts as standard behaviours or skills for the discipline. The examination also produces ways to identify people by labelling them. John Fiske (1993) provides an example of how gathering information about workers in an airline reservation centre is used to establish "normal" work efficiency as well as the categorization of workers. One worker had a 93.55 percent "utilization" by virtue of handling 79 calls in the day, spending 3.53 minutes on each call, and completing her after-call work in about 23 seconds. Since the normal utilization for workers at the reservation centre was 96.5 percent, normal calls per day were between 150 and 200, and time spent on after-calls was not more than 0.3 of a minute, this worker was labelled as inefficient. As Fiske indicates, standards are established by "a monitoring knowledge system. [Without standards] the knowledge of any one individual can be neither evaluated nor ranked, and thus cannot be applied ... as rewards or sanctions" (1993, p. 74).

The examination re-establishes or repositions the standards of a discipline and produces documented information about individuals and the differences between them. Another way in which disciplines produce knowledge about individuals in relation to standards occurs when participants in a discipline are required to talk about their experiences within the discipline. In what Foucault refers to as "the confessional," participants tell or perhaps write their experiences and an authority records the information along with his or her expert interpretation of the information. This is followed by an intervention "in order to judge, punish, forgive, console, and reconcile ... and [to] ... produce ... intrinsic modifications in the person who articulate[d] it" (Foucault 1980b, pp. 61–62). Sport psychologists, for example, make use of confessionals in a number of ways, including paper-and-pencil tests in which athletes indicate (confess) their responses to a variety of possibly stressful situations.

Implicit in the confession is the assumption that individuals attain self-knowledge by confessing to experts who interpret the confession for them. It is also assumed that it is possible to improve the confessor by interventions designed to bring the individual closer to standards for the discipline. In sport psychology confessionals, athletes come to know themselves and are known by others through the following labels: confident, hesitant, aggressive, and/or "choker." In a similar way, those who confess their experiences of being unable to meet the standards of normalized movement tasks or activities are labelled by experts as awkward, clumsy, unskilled, incompetent, and/or disabled.

As noted in Chapter 9, the more examinations we pass, the more normal we become (Fiske 1993, p. 75) and the more we confess, the more normal we become. Both the examination and the confessional entail interventions by experts to change individuals so that they meet the standards of a discipline. When the interventions are successful, normalization is a consequence. Normalization is an effect of the "constant pressure to conform to the same model, so that they might all be ... like one another" (Foucault 1979, p. 182).

NORMALIZATION AND THE SOCIAL CONSTRUCTION OF DISABILITY

Modern institutions emerged in the West in the 17th and 18th centuries as a way to control large numbers of people in public institutions. Social control was made possible by procedures produced by disciplines that attempted to normalize and homogenize people by controlling the space and time in which tasks were performed. A notion of the "normal" to signify that which conforms to and does not deviate from a standard coincided with the emergence of the disciplines and gained sophistication with developments in statistics and probability theory during the 19th century (MacKenzie 1981; Hacking 1987; Hacking 1990; Davis 1995). Historical records show that people with physical and mental impairments have lived in every age, and that their status has shifted according to how these impairments have been understood (Winzer 1997). However, prior to the 19th century there was no concept of normal and abnormal, nor was there a concept of the disabled in relation to a standard (Davis 1995, p. 24).

The work of statistician Adolphe Quetelet (1796–1847) was central to the conceptualization of the "normal" to signify what is usual or typical. Quetelet proposed that the method astronomers used to locate a star—the "law of error"—could be applied to frequency distributions of human and social phenomena. Astronomers found that most sightings of a star fell in the centre of a bell curve. They considered those sightings that fell to the sides of the curve to be errors. According to Quetelet, physical characteristics, as well as moral and social behaviours, could be plotted and determined utilizing this law of error. Quetelet constructed the notion of the "average man" from the "true mean" of human attributes (Hacking 1990; Davis 1995). He thought the average or the "normal" signifies what is usual or typical, as well as the way things ought to be. In contrast, "errors" were abnormalities, deviations, or extremes (Hacking 1990; Davis 1995).

The norm divides the population into standard and non-standard subpopulations. Quetelet wrote, for example, that "deviations more or less great from the mean have constituted ... ugliness in body as well as vice in morals and a state of sickness with regard to the constitution" (cited in Porter 1986, p. 103). In Lennard Davis's (1995) words, "the idea of the norm pushes ... variation of the body through a stricter template guiding the way the body 'should' be" (p. 34). The emergence of a notion of normalcy is what, then, creates the "problem" of the disabled person (Davis 1995, p. 24). Indeed, the very meaning or signification of the normal has become tied to a concept of disability (Davis 1995, p. 2). Adapted physical activity has not been immune to this conceptualization of disability. The American *Adapted Physical Activity National Standards* (1995) indicates, as an example, that practitioners are to understand that "the meaning of obtained test scores that range two or more standard deviations below the mean [are] related to individuals with disabilities" (p. 63).

While Quetelet's focus was on central tendencies, Sir Francis Galton (1822–1911), founder of the biometric school of statistical research, was interested in distributions and deviations from the mean (Hacking 1990). And, while Quetelet considered "average" or "normal" human characteristics to be how things ought to be, Galton regarded the "normal" as an indication of mediocrity requiring improvement (Hacking 1990). Galton thought it problematic to consider all extremes in human characteristics as errors or abnormalities (MacKenzie 1981; Davis 1995). He claimed that certain attributes he valued—such as tallness, intelligence, ambitiousness, strength, and fertility—were positive distributions of a trait and not errors. Galton divided the bell curve (renamed the normal distribution curve) into quartiles that established a ranking system for characteristics. Distributions around the norm were no longer regarded as equal: the average, now referred to as the median, represented mediocrity. Those in the lower quartile were posited as deviant or abnormal and as objects of intervention, while those in the upper quartile represented progress, perfectibility, and normality (Davis 1995).

Quetelet's appropriation of the law of error to explain stability in social statistics and Galton's imposition of his values about human development onto the bell curve have had profound effects on how ability and disability are understood. Far from being a neutral, objective enterprise, statistics as practised by Galton and Quetelet produced social meaning about the "normal" and the "abnormal," "ability" and "disability," and created categories such as the "intelligent," the "deviant," and the "disabled" that had implications for tasks in many different social contexts from classrooms to playgrounds, from boardrooms to factory floors. Labels set out in advance how people can take up these tasks and how they will be judged when they do.

The belief that people must alter themselves to achieve standards established for a task, or that they must change to participate in tasks designated as normal for a culture, is another way to understand how ability and disability are socially constructed. When social structures support those who participate in tasks that have been designated as normal or mainstream, and reward those who reach or exceed the standards for performance in these tasks, those who value different tasks or who do not meet the standards of mainstream tasks are disabled by these social structures. Central to this point is understanding distinctions that have been made between impairment, disability, and handicap. The United Nations, until very recently, defined these terms as follows:

- *Impairment*: Any loss or *abnormality* of psychological, physiological, or anatomical structure or function.
- *Disability*: Any restriction or lack (resulting from impairment) of ability to perform an activity in the manner or within the range considered *normal* for a human being.

- *Handicap*: A disadvantage for a given individual, resulting from impairment or disability, that limits or prevents the fulfillment of a role that is *normal*, depending on age, sex, social, and cultural factors, for that individual. (United Nations Decade of Disabled Persons 1983–1992 (1983), p. 2)

Handicap is therefore a function of the relationship between disabled people and their environment. It occurs when they encounter cultural, physical, or social barriers that prevent their access to the various systems of society that are available to other citizens. Thus, handicap is the loss or limitation of opportunities to take part in the life of the community on an equal level with others (United Nations Decade of Disabled Persons 1983–1992 1983, pp. 6–7).

While these distinctions made possible the consideration of debilitating chronic illnesses (Wendell 1989, p. 107) by defining impairment and disability in physical terms and handicap in cultural, physical, and social terms, the 1983 UN document made an arbitrary distinction between physical and social aspects of disability. In contrast, activists from the disability movement distinguish between impairment and disability, but see no need to distinguish further between disability and handicap. As Oliver (1996) indicates, to be impaired is to lack "part of or all of a limb, or have a defective limb, organ, or mechanism of the body ... [whereas] disability [is] the disadvantage or restriction of activity caused by a contemporary social organization which takes little or no account of people who have ... physical impairments" (p. 22). Recently, the World Health Organization of the United Nations has heeded concerns about effects of the social environment on how we understand disability and it now defines disability as "the outcome or result of a complex relationship between an individual's health condition and personal factors, and of the external factors that represent the circumstances in which the individual lives" (World Health Organization 2000, p. 20). Rather than classify people, this new approach to disability seeks to describe the situation of each person "within the context of environmental and personal factors" (p. 11).

> An environment with barriers, or without facilitators, will restrict the individual's performance; other environments that are more facilitating may increase that performance. Society may hinder an individual's performance because either it creates barriers (e.g., inaccessible buildings) or it

does not provide facilitators (e.g., unavailability of assistive devices). (World Health Organization 2000, p. 20)

This new position of the World Health Organization coincides with those writing within the disability movement who have indicated that "not only the 'normal' roles for one's age, sex, society, and culture, but also 'normal' structure and function and 'normal' ability to perform an activity, depend on the society in which the standards of normality are generated" (Wendell 1989, p. 107). Such factors as "social expectations, the state of technology and its availability to people in that condition, the educational system, architecture, attitudes toward physical appearance, and the pace of life" affect the point at which variation from the norm becomes a disability (Wendell 1989, pp. 107, 109). Notions such as "success," "competence," "excellence," "merit," and "ability" acquire meaning only in contexts in which some tasks and their associated skills, attributes, or characteristics are valued more than are others. As Ransom comments, what counts as normal "'falling short of the norm,' 'subnormal,' shades off into the value judgment 'bad,' 'abnormal,' 'retarded.' The 'normal' becomes normative" (1997, p. 51).

How and whether one is disabled or enabled by a social context depends on "the relationship of a[n] ... impairment and the political, social, even spatial environment that places that impairment in a matrix of meanings and significations" (Davis 1995, p. 3). Indeed, as McDermott and Varenne (1995) indicate, cultures "actively organize ways for persons to be disabled" (p. 337), "The difficulties that people in wheelchairs (or city shoppers with carts ...) face with curbs and stairs tell us little about the physical conditions requiring wheelchairs or carts," according to McDermott and Varenne, "but a great deal about the rigid institutionalization of particular ways of handling gravity and boundaries between street and sidewalk as different zones of social interaction" (pp. 327–328).

When some are at a disadvantage as a result of how a social context is organized, it is possible to claim that disability is an *effect* of the social context or, in other words, that disability is socially constructed. Martha's Vineyard of the 18th and 19th centuries is a striking example of an absence of disability in a community, even though there were a number of people with physical impairments. What was unusual about this community was not only that many people in the community were deaf but also that almost everyone in the community used sign language (Groce reported in McDermott

& Varenne 1995, p. 328). Surviving members of the community could not always remember who had been deaf because almost everyone in Martha's Vineyard used sign language, including hearing people with other hearing people (Groce reported in McDermott & Varenne 1995, p. 328). This is an example of how it may be possible in some situations to "eliminate the category of the disabled altogether, and simply talk about individuals' physical abilities in their social context" (Wendell 1989, p. 108).

What is apparent from the discussion to this point is that someone can be disabled in relation to the standards established for certain tasks supported by social structures, yet not have a physical impairment. Impairment is not a necessary condition for someone to be judged as incompetent, unsuccessful, unskilled, unfit, inadequate, or, in short, abnormal. To be judged in this way requires only that one has failed to meet the expectations or standards of tasks that are socially supported. In the section that follows, I am interested in the extent to which the discipline of adapted physical activity is committed to normalizing behaviours and skills in what have been constructed as normal tasks.

NORMALIZATION, DISABILITY, AND THE DISCIPLINE OF ADAPTED PHYSICAL ACTIVITY

Adapted physical activity, like other disciplines, entails both meanings of discipline—discipline as a body of knowledge and discipline as social control. The discipline of adapted physical activity produces knowledge about people who are considered to be lacking in some way. These people may or may not have impairments. Like other disciplines, the work of adapted physical activity involves evaluation, ranking, and interventions to change people. It is important to emphasize that the discipline of adapted physical activity is not unique in its relationship to normalization. The impetus to normalize is central to all modern institutions and their related disciplines. The issue of normalization may be more focused in adapted physical activity than some other disciplines, however, because an emphasis of many adapted physical activity programs is to normalize participants by including them in mainstream tasks.

What distinguishes adapted physical activity from many other disciplines is that expert intervention is not designed to make everyone equally skilful. Rather, interventions are intended to make it possible for everyone to engage in a range of similar tasks—those designated "normal" for a culture. However, it is important to understand that attempting to include people in the *same* activities is a type of normalization.

The goal of normalization in adapted physical activity is to "make available to differently abled individuals conditions as close as possible to that of the group norm (average)" (Sherrill 1993, p. 68). Normalization theory is used in adapted physical activity in relation to "disabilities in which persons are perceived as looking or behaving differently" (1993, p. 132). The following three principles are central to normalization theory as proposed by Wolf Wolfensberger in 1972:

> 1. Behavioural and appearance deviancy can be reduced by minimizing the degree to which persons with disabilities are treated differently from able-bodied persons.
> 2. Conversely, deviancy is enhanced by treating persons as if they were deviant.
> 3. To the degree that they are grouped together and segregated from the mainstream of society, individuals will be perceived as different from others and will tend to behave differently. (Wolfensberger in Sherrill 1993, p. 132)

The goal is to make disability or difference less noticeable by having everyone participate in "normal" activities or tasks. Sherrill argues that normalization is not intended to make a person like everyone else (1993, p. 68). What it does mean, she says, is that everyone is expected to adapt so that games resemble those played by the able-bodied as much as possible (1993, p. 68). Whether segregated from or included in regular classrooms, the goal is to have everyone engage in the same tasks and share the same values about what these tasks should be.

Wolfensberger developed an instrument called "passing" to evaluate how well services normalize participants into what are considered to be "normal" tasks (Sherrill 1993, p. 132). We should remember, however, that the use of the term "passing" in other cultural contexts is used to signify that someone in a minority attempts to be mistaken as someone in the majority—the attempt, for example, of a Native to pass as White, or a gay man to pass as straight. In these contexts, however, passing is a double-edged sword that allows the passing person to participate in the privileges of the mainstream culture, but only by denying his or her own identity.

There is an assumption predominant in adapted physical activity that everyone should participate in the same tasks or activities even if there is not an expectation that they attempt to meet "normal" standards for these tasks. "Normal" tasks or activities are those that most people do. However, when the tasks that most people do is the measure of whether someone is "normal," not only are categories that deviate from the norm created (such as the disabled), it is difficult to notice other ways of participating in the world. As McDermott and Varenne (1995) point out, "mainstream or 'normal' criterion becomes gradually accepted for assessing members of minorities as deprived and disabled because they do not take part in mainstream activities" (p. 336).

How might the discipline of adapted physical activity negotiate the tension between a commitment to improving the lives of people and the homogenizing effects of normalizing tasks? Furthermore, how can adapted physical activity resist or disrupt the impulse to normalize while making it possible for a range of people to participate in a range of physical activities? One way that the discipline of adapted physical activity is already doing this is through the recognition that not all people who are "different," including those with impairments, require adapted physical activity (personal communication, G. Reid, November 1, 1999). They are doing just fine without interventions perhaps because they live in a social context, such as Martha's Vineyard, where impairment or other "differences" do not disable them.

Since Michel Foucault was the person who called our attention to the emergence of a society of normalization, it might be helpful to note how Foucault thought normalization might be countered. Foucault thought that to be engaged in ethical practice is to become aware of *how* one's actions and behaviours are shaped by standards. This awareness provides information from which one can either refuse a particular set of standards or refuse a passive acceptance of them (Foucault 1984). Refusing passive acceptance of rules, codes, and standards allows one to push the limits of what is considered to be "normal" and create new ways of living in the world.

In the case of adapted physical activity, one might refuse the assumption that certain tasks are acceptable for everyone. Refusal might also include asking whether human life is appropriately understood as the accomplishment of a set of prescribed tasks and noticing instead that human living "requires dealing with indefinite and unbounded tasks while struggling with the particular manner in which they have been shaped by the cultural process." This might lead to a recognition that what comes to count as competence in the tasks created by discipline "is a fabrication, a mock-up, and ... [that] the most arbitrary tasks can be the measure of individual development" (McDermott & Varenne 1995, p. 337).

Refusing normalization is not easy work because a society of normalization is comprised of other disciplines that are also intent on normalization. Everything in modern society conspires to normalize. However, if you believe as I do that the impulse to normalize is one of the major ethical issues of these times, it is important to refuse the ways in which normalization eliminates difference and diversity. And, while it is necessary to acknowledge and celebrate difference, we must also notice that what comes to be accepted as different behaviour, skill, or even bodies is socially constructed when we establish and maintain some tasks as "normal" tasks for a culture.

SUMMARY

This chapter examined the features of a "society of normalization" and explored implications for adapted physical activity of the impetus to normalize. It was shown how someone becomes disabled when the cultural context in which he or she lives does not accommodate his or her difference from the norm, and it was pointed out that differences that disabled people have may or may not be because of impairments. Unlike other disciplines that intervene to eliminate difference in order to make participants equally skilful, practitioners of adapted physical activity intervene to make it possible for everyone to be included in similar tasks. This, however, is also to normalize participants. Perhaps, a future direction for researchers and practitioners of adapted physical activity is to consider how to make it possible for people with impairments to gain the benefits of physical activity without also privileging those activities that are regarded as standard, or "normal," for people, to enjoy.

ACKNOWLEDGEMENT

Some of the material in this section has previously appeared in Shogan (1998). I would like to thank the *Adapted Physical Activity Quarterly* for allowing me to use this material. In that essay I acknowledged Sheryl McInnes for introducing me to the history of statistics and probability theory.

REFERENCES

Adapted Physical Activity National Standards. (1995). http://www.cortland.edu/
APENS/

Davis, L.J. (1995). *Enforcing normalcy: Disability, deafness, and the body*. London & New York: Verso.

Fiske, J. (1993). *Power plays power works*. London & New York: Verso.

Foucault, M. (1979). *Discipline and punish: The birth of the prison*. Translated by A. Sheridan. New York: Vintage.

Foucault, M. (1980a). Two lectures. In C. Gordon (Ed.), *Power/knowledge: Selected interviews and other writings 1972–1977* (pp. 78–108). New York: Pantheon.

Foucault, M. (1980b). *The history of sexuality: Vol. 1. An introduction*. Translated by R. Hurley. New York: Vintage.

Foucault, M. (1984). What is enlightenment? In P. Rabinow (Ed.), *The Foucault reader*. New York: Pantheon.

Hacking, I. (1987). Was there a probabilistic revolution, 1800–1930? In L. Kruger, L. Daston & M. Heidelberger (Eds.), *The probabilistic revolution: Vol. 1. Ideas in history* (pp. 45–55). Cambridge: MIT Press.

Hacking, I. (1990). *The taming of chance*. Cambridge: Cambridge University Press.

MacKenzie, D.A. (1981). *Statistics in Britain 1865–1930: The social construction of scientific knowledge*. Edinburgh: Edinburgh University Press.

McDermott, R. & Varenne, H. (1995). Culture as disability. *Anthropology and Education Quarterly 26*(3), 324–348.

Nideffer, R. (1980). Attentional focus: Self-assessment. In R. Suinn (Ed.), *Psychology in sport: Methods and applications* (pp. 281–290). Minneapolis: Burgess.

Oliver, M. (1996). *Understanding disability: From theory to practice*. New York: St. Martin's Press.

Porter, T.M. (1986). *The rise of statistical thinking 1820–1900*. Princeton: Princeton University Press.

Rabinow, P. (1984). *The Foucault reader*. New York: Pantheon.

Ransom, J.S. (1997). *Foucault's discipline: The politics of subjectivity*. Durham & London: Duke University Press.

Reid, G. (1999). Personal communication, November 1.

Sherrill, C. (1993). *Adapted physical activity, recreation, and sport: Crossdisciplinary and lifespan* (4th ed.). Madison: W.C.B. Brown and Benchmark.

Shogan, D. (1998). The social construction of disability: The impact of statistics and technology. *Adapted Physical Activity Quarterly 15*, 269–277.

Shogan, D. (1999). *The making of high-performance athletes: Discipline, diversity, and ethics*. Toronto: University of Toronto Press.

United Nations Decade of Disabled Persons 1983–1992. (1983). *World program of action concerning disabled persons*. New York: United Nations.

Wendell, S. (1989). Toward a feminist theory of disability. *Hypatia: A Journal of Feminist Philosophy 4*(2), 104–124.

Winzer, M.A. (1997). Disability and society before the eighteenth century. In L.J. Davis (Ed.), *The disability studies reader* (pp. 75–109). New York: Routledge.

Wolfensberger, W. (1972). *The principle of normalization in human services*. Toronto: National Institute of Mental Retardation through Leonard Crainford.

World Health Organization. (2000). *ICIDH-2: Internal classification of functioning, disability, and health*. Prefinal draft full version. Geneva: Author.

11 QUEERING PERVERT CITY

In 1997, junior hockey coach Graham James was sentenced to three-and-a-half years in prison for abusing Sheldon Kennedy and another unnamed player whom James coached as junior players. Sheldon Kennedy was well known as a National Hockey League (NHL) player and this, together with the fact that hockey is considered by some to be Canada's national pastime, created great interest not only in the people involved in the scandal but in the places in which the abuse was reported to have happened. One of these places, Swift Current, Saskatchewan, received most of the media attention because it was here that James, Kennedy, and Kennedy's teammates achieved their greatest success, winning the Memorial Cup for junior hockey supremacy and producing a number of stars for the NHL.

While much can be written about this episode in Canadian sporting history, including how sexual abuse in sport emerged as an ethical issue worthy of attention,[1] in this chapter I am interested in how representations of the James scandal by the popular media relied on a dominant cultural story (Hall 1997; Kincaid 1998) about sexual abuse of children and youth in dysfunctional families. I focus on how newspaper representations constructed meaning about the events, people, and place associated with the scandal from a pervasive cultural narrative that gave "form to ... our ways of seeing children, sexuality, and transgression" (Kincaid 1998, p. 5). Demonstrating how the scandal was represented in the media is not intended as a denial of events that took place in Swift Current. Rather, it is an attempt to make apparent how newspaper representations of these events invoked a dominant cultural story about sexual abuse in dysfunctional families and, in this particular case, represented Swift Current *as* a dysfunctional family, a complicit yet innocent bystander in the sexual abuse of junior hockey players coached by James.

Once the story broke that James had been charged with assaulting junior hockey players, and particularly when Sheldon Kennedy, by then an NHL player, came forward to talk publicly about what had happened, news media across North America became interested in Swift Current. *The Globe and Mail,* for example, described Swift Current this way:

> To understand why the James affair has hit Swift Current so hard, you first need to understand how small the city is and how big the sport.
>
> Swift Current is the sort of place where people are excited that Tommy Hunter is coming this month to perform.... It's the sort of place where people are still known by what church they belong to, where you could drive down the fiendishly cold main street last week and see a whole row of cars left running and unlocked.
>
> ... In such a climate, those who play for the Broncos are local heroes who stand a chance of living the Canadian dream of playing in the NHL, feted guests of honour at fowl suppers, and community leaders with a stature far beyond their years. (Mitchell 1997, p. A6)

Swift Current was also described by the media as angry and betrayed (Brownridge 1997a, p. A2), a town of deep shame, and "Pervert City," as one of my colleagues referred to it when I indicated that that was where I was born. Swift Current was reduced simultaneously to a city of perversion and bucolic innocence: a place with "its heart broken, its shoulders slumping, every bone in its body aching as it searches within itself for answers" (Drinnan 1997, p. B1). As I explain, these contradictory representations can coexist within a cultural narrative about sexual abuse in dysfunctional families.

In what follows, I first read newspaper representations of Swift Current as a dysfunctional family through a familiar cultural story about sexual abuse that highlights notions of complicity, duplicity, and innocence. However, in order to confound representations of Swift Current as a place fixed by this cultural story, I intervene with my own understanding of this place. As a queer youth who lived in Swift Current in the 1950s and 1960s, I was often smitten by adults who were my mentors. By interjecting some of my experiences, I hope to disrupt the cultural story of Swift Current as a dysfunctional family, as well as open up notions of authority, innocence, and sexual abuse to other possibilities. I offer my experiences not to assert the truth of this place, thus applying a different but still singular set of meanings to Swift Current and the relationships of the people who live and have lived there (Scott 1992; Sedgwick 1993).

Rather, this is a deconstructive move. Referring to writing about her experiences with the diagnosis and medical treatment of breast cancer, Eve Kosofsky Sedgwick indicates that "it's hard not to think of this ... experience as ... an adventure in applied deconstruction" (1993, p. 12). Sedgwick's experiences call into question neatly packaged oppositions between safety and danger, fear and hope, past and future, thought and act, and the natural and the technological and, in doing so, disrupt precise definitions of identity, gender, and sexuality (1993, pp. 12, 13). Likewise, recounting some of my experiences of sexuality as a youth living in Swift Current, including my pursuit of my coach, has the potential to call into question oppositions between innocence and dysfunction, the normal and the perverted, and insiders and outsiders and, in so doing, disrupt the tidy stories told about sexual abuse of innocent youth in dysfunctional families (or places). I intend the intervention of my experiences as a queer reading of this place called "pervert city," where queer suggests that "meanings ... can be at loose ends with each other" (Sedgwick 1993, p. 6). In turn, I hope to show that Swift Current exceeds representations of it as a healthy, family town and that it also surpasses representations of it as a town of perversion or dysfunction.

Before proceeding with the popular media and my own reading of Swift Current, I first present a chronology of the scandal involving James and Kennedy.

THE SCANDAL

Graham James began his coaching career in Manitoba in the late 1970s and by the beginning of the 1980s he had become a Junior A hockey coach. He first encountered Sheldon Kennedy at a hockey school in 1982 when Kennedy was 13 years old. In 1984, Graham James recruited Kennedy to his Winnipeg team and, when this team was moved to Moose Jaw, James arranged to have Kennedy move with him. According to Kennedy, James began sexual contact with him not long after his arrival in Winnipeg. While in Moose Jaw, the expectation that Kennedy would go to James's apartment every Tuesday and Thursday began and continued until Kennedy was 19 years old.

James was dismissed from the Moose Jaw team for suspected improprieties that were revealed only when the abuse story broke. He moved Kennedy with him to Winnipeg for a short time and then in 1986 he became the head coach of the Swift Current Broncos. He ensured that Kennedy joined him there. In 1986, a bus accident killed four of the Bronco players and James was credited with helping the surviving players through the ordeal (Robinson 1998, p. 160). In 1989, the Swift Current Broncos won the Memorial Cup with the most successful record ever in the Canadian Hockey League. Sheldon Kennedy had outstanding seasons both in 1988 and in 1989 and was named to the national junior team in 1988.

Kennedy was drafted by the Detroit Red Wings in 1989 and acquired a reputation as someone emotionally out of control. He was convicted of reckless driving and charged with drug possession, and he was traded a number of times. Meanwhile in Swift Current, James continued his success as a winning coach and his popularity as a colourful personality. However, at the end of the 1993–1994 season, James's contract was not renewed. He subsequently appeared in Calgary where he became part owner, general manager, and head coach of the Calgary Hitmen (Robinson 1998, p. 164). In 1997, while Kennedy was a player for the Boston Bruins, he went public with his story.

In 1997, Graham James was sentenced to three-and-a-half years in prison. He was released from prison in July 2000 and, to the consternation of the Canadian Hockey Association and of many in the sporting public, James became a coach with the Spanish national team.

READING REPRESENTATIONS OF SWIFT CURRENT THROUGH STORIES OF SEXUAL ABUSE

Experts in psychology, social work, and other human sciences have had a prominent role in producing a story about sexual abuse in dysfunctional families that has become familiar in this culture (see Armstrong 1984; Crewsdon 1988; La Fontaine 1990; Miller 1983; Rush 1980). This is a story of sexual abuse in a "'family system' gone wrong [where] each family member own[s] a piece of the problem" (Dinsmore 1991, p. 15). According to Pat Gilmartin, family pathology is not regarded as an "idiosyncratic behaviour of a single member of that unit; rather, the family system is implicated as causing and perpetuating whatever problem that exists" (1994, p. 82). Family members are all implicated in the abuse as victims, perpetrators, gullible innocents, or complicit third parties (Butler 1985).

As I have said, newspaper reporters' attempts to understand what happened in Swift Current were cast in terms of this familiar story about sexual abuse in dysfunctional families. Both official city information sources and outside media represent Swift Current as valuing families. The city Web site, for example, indicates that "Swift Current is a city of families and friends. Our continuing efforts to maintain a high quality of life and opportunity for our neighbours is only rivalled by our desire to welcome new families to Swift Current and make new friends" (Swift Current Community Information 2001). Swift Current not only values family, it *is* a family, according to some. For example, Joe Arling, a hotel owner and member of the board of directors of the Broncos, was reported in 1997 to say,

> This is a community with very strong morals and beliefs. It has very strong family values and in a way, it's a family itself. To me, what Graham did was a violation of trust and position, just like priests and teachers have abused their positions. Hockey just happened to be the venue, in this case. But like anywhere, there'll be significant hurt here. No one would have expected it to happen in this community. (quoted in Gillis 1997a, p. H2)

Swift Current is a family, but a dysfunctional one. Moreover, people in Swift Current were represented as recognizing the dysfunction of the community: "One thing's certain, this farming, railway, and oil community—a well-spring of dedicated, sometimes brilliant hockey players—will never feel the same about itself. Or its and Canada's favourite game" (Gillis 1997b, p. A2).

As a dysfunctional family, Swift Current was represented as complicit in the sexual abuse of the junior hockey players who lived there. In some accounts James was cast as a member of this dysfunctional family that made possible the abuse of Kennedy and other junior hockey players: "while preying on boys for his confessed sexual gratification, James could not operate alone. He had help and lots of it. Passive, blind, hopelessly naïve help from those who most trusted the junior hockey coach: parents, billets, league and team administrators, and teammates" (Ormsby 1997, p. D3).

Many reporters and some residents of the city were reported to have thought it was impossible that no one knew that the sexual abuse was happening in Swift Current. Two residents of the Saskatchewan city were quoted as saying: "I just can't imagine how somebody could live with these players and not try to figure out why they were spending so much time with the coach"; "What do you mean nobody knew? I'm sure people knew, but they just didn't do anything" (quoted in Gillis 1997c, p. A4). Another account went so far as to surmise that the team organization refused therapy for team players after the tragic bus accident in 1986 left four players dead because they were afraid that "the terrible truth about James's sexual shenanigans [would] surface" (McConachie 1997, p. B1). In these representations, Swift Current assumed the role of the mother within the dysfunctional family: the "invisible third partner," "colluding" in the sexual interaction between the abuser and the child or abandoning the child to the abuser (see Butler 1985, pp. 102, 113). It is assumed in this conventional story about sexual abuse that abuse would not have occurred if the mother, in this case Swift Current, had not created a particular emotional climate through "commission and omission" (Butler 1985, p. 114).

Central to the story of sexual abuse in dysfunctional families is the gullibility of at least some family members. Reporters represented Swift Current as innocently caught up in and bewildered by the events:

> Meanwhile, the citizens of Swift Current will never understand how or why all of them came to be victims, too. But that's what happens when sexual abuse, society's dirty little secret, rears its ugly head in your community. There are good people in Swift Current, good people, salt-of-the-earth people, who are torturing themselves, trying to understand what it is that went on behind closed doors in their community and why they weren't able to recognize the signs. (Drinnan 1997, p. B1)

The trainer of the Broncos was reported to say, "I've been lying awake every night thinking, 'Did I miss something? Were there signs I didn't see?' But there just weren't any hints" (quoted in Gillis 1997b, p. A2).

The cultural story of sexual abuse in dysfunctional families includes accounts of loyalty of members to the abuser (see esp. Butler 1985, p. 121). The loyalty of some Swift Current residents to James was central to some media depictions. When faced with the allegations about James, team president John Rittinger was reported to have said that, "the Graham I know was always a pleasant, humorous fellow. It's impossible for me to believe that a man of his intelligence would get involved in something like this. I couldn't be more devastated by this if Graham had died. I couldn't feel worse by this if it was my own family" (quoted in Todd 1997, p. G2). There were many letters of support submitted at James's trial by former players and administrators of the Broncos' organization

(Robinson 1998, p. 168). This loyalty to James was interpreted as just another indication of the dysfunction of the city.

Gilmartin indicates that social-psychological explanations of sexual abuse of children in families "keeps the focus on individual families as the problem and ignores the societal power imbalances which many families mimic" (1994, p. 87). Much of the reporting about the James case, while differing about whether Swift Current was complicit, innocent, or both, nevertheless represented this place as an aberration among Canadian cities. Administrators of hockey sport-governing bodies were also keen to make the point that what happened in Swift Current was not representative of hockey culture. Hockey authorities were quick to represent the James case as an isolated incident and not reflective of junior hockey (see Todd 1997, p. G2). However, accounts such as Laura Robinson's in *Crossing the Line: Violence and Sexual Assault in Canada's National Sport* document how abuse of and by hockey players may be central to hockey culture. Robinson argues that abuse in hockey is institutionalized and that abuse takes many forms, including pressure on young players to excel and conform, hazing rituals, and sexual abuse.

A common representation by the media of the James affair was that James duped Swift Current by fooling them with his charm and knowledge of hockey.

> This was a man of contradictions.... James was a pillar of the community. He was a role model. He was on the Broncos' bus that ugly night 10 years ago and he helped the community mend its broken heart, the same heart he would smash to smithereens. He picked that team up by the skatelaces and took it to a Memorial Cup championship just three years later. It was a miracle that put Swift Current on the map. Now it turns out he was the devil in disguise. (Drinnan 1997, p. B1)

In this representation, James is not one of the family. He is an outsider, described by one of the players' billets as "an import to the community" (quoted in Gillis 1997b, p. A2). The mayor of the city at the time also distanced the community from James by indicating that, "this is an isolated event by perhaps a deranged person. Certainly, it doesn't reflect the community" (quoted in Vanstone 1997, p. A1).

While, for the most part, the mainstream media did not link the charges of abuse to James's homosexuality, they did portray him as "a very private man, rarely seen socially" (Brownridge 1997a, p. A1). The *Alberta Report*, a right-wing, Christian fundamentalist news weekly, accused other media of downplaying James's homosexuality and ignoring what they portrayed as "the known link between homosexuality and pedophilia" (Sillars 1997, p. 34). Albert Howlett, a Bronco supporter, shared the indignation: "You pretty near have to put him down near the lowest class of person you can be. What he did with those boys was terrible" (quoted in Vanstone 1997, p. A1).

Many in the city were reported to have known about James's homosexuality, with the effect that reporters did not take seriously the representation of the city by one of its citizens as a naïve, small Bible-belt town (Mitchell 1997, p. A6). A former Bronco director was reported to say that: "There were rumours about Graham's sexual orientation, but never any suggestion he was sexually abusing players.... Innuendo, suspicion and rumour was all there was, and until someone comes forward, there's really nothing you can do. If you decided to end a coaching contract on something like that, human rights would be all over you" (quoted in Gillis 1997b, p. A2). In another report, the following was attributed to the director: "Some of the club's inner circle suspected that Mr. James was a homosexual but they were broad-minded enough not to assume that a gay man also had a taste for the youths under his control" (Mitchell 1997, p. A6). That the "homophobic world of junior hockey" (Todd 1997, p. G2) would be so open to homosexuality stretched the limits of credulity for most reporters. One asked rhetorically, "Could it be that as long as you're winning and developing NHL stars, people look the other way? Could it be that James would have been found out long ago if he was a losing coach?" (Todd 1997, p. G2).

A flurry of articles identifying other "homosexual" coaches who had been "known" to prey on players (see Houston & Campbell 1997, p. A1; Spector 1997a, p. A1; Stock & Crowley 1997, p. A1) belied the representation of James as an exception. Many of these coaches were dead and not in a position to defend themselves. Most attention was paid to Brian Shaw, former coach, general manager, and owner of the Edmonton Oil Kings and Portland Winter Hawks. The *Edmonton Journal* also carried a front-page story with pictures about Peter Spear, who died in 1988, and who allegedly abused at least one of his players (Spector 1997a, p. A1). None of these accounts of homosexuality in hockey, including the disingenuous reference to looking the other way, acknowledged what many of the reporters must have witnessed: the homoeroticism of the locker room. As Brian Pronger indicates, "locker rooms are places where orthodox men like to hang around naked, talking and joking with each other" (1992, p. 76). In response to the revelation that James regularly showered with his players after practices, Western Hockey League coach Mike Babcock reported that, in the aftermath of the scandal, he and his assistant coaches had talked about whether they should continue to shower with players when the team was on the road (Stars Looking to Shine over Hockey Scandal 1997, p. E2). If there were indications of James's sexual interest in Bronco players, they may have been indistinguishable from homoerotic interactions taken for granted on male sporting teams.

The story about sexual abuse in families and family-like settings is unable to account for homoerotic behaviour on male athletic teams nor can it contain Kennedy's or James's understanding of what happened between them. When asked about his willingness to go to where James was coaching after the first sexual encounter, Kennedy responded, "Well, yeah ... I was scared sh__less ... I knew right after, but there was nothing I could do because I wanted to play" (Player's Self-Esteem Sank after Years of Abuse 1997, p. D10). Jimmy Devellano, who drafted Kennedy from Swift Current, was one of many people surprised by Kennedy's accusations because, according to Devellano, Kennedy "always talked about Graham so sincerely" (Simmons 1997, p. B1). A former Bronco vice-president said he was told that James was "doing it" with Kennedy: "I figured that if they were doing it, they were doing it with consent" (quoted in Vanstone 1997, p. A5). Kennedy later said that he believed that James was in love with him. He also indicated that James knew what he was doing and "he should have known that it wasn't accepted, because I had mentioned many times that I hated it" (quoted in Board 1997, p. D1). Kennedy said that he could not tell anybody because "I was so scared to come out and admit it happened to me. I was scared to say I was with another man" (Learning to Live Again 1997, p. A2). James commented after his trial that he realized that Kennedy was not comfortable with the sex, but he tolerated it because "he legitimately cared. Not about THAT (the sex) obviously. He cared. He knew I was lonely and, you know, that sort of registered as desperation" (quoted in Spector 1997b, p. D6). When asked in an interview from prison whether he realized that what he was doing was wrong, James responded, "when you're attracted to somebody, you're blinded, and you try to justify things, and you figure if you can do enough for somebody then somehow that makes up for it" (quoted in "Caring" Coach Tells His Story 1997, p. K2); "I suppose you don't think these things ... will be brought out into the general public. It's like anybody's sex life—it goes out in the general public [and] it doesn't look too flattering" (quoted in James Says He Feels Betrayed by Kennedy 1997, p. E2).

Irrespective of the homoeroticism of the locker room or what James or Kennedy had to say, media representations of Swift Current and the people who live there sustained an understanding of sexual abuse consistent with conventional stories of abuse in dysfunctional families. This is a story of innocence, collusion, duplicity, and gullibility. Yet Swift Current and the events that took place there are open for other readings.

ANOTHER READING OF SWIFT CURRENT

As it turns out, many of the places in which the events that implicated James and Kennedy occurred were places I had inhabited under different conditions 20 years earlier. During high school, I lived in a house on Jubilee Drive in the northeast side of the city. This house was later sold to Colleen and Frank McBean, who billeted Bronco players through the 1990s. Kennedy was one of these players.

Kennedy would have left the side door into the car park every Tuesday and Thursday evening to go to Graham James's house. Was his room the southeast bedroom where I had spent so much time as a 15-year-old thinking about my first girlfriend? This girlfriend was 18 and, under today's laws, would be considered an adult. As I found out later, she was two-timing me with her female college coach.

Many reporters have wondered how the people of Swift Current, especially those billeting players, could not have known that a player was sexually involved with the coach. They surmised that people must have known or were too simple or naïve to have guessed. I often went to my basketball coach's apartment, usually unannounced, hoping to seduce her. I was oblivious to whether the neighbours knew. My coach's careful closing of the curtains upon my arrival was reason for me to be hopeful of what might happen but, as I think about it now, she was likely very aware that some would think that a player should not be in her coach's home unsupervised at night. Only she and I were aware that the 17-year-old girl was pursuing the 25-year-old coach. Applied to me, the story of innocence and dysfunction would have shrunk a "smart and

active older adolescent ... into a child, a generic 'essence-of-child'"
(Kincaid 1998, p. 31).

My mother did not ask me questions about spending time with my
coach. Instead, my mother often helped me buy chocolate bars for her.
Nor did she have much to say about the black eye my coach accidentally
gave me when we were wrestling in the locker room. This black eye would
have been very difficult for my coach to explain if someone had chosen
to cast my relationship with her as inappropriate. In some accounts, James
was accused of threatening Kennedy with a gun. James had this to say
about the gun: "There was a gun in a sense of a Clousseau-Kato type
thing. He'd chase me until I could find something to stop him, and vice
versa. Then we'd laugh about it. That's all there was to it" (quoted in
Spector 1997b, p. D6).

Was my mother complicit in my sexual encounters with girls my own
age? Was she implicated in my active pursuit of a young woman in authority who, arguably, in sexual terms was more innocent than I was? My
mother told me much later that she did not have the language to broach
my sexuality with me. According to the familiar story, this inability to
talk about what may have appeared as an unusual relationship with my
coach is evidence of the dysfunction of my family. As the titles of books
that support this story reflect, silence is considered to be central to dysfunction (Butler 1985; Miller 1983; Rush 1980). I had a sense then, however,
that by helping me buy small presents for my coach, my mother communicated her tacit approval of me.

Agonizing about what the adults should or should not have known or
done cannot account for the complications of people's lives. Colleen and
Frank McBean, for example, began billeting Bronco players, including
Kennedy, after losing two of their sons in a tragic vehicle accident. How
and if this tragic event affected the decisions that were made in relation
to the boys in their care cannot be captured by implying that they somehow colluded in what was later understood as Kennedy's abuse. They
may have been unable to make explicit what was later construed as a
terrible abuse of authority by a coach whose "victim" left his home twice
a week, every week, for four years to visit the coach.

Swift Current and its people cannot be captured by stories about
dysfunction and innocence, nor can the relationships between the adults
and youth who live and have lived there. Many of my memories of living
as a child and teenager in Swift Current reproduce this as a time and place

marked by innocence, exuberance, creativity, and fun. But I know that these memories make sense to me in contrast to the heaviness that often accompanies adulthood. With little effort, however, I can also remember the stranger in the car who persisted in trying to give me a ride home when I was five; the woman who did some sewing for my mother who was found dead in the Swift Current creek; the rape of one of my sister's friends; the way the kids at school treated the children of one family because they were poor and Arab and lived in the valley; the man who turned out to be a woman who drove the "honey wagon" (the name for the horse-drawn wagon that carried the excrement from the outdoor toilets used by the people in the valley); children throwing rocks at the man with cerebral palsy who dared to try to walk in his neighbourhood; what I now understand to be the racism that pervaded the speech of the adults around me; or the awesome wrath of one of my teachers when I was 10 because I persisted in playing hockey with the boys.

Years later, my mother apologized for not doing something more to ease what she thought must have been a horrible time for me living in Swift Current. But it was not a horrible time. Rather, it was then and there that I found other girls like me and we engaged in sexual lives not remotely imagined in representations of Swift Current as a quaint, quiet family town or as a dysfunctional city complicit in the sexual abuse of its young people. Still, I am surprised at the apparent casualness to homo-sexuality expressed by at least some in the community during the James scandal. In the 1960s, I would have sworn that, except for those of us engaged in these thrilling subterranean practices, no one had a clue that people did these things. At least some people did know about these prac-tices when I lived there, including my mother, as did some during the time James and Kennedy were living in Swift Current. Yet, dominant cultural stories about families, sexuality, relationships, and innocence still circu-late, making it difficult to understand events, people, and places in anything but the terms of these stories. What has changed, however, is that queer stories are being told about the relationships between people that occurred in these places. These queer stories situate dysfunction not in individuals or places but in a cultural story that simplifies complicated lives. The dysfunction of the cultural story is that it permits only two main roles, "monster and victim ... along with supporting parts for police, judges, juries, therapists, parents, friends, journalists, and lawyers" (Kincaid 1998, p. 30).

I want to emphasize that I am not saying that my experiences in Swift Current prove somehow that Kennedy was not traumatized by the sexual encounters he had with James. Rather, I want to show that the stories about dysfunctional families and the innocence of youth are too simple to capture the complexity of relationships, events, and people. In their simplicity, they have the effect of fixing what we can know about a place, people who live there, and events in a way that is "intolerant and relentless" (Kincaid 1998, p. 30). A queer reading of this place called "pervert city" renders a little less tidy the meaning of this place and its events.

NOTE

1 Where little attention was paid to this issue before, despite frequent concerns expressed by female athletes in relation to their male coaches, it took NHL player Sheldon Kennedy's story to produce policy, handbooks, Web sites, hot lines, skateathons, TV movies, and other ways of dealing with these issues.

REFERENCES

Armstrong, Louise. (1984). *Home front: Notes from the family war zone.* New York: McGraw-Hill.

Board, Mike. (1997). Kennedy describes his life as a lonely hell. *The Gazette*, Montreal, (January 7), D1.

Brownridge, David. (1997a). A feeling of betrayal. *The Leader Post*, Regina (January 4), A1.

Brownridge, David. (1997b). Assault charges stun Swift Current. *The Star Phoenix*, Saskatoon (January 4), A2.

Butler, Sandra. (1985). *Conspiracy of silence.* Volcano: Volcano.

"Caring" coach tells his story. (1997). *Edmonton Sun* (January 7), 12.

Crewsdon, John. (1988). *By silence betrayed: Sexual abuse of children in America.* New York: Little Brown & Co.

Dinsmore, Christine. (1991). *From surviving to thriving: Incest, feminism, and recovery.* New York: State University of New York Press.

Drinnan, Gregg. (1997). Swift Current tries to heal its wounds. *The Leader Post*, Regina (January 9), B1.

Gillis, Charlie. (1997a). Hockeytown, Canada searches its soul. *The Edmonton Journal* (January 11), H1–H2.

Gillis, Charles. (1997b). James incident steals city of its innocence. *The Star Phoenix*, Saskatoon (January 14), A2.

Gillis, Charles. (1997c). Sex assaults shock prairie town. *The Gazette*, Montreal (January 12), A1, A4.

Gilmartin, Pat. (1994). *Rape, incest, and child sexual abuse.* New York: Garland.

Hall, Stuart (Ed.). (1997). *Representation: Cultural representations and signifying practices*. London: The Open University.

Houston, William & Campbell, Neil. (1997). Ex-WHL boss abused players. *The Globe and Mail* (January 9), A1.

James says he feels betrayed by Kennedy. (1997). *The Vancouver Sun* (January 8), E2.

Kincaid, James R. (1998). *Erotic innocence: The culture of child molesting*. Durham: Duke University Press.

La Fontaine, Jean.(1990). *Child sexual abuse*. Cambridge: Polity Press.

Learning to live again. (1997). *The Leader Post*, Regina (January 7), A1, A12.

McConachie, Doug. (1997). Independent investigation needed by WHL. *Saskatoon Star Phoenix* (January 15), B1.

Miller, Alice. (1983). *Thou shalt not be aware*. New York: Farrar, Straus & Giroux.

Mitchell, Alana. (1997). Swift Current's hockey pride left in tatters. *The Globe and Mail* (January 14), A6.

Ormsby, Mary. (1997). Be vigilant to protect vulnerable youngsters. *The Toronto Star* (January 4), D3.

Player's self-esteem sank after years of abuse. *The Vancouver Sun* (January 7), D10.

Pronger, Brian. (1992). *The arena of masculinity: Sport, homosexuality, and the meaning of sex*. Toronto: University of Toronto Press.

Robinson, Laura. (1998). *Crossing the line: Violence and sexual assault in Canada's national sport*. Toronto: McClelland & Stewart.

Rush, Florence. (1980). *The best-kept secret: Sexual abuse of children*. Englewood Cliffs: Prentice-Hall.

Scott, Joan. (1992). Experience. In Judith Butler & Joan Scott (Eds.), *Feminists theorize the political* (pp. 22–40). New York: Routledge.

Sedgwick, Eve Kosofsky. (1993). *Tendencies*. Durham: Duke University Press.

Sillars, Les. (1997). Hockey pays the price for gay tolerance. *The Alberta Report* (January 20), 30–34.

Simmons, Steve. (1997). Many tried to help a troubled Kennedy. *The Star Phoenix*, Saskatoon (January 8), B1.

Spector, Mark. (1997a). Scars that last a lifetime. *The Edmonton Journal* (January 9), A1, A9.

Spector, Mark. (1997b). Kennedy disclosure a betrayal: James. *Star Phoenix*, Saskatoon (January 9), D6.

Stars looking to shine over hockey scandal. *The Leader Post*, Regina (January 22), E2.

Stock, Curtis & Cowley, Norm. (1997). The saddest power play. *The Edmonton Journal* (January 7), A12.

Swift Current Community Information. (2001). December 1 [http://www.city.swift-current.sk.ca/info/index/htm].

Todd, Jack. (1997). Junior hockey looks other way. *The Gazette*, Montreal (January 4), G2.

Vanstone, Rob. (1997). Shadow over a hockey town. *The Leader Post*, Regina (January 11), A1.

COPYRIGHT ACKNOWLEDGEMENTS

Chapter 6, "Hybrid Athletes," is a revised version of the chapter "Hybrid Athletes," in Debra Shogan, *The Making of High Performance Athletes: Discipline, Diversity, and Ethics* (Toronto: University of Toronto Press, 1999). Reprinted with permission from the publisher.

Sections of the introduction to Section 3, "A New Sport Ethics," were previously published in Debra Shogan, *The Making of High Performance Athletes: Discipline, Diversity, and Ethics* (Toronto: University of Toronto Press, 1999). Reprinted with permission from the publisher.

Chapter 8, "A New Sport Ethics: Taking König Seriously," was originally published as Debra Shogan and Maureen Ford, "A New Sport Ethics: Taking König Seriously," in *International Review for the Sociology of Sport* 35/1 (2000): 49–58. © 2000 by International Sociology of Sport Association and Sage Publications. Reprinted with permission from Sage Publications.

Chapter 9, "Disciplinary Technologies of Sport Performance," is a revised version of the chapter "Production of 'The Athlete': Disciplinary Technologies of Sport," in Debra Shogan, *The Making of High Performance Athletes: Discipline, Diversity, and Ethics* (Toronto: University of Toronto Press, 1999). Reprinted with permission from the publisher. It was subsequently published as Debra Shogan, "Disciplinary Technologies of Sport Performance," in *Sport Technology: History, Philosophy and Policy* 21 (2002): 93–109. © 2002 by Elsevier Science Ltd. Reprinted with permission from Elsevier.

Chapter 10, "The Social Construction of Disability in a Society of Normalization," was originally published as Debra Shogan, "The Social Construction of Disability: The Impact of Statistics and Technology," in *Adapted Physical Activity Quarterly* 15(3): 269–277. © 1998 by Human Kinetics Publishers, Inc. Reprinted with permission from Human Kinetics (Champaign, IL). It was subsequently published as Debra Shogan, "The Social Construction of Disability in a Society of Normalization," in Robert D. Steadward, Garry D. Wheeler, E. Jane Watkinson, eds., *Adapted Physical Activity* (Edmonton: University of Alberta Press, 2003). Reprinted with permission from the publisher.

Chapter 11, "Queering Pervert City," was originally published as Debra Shogan, "Queering 'Pervert City'," in *Torquere: Journal of the Canadian Lesbian and Gay Studies Association/Revue de la Société canadienne des études lesbiennes et gaies* 4-5 (2002–03). Reprinted with permission from the publisher.

INDEX